Anonymous

Picturesque Chicago and Guide to the World's Fair

Anonymous

Picturesque Chicago and Guide to the World's Fair

ISBN/EAN: 9783744718837

Printed in Europe, USA, Canada, Australia, Japan

Cover: Foto ©ninafisch / pixelio.de

More available books at **www.hansebooks.com**

AND

GUIDE TO THE WORLD'S FAIR

ISSUED BY

THE RELIGIOUS HERALD,

AND

PRESENTED TO ITS SUBSCRIBERS AS A

SOUVENIR

OF

FIFTY YEARS PUBLICATION OF THE PAPER.

PROFUSELY ILLUSTRATED

CONTENTS.

PART I.
THE CITY OF CHICAGO.

PAGE

A Sketch of the City of Chicago   1

PART II.
IMPORTANT BUILDINGS AND POINTS OF INTEREST.

Auditorium Building	42
Auditorium Theatre	42
Central Music Hall	42
Auditorium Hotel	43
Grand Pacific Hotel	45
Palmer House	45
Permanent Art Building	45
Art Collections	46
Grand Opera House	46
Havlin's Theatre	46
Board of Trade Building	46
Libby Prison Museum	48
City Hall	49
Cook County Court-House	49
First National Bank	50
Chamber of Commerce Building	52
Tacoma Building	52
Temperance Temple	52
Bridges	53

	PAG
Viaducts	5
"Rookery"	5
Masonic Temple	5
Potter Palmer	5
Grant Statue, Lincoln Park	6
Haymarket Massacre	6
Haymarket Square	6
Logan Statue	6
Michigan Avenue	6
Grand Boulevard	6
Michigan Boulevard	7
New Building of Chicago Herald	7
Ashland Block	7
Columbus Building	7
Water Works	7
Von Linne Statue	7
Water Towers	7
Post-Office	8
Union Stock Yards	8
Grain Elevators	8
Washington Park Club	8
Armour Mission	9
University of Chicago	9
Chicago Light	9
Crib and Breakwater Lights	9
Grosse Point Light	9
The Public Library	9
Hotels	9
Chicago Athenæum	9
Cook County Hospital	9
First Regiment, I. N. G.	10
Prairie Avenue	10
Farwell Hall	10
McCormick Harvesting Machine Company	10
Newspapers	10
Columbian Association	10
German Society of Chicago	11
Ogontz Association	1
Baptist Missionary Training School	1
Railroad Transportation	1

	PAGE
ILLINOIS CENTRAL RAILROAD	120
WISCONSIN CENTRAL LINES	120
GRAND CENTRAL DEPOT	122
THE UNION DEPOT	123
PULLMAN	124
PULLMAN PALACE CAR COMPANY	141

PART III.

THE PARK SYSTEM.

CONSERVATORIES	152
SOUTH PARKS	158
DOUGLAS PARK	158
DREXEL BOULEVARD	158
GARFIELD PARK	160
JACKSON PARK	162
LAKE SHORE DRIVE	162
LINCOLN PARK	166
LINCOLN PARK PALM-HOUSE	168
MICHIGAN AVENUE BOULEVARD	168
OAKWOOD BOULEVARD	168
WASHINGTON BOULEVARD	168
WASHINGTON PARK	170

PART IV.

THE WORLD'S COLUMBIAN EXPOSITION.

BIRD'S-EYE VIEW OF EXPOSITION	190
DESCRIPTION OF THE ADMINISTRATION BUILDING	192
DESCRIPTION OF THE GOVERNMENT BUILDING	195
DESCRIPTION OF THE NAVAL EXHIBIT	197
DESCRIPTION OF THE WOMAN'S BUILDING	201
DESCRIPTION OF THE MACHINERY HALL	207
DESCRIPTION OF THE MANUFACTURERS' AND LIBERAL ARTS BUILDING	210

	PAGE
DESCRIPTION OF THE ELECTRICAL BUILDING	21
DESCRIPTION OF THE TRANSPORTATION BUILDING	21
DESCRIPTION OF THE HALL OF MINES AND MINING	22
DESCRIPTION OF THE AGRICULTURAL BUILDING	23
THE LIVE STOCK EXHIBIT	23
FORESTRY	24
THE DAIRY	24
THE HORTICULTURAL BUILDING	24
FLORICULTURE	24
THE FISHERIES BUILDING	24
LIVE FISH DISPLAY	25
THE ART PALACE	25
THE CASINO AND PIER	26
THE STATE BUILDINGS AND EXHIBITS	26
THE TERRITORIES	27
A GROUP OF STATE BUILDINGS	27
OTHER BUILDINGS	27
SPECIAL ATTRACTIONS	28
ARCHÆOLOGY AND ETHNOLOGY	28
GOVERNMENT EXHIBIT	28
INDIAN EXHIBIT	28
NOVEL, QUAINT AND CURIOUS THINGS	28
PHYSICIAN'S BUREAU OF SERVICE	28
MODEL POST-OFFICE BUILDING	28
LITTLE SHIP "SANTA MARIA"	28
STREET IN CAIRO	28
PALAIS INDIAN TEA HOME	28
FOREIGN EXHIBITS	29

LIST OF ILLUSTRATIONS.

	PAGE
BIRD'S-EYE VIEW OF THE CITY OF CHICAGO . . . . Frontispiece.	
TACOMA BUILDING	3
GRAND PACIFIC HOTEL	7
PLYMOUTH CHURCH	11
THE CITY HALL	15
INTERIOR VIEW OF AUDITORIUM HOTEL	19
INTERIOR VIEW OF THE CASINO	23
DINING-ROOM OF THE AUDITORIUM HOTEL	27
INTERIOR OF BOARD OF TRADE	31
HAVLIN'S THEATRE	35
CORNER OF STATE AND MADISON STREETS	39
INDIAN MONUMENT	41
AUDITORIUM HOTEL	43
INTERIOR VIEW AUDITORIUM HOTEL	44
DINING-ROOM OF THE PALMER HOUSE	47
LIBBY PRISON MUSEUM	48
RELIC OF OLD COURT-HOUSE AFTER THE FIRE	50
THE TEMPLE—WOMAN'S CHRISTIAN TEMPERANCE PUBLISHING HOUSE . . .	51
INTERIOR OF PRESENT ROOKERY BUILDING	54
THE ROOKERY BUILDING	55
LINCOLN STATUE	57
RESIDENCE OF POTTER PALMER	59
GRANT STATUE	62
RESIDENCE OF MR. C. V. FARWELL	63
GRANT STATUE	64
POLICEMAN'S MONUMENT	65
HAYMARKET SQUARE—POINT OF ANARCHIST RIOT, MAY, 1886	67
THE LAFAYETTE STATUE	68
GRAND BOULEVARD	70
MICHIGAN AVENUE BOULEVARD	71
CHICAGO HERALD OFFICE	73
VIEW ON STATE STREET	75

LIST OF ILLUSTRATIONS.

	PA
VON LINNE STATUE	
SCHILLER MONUMENT	
CHICAGO WATER WORKS	
SOL'S CLOCK	
JACKSON PARK BRIDGE	
STOCK YARDS	
SCENE IN LINCOLN PARK	
GARFIELD PARK	
ARMOUR ELEVATOR	
INDIAN MONUMENT	
WASHINGTON PARK FOUNTAIN	
A SCENE ON THE CANAL	
OAKWOOD DRIVE	
DREXEL MONUMENT	
THE METROPOLE HOTEL	
JACKSON PARK PAVILION	
WORLD'S FAIR GLOBE	
SEA WALL	
SCENE IN LINCOLN PARK	1
CHURCH OF THE MESSIAH	1
SOL'S CLOCK	1
JACKSON PARK BEACH	1
SOUTH PARK FLAG	1
GATES AJAR	1
DEARBORN STREET DEPOT	1
SOUTH PARK LAKE	1
SCENE IN THE DOCK	1
DEARBORN AVENUE CHURCH	1
FLORAL DESIGN IN SOUTH PARK	1
IN THE STOCK YARDS	1
SCENE IN LINCOLN PARK	1
THE SHELDON RESIDENCE	1
SOUTH PARK SCENERY	1
ST. JAMES' CHURCH	1
LINCOLN PARK LAKE	1
STOCK YARDS	1
WORLD'S FAIR GLOBE	1
SOL'S CLOCK	1
BEACH FRONT	1
FLORAL DESIGN	1

LIST OF ILLUSTRATIONS.

xi

	PAGE
CENE IN SOUTH PARK	135
N THE BEAR PITS	136
,INCOLN PARK FLOWERS	138, 159
,INCOLN MONUMENT	139
)OUGLAS MONUMENT	142
N THE ZOO	143–148
,INCOLN PARK LILY-BEDS	144
;ARTLETTE RESIDENCE	145
,MONG THE LILIES	147
'OMMERCIAL NATIONAL BANK, DEARBORN STREET	149
OUTH PARK LILY PONDS	151
'HE CONSERVATORY	152
,AKE SHORE DRIVE	153
;CENE IN LINCOLN PARK	155–156
ONES RESIDENCE	157
N GARFIELD PARK	160
JICKERSON RESIDENCE	161
ABSTRACT BUILDING	165
N LINCOLN PARK	167–170
AUDITORIUM BOXES	169
3OARD OF TRADE	172
3IRD'S-EYE VIEW OF EXPOSITION GROUNDS	174
;HIPPING YARDS	179
MENADNOCK BUILDING	182
:HAMBER OF COMMERCE	185
NTERIOR OF AUDITORIUM THEATRE	188
ADMINISTRATION BUILDING	193
3OVERNMENT BUILDING	196
PRAIRIE AVENUE	199
WOMAN'S BUILDING	202
:HICAGO UNIVERSITY – WHEN COMPLETED	205
MACHINERY HALL	208
MANUFACTURES AND LIBERAL ARTS	211
ELECTRICAL BUILDING	214
CENTRAL MUSIC HALL	217
TRANSPORTATION BUILDING	220
MINES AND MINING BUILDING	224
ART INSTITUTE	227
MASONIC TEMPLE	230
AGRICULTURAL BUILDING	233

POST-OFFICE . . . .
LA SALLE STREET . . . .
WASHINGTON PARK RACE TRACK . . . .
HORTICULTURAL BUILDING . . . .
FISH AND FISHERIES BUILDING . . . .
STREET SCENE . . . .
ART PALACE . . . .
AUDITORIUM CURTAIN . . . .
PALMER HOUSE . . . .
RANDOLPH STREET . . . .
GREAT NORTHERN HOTEL . . . .
PULLMAN BUILDING . . . .
ILLINOIS CENTRAL R. R. TRACKS . . . .
MARSHALL FIELD'S BUILDING . . . .
AUDITORIUM OFFICE . . . .
GUNTHER'S CONFECTIONERY . . . .
ARMORY . . . .
LAKE FRONT, MICHIGAN AVENUE . . . .
ASHLAND BANK . . . .
FIRST NATIONAL BANK . . . .

PREFACE.

THE story of Aladdin and his lamp is among the most wonderful in the literature of fable, and in history the story of Chicago stands among the most marvellous for great and rapid growth in the annals of the Old and New World. Chicago has sprung into existence "like magic." Its history proves the old adage that truth is sometimes stranger than fiction.

All eyes are now turned towards this great city of the West because therein is to be held, in 1892–1893, THE WORLD'S COLUMBIAN EXPOSITION, by which the nations of the earth are to unite in celebrating the 400th anniversary of one of the greatest events in all history—the discovery of America by Christopher Columbus, October 12, 1492.

In this volume will be found not only a minute account of the GREAT EXPOSITION, but also a historical sketch of Chicago, and a description of that city as it is to-day in its greatness.

Many books have been written upon these subjects, but in this one volume are collected all the most important facts, which are presented in a very attractive and entertaining way, and which makes this work rank among the very best of its kind.

THE PUBLISHERS.

IMPORTANT BUILDINGS

AND

POINTS OF INTEREST IN THE CITY OF CHICAGO.

MICHIGAN AVENUE.

PICTURESQUE CHICAGO

AND

GUIDE TO THE WORLD'S FAIR.

PART I.

A SKETCH OF THE CITY OF CHICAGO.

MATTHEW ARNOLD has called the American people uninteresting because "they had no ancient monuments of man's industry and devotion; no historic past to inspire reverence and kindle imagination; nothing to throw a misty haze over the crude strong realism of the present." I would like first to ask a question. "Does he consider, for instance, the building of a city like the subject of our sketch, to be done without industry and devotion?" Beyond doubt there were both in the very highest degree; true their product is not very ancient, but what is there in the *natural* order of things that would put such a premium on the one and such a discount on the other. And as for reverence; I wonder if there is more reverence, true and sincere, in the breasts of the English nation for their entire historic past than there is in the hearts of the American people for the history of the few short years embraced by the greatest of all wars, the war of the Revolution. Imagination! It isn't possible for a single person within the bounds of such a country, compelled by the force of circumstances to daily remember our past, to live in our present, and to contemplate our future, to be without an imagination the most vivid.

I acknowledge, and with pride, that as a nation our imagination has been schooled by necessity to be practical as well as theoretical but for all that it is imagination, purest and best. Who is th greater, a man like Moore who dreams of a Utopia, or one who bring his imagination within the bounds of reason and creates one?

Faults we have, and many of them; mistakes we have made, an grievous ones; but to be turned down as commonplace and uninter esting, impossible! Mr. Arnold, your criticism is a poor one, poore for you than for us.

Let us leave Mr. Arnold and his unjust criticism and see if w can find something of interest and profit in a short description of on of our greatest cities; a city the story of whose building will one da vie with "Aladdin and his lamp." It has been said, and truly, "tha there is not on record an achievement of human intellect, skill an industry that will bear comparison with the transformation of a dis mal swamp in the midst of a trackless desert, within the space of human life, into one of the mightiest and grandest cities of the globe.'

We will pass over the discovery of the present site and its earl history very briefly.

The world first became acquainted with the Chicago river, c portage, by a map made by the Frenchman, Joliet, who discovered i in 1673. The first settler was a fugitive San Domingo slave, name Pointe De Sable. How he escaped his master and reached Louisiana and afterwards made his way through the wilderness to this point i not known, but that he was settled in a cabin at the mouth of th Chicago river and was leading the life of a trapper there in 1779, i a settled fact. Quite a settlement sprang up. Le Mai bought ou De La Sable. Under him the business and the settlement improved He in turn was bought out, in 1804, by Jno. Kinzie, the first "promi nent citizen."

About this time the government owned a small tract of lan here, six miles square, ceded to it by the Indians. On this land, i the midst of the wilderness, owned by the Indians and claime by both English and French, Fort Dearborn was erected. Thi

TACOMA BUILDING.

move was bold if not reckless. Under the stress of the disastrou[s]
defeats and the general uprising of the Indians in the Northwes[t]
during the war of 1812, the fort was evacuated, and most of th[e]
retreating garrison were killed by the Indians. This broke up, for [a]
time, the settlement of the Chicago portage. The fort was rebuilt i[n]
1814. The government at this time also ordered a survey of th[e]
water courses between the Chicago and Illinois rivers. Jno. Kinz[ie]
and family returned, and again the place had white inhabitants.

In 1830 Chicago was still what it always had been—a militar[y]
post and fur station. It boasted twelve habitations. The old lo[g]
fort (with its garrison of two companies of United States troops), th[e]
fur agency, three taverns (patronized largely by idle, drunken I[n]
dians, who made things lively as long as their fur money lasted), tw[o]
stores (also largely patronized by Indians), a blacksmith shop, th[e]
house for the interpreter of the station, and one occupied by Indi[an]
chiefs. It boasted a large and varied population, never the same tw[o]
days in succession, yet always the same. Most of them were Indian[s]
to be sure, but then there was little else there but Indians and—mu[d.]
Some historian has said that at that time as many Indian tra[ils]
marked the prairie and concentrated at the agency house as there a[re]
railroads now terminating in the city of Chicago.

Once a year John Jacob Astor sent a schooner to the post to co[n]
vey supplies to it and to take away the year's product of fur. On[ce]
a week in summer, and twice a month in winter, a mail rider broug[ht]
the news of the great world to this little outpost of humanity.

Let us pause a moment and glance at two pictures (1832-[9]
drawn by Mr. Kirkland in his "Story of Chicago." Point of obs[er]
vation, the top of the old block-house.

1832—"a lonely, weedy streamlet flows eastward past the fo[rt,]
then turns sharp to the right and makes its weak way by a shallo[w]
fordable ripple, over a long sand-bar, into the lake a half mile to t[he]
southward. At his feet, on the river bank, stands the United Sta[tes]
agency storehouse. Across the river, and a little to the eastward,
the old Kinzie house, built of squared logs, by Pointe De Sab[le]

nearly forty years ago: now repaired, enlarged and improved by its owner and occupant, John Kinzie. A canoe lies moored to the bank in front of the house; when any of the numerous Kinzies wish to come to the fort they can paddle across; when any one wishes to go over he can halloo for the canoe. Just west of Kinzie's house is Duillemette's cabin, and still further that of John Burns. Opposite Burns' place (near South State Street), a swampy branch enters the river from the south; and on the sides of this branch there is a group of Indian wigwams. The north side of the river is all woods, except where little garden-patches are cleared around the human habitations. The observer may see the forks of the stream a mile to westward, but he cannot trace its branches, either 'River Guave' to the north, or 'Portage River' to the south, for the trees hide them. Near him, to the west and south, sandy flats, grassy marshes and general desolation are all he can see. (Will that barren waste ever be worth more than a dollar an acre?)"

1892.—"Close at hand one sees the streamlet, now a mighty channel, a fine, broad, deep water-way running straight between long piers out into the lake; and stretching inland indefinitely; bordered by elephantine elevators; spanned by magnificent draw-bridges each built of steel and moved by steam; carrying on its floods propellers of 100,000 bushels of grain capacity. Looking north, west and south, he sees serried ranks of enormous buildings towering for miles and miles, each one so tall as to dwarf the fort and block-house to nothingness. He sees hundreds of miles of paved streets, thronged with innumerable passengers and vehicles moving hither and thither, meeting and impeding each other, so that sometimes so many try to pass that none can pass; all must wait until the uniformed guardians of the peace bring order out of chaos. Every acre of ground in sight is worth millions of dollars."

The real history of the place begins here. The tide of emigration turned toward the west. Her waste places were taken up rapidly under the "Homestead Act"; Chicago began to assume the appearance of a thrifty village; and from that time on, though interrupted now and then by dreadful calamities, her course has been stead upward and onward.

In 1833 there were no less than fifty families trying to solve th two great problems of how to rid themselves of Indians and mu The Indians were finally disposed of in '35 by the common Unc who bought their land and sent them beyond the Mississippi, an Chicago was rid of them forever. "Walking in the imposing stree of Chicago to-day, how difficult to realize that fifty years have hardl elapsed since the red men were dispossessed of the very site o which the city stands, and were toted off in forty days to point now reached in fifteen hours." How they solved the mu problem we will explain later.

In 1834, when the whole town turned out on a wolf hunt an succeeded in killing about fifty, the records give the number of in habitants as 2,000. In 1835 there were 3,000. Mr. Parton in speak ing of this time gives a graphic sketch of the town and the peopl which we will quote at length.

"The motive must have been powerful which could induce suc} large numbers of people to settle upon that most uninviting shore A new town on a flat prairie, as seen from car windows, has usuall; the aspect which is described as God-forsaken. Wagon-wheels hac obliterated the only beauty the prairie ever had, and streaked it witl an excellent article of blacking. There may have been twenty littl(wooden houses in the place; but it is 'laid out' with all the rigo: of mathematics; and every visible object, whether animate or inani mate,—the pigs that root in the soft, black, prairie mire, the boys. the horses, the wagons, the houses, the fences, the school-houses, the steps of the stores, the railroad platform, are all powdered or plasterec with disturbed prairies. If, filled with compassion for the unhappy beings whom stern fate seems to have cast out upon that dismal plain, far from the abodes of men, the traveler enters into conversa tion with them, he finds them all hope and animation, and disposed to pity *him* because he neither owns any corner lots in that future metropolis, nor has intellect enough to see what a speculation it

GRAND PACIFIC HOTEL.

would be to buy a few. What a pity! You might as well pity the Prince of Wales because he is not yet king."

But, for all the hope and animation of the inhabitants, for many years in all prairie towns it was shunned the most by those who were looking for the pleasant and the beautiful and, no wonder, if there be any truth in the following quotation also from Mr. Parton. "The prairie on that part of the shore of Lake Michigan appears to the eye as flat as the lake itself, and its average height above the lake is about six feet. A gentleman who arrived at Chicago from the South in 1833, reports that he waded the last eight miles of his journey in water from one to three feet deep,—a sheet of water extending as far as the eye would reach over what is now the fashionable quarter of Chicago and its most elegant suburbs. Another traveler records, that, in 1831, in riding about what is now the very center and heart of the business portion of the city, he often felt the water swashing through his stirrups. Even in dry summer weather that part of the prairie was very wet, and during the rainy season no one attempted to pass over it on foot. 'I would not have given sixpence an acre for the whole of it,' said a gentleman, speaking of land much of which is now held at one thousand dollars a foot. It looked so unpromising to farmers' eyes, that Chicago imported a considerable part of its provisions from the eastern shores of Lake Michigan as late as 1838 This Chicago now feeds States and Kingdoms."

Many people ignorant of its real situation are at a loss to account for the startling growth of the place. If they will follow us for a brief space we will try to show them not only that it is not mysterious but that under existing circumstances it could not have been otherwise The only recommendation the place gave to the first settlers was the inlet which offered a chance for a harbor on the coast of a very stormy and dangerous lake, an advantage offered by no better sites. The inlet, or river as it is called, is simply a cutting of the lake into the soft prairie; it was 100 yards wide and ran three quarters of a mile straight into the prairie where it divided into two branches, one running north and the other south and both parallel with the lake shore

These branches extended several miles each. It was originally twenty feet deep, but the mouth was so obstructed that only very small vessels could enter; but nature had done her share and it only wanted the engineer and the dredge to make it capable of receiving the largest ships that sail the lake and to give to the city forty miles of wharves.

Situated at the southern end of Lake Michigan, from eight hundred to nine hundred miles from the principal ports on the Atlantic seaboard; twenty-four hundred and fifty miles from San Francisco, directly on the natural highway from East to West, and from the great northwestern States to the Atlantic; having all the advantages of a seaport town combined with those of a great inland feeder, it is not strange Chicago has grown with the development and accessibility of that wonderful region, of which it is the great depot, exchange, counting-house and metropolis.

Well might these prairies so long considered a wilderness and left to the trapper, the Indian and the buffalo, be called the "treasure-house" of nature, for there is no known spot on this globe where she has been so lavish in the variety and quantity of what man needs for the sustenance and the decoration of his life, or where she has placed fewer and smaller obstacles in his way. "That is the region where a deep furrow can be drawn through the richest mould for thirty miles or more, without striking a pebble, a bog, or a root; and under almost every part of which there is deposited some kind of mineral—coal, clay, stone, lead, iron—useful to man. Besides being well watered by rivers, nowhere is it so easy to make artificial highways—roads, railroads and canals."

The climate although occasionally extremely warm or cold is on the whole remarkably pleasant and healthy. The air is cool and bracing through most of the summer; hot nights are rare. In fact, there is none better. There is, no doubt, a great deal of truth in the theory that the wonderful growth of the city can be attributed in part to the stimulating atmosphere which arouses all the latent energy in the human system and makes possible the hard mental and physical labor of the people.

In 1837 the whole country was depressed and Chicago did 1 escape; for five years there was no increase in her population. F real estate boom fell flat; corner lots, river fronts and lake bord(found no buyers. It is said that there are millionaires in Chicago day only because they could not sell their land at any price duri those years of depression and despondency.

It was during this dark period (1837 to 1842) that Chicago ma her first shipments of salt meat and wheat. In 1838 some reckl(fellow shipped thirty-nine two-bushel bags of wheat across the lak next year 4,000 bushels were exported; the next 10,000; and in 18. it jumped to 600,000. The grain was brought in great canvas-cover wagons, prairie schooners, from the surrounding country, some of coming as far as one hundred and fifty miles and shipped by the lak Before Chicago had a railroad or a canal she shipped two and a hí millions of bushels of grain in one year and sent back most of tl wagons that brought it loaded with merchandise.

The canal connecting the Chicago river with the Illinois, a1 through that river the Mississippi, was finished in 1848. Tl opened up a large area hitherto not profitable to cultivation.

A scheme for a railroad to Elgin was proposed, but opposed l almost every one; they argued that if a road was built to Elgin tl farmers would sell their grain and buy their merchandise there, a1 thus ruin the town. How blinded to their own interests! They d not see their entire success depended on their accessibility to tl Eastern States and to the great prairie world. At last, after mar difficulties, the road was put through by the perseverance of a fe men. Compare the policy of the people then and now.

"When in 1853 the road paid a dividend of 11 per cent. and was found that Chicago had trebled its population in six years aft(the opening of the canal, and that every mile of railway had pour(its quota of wealth into Chicago's coffers, then the truth took posse sion of the whole mind of the city and became its fixed idea, thí every acre with which it could put itself into easy communicatio must pay tribute to it forever. From that time on there has been r

PLYMOUTH CHURCH.

pause, no hesitation; she saw her vocation was to put every goc acre in all that region within ten miles of a railroad, and to conne every railroad with a system of ship-canals terminating in the Missi sippi or the Atlantic Ocean." Since then all the surplus force ar revenue of Chicago has been expended in making itself the centre the great system of railroads and canals that it is to-day.

"The Forties saw the beginning, in a small way, of nearly a the great institutions Chicago now enjoys. In 1841 the first wate works were built. The first propeller was launched in 1842, which year the exports were for the first time greater than the in ports. The first book compiled, printed, bound and issued is said have been in 1843. The first meat for the English market w. packed in 1845. In 1846 the River and Harbor convention me and Chicago was made a port of entry. In 1847 the first permane theatre was opened (Rice's, south side of Randolph street, betwee State and Dearborn streets), and McCormick's reaper factory w started. In 1848 the first telegram was received, being a messa; from Milwaukee, and later the 'Pioneer,' the first locomotive, w. landed from the brig 'Buffalo' and started out on the Galer railway. In the same year the Board of Trade was established ar the canal opened. In 1849 the 'Chicago & Galena Union Railroac was opened to Elgin." Certainly this is a good showing for t(years.

Let us notice here briefly this first railroad, for without th power of steam to annihilate distance all her natural advantag would count for little. As mentioned above, the first locomotive arriv in 1848 on the brig "Buffalo." It was a small affair, built by Bal win, of Philadelphia, weighed only ten tons and had two drive: instead of four, six or eight, now used. The entire equipment of t road consisted of this engine, five flat cars and one box car. On N vember 20 the first train drew out of Chicago amid the cheers of t people who had little to lose and the forebodings of most of those w had much. At the present time over ninety thousand miles of railro centers in Chicago. She is "the greatest railway depot in the u;

verse—more passengers arrive and depart, more merchandise is received and shipped there daily than in any other city on the globe." 1849 was the year of the great flood; all the bridges were swept away, vessels and canal boats broken into kindling by the ice and the wharves ruined. The *Democrat* stated the losses as follows: Damage to bridges, $15,000; to vessels, $58,000; to canal boats, $30,000; to wharves, $5,000. Total, $108,000. In this age, when the cost of a single bridge or vessel far exceeds the total, the loss seems inconsiderable, but to a thoughtful person there is a deal of history in it.

At this time the long disputed and vexing question of the respective rights of landsmen and sailors came to a judicial adjustment. When Lake Street Bridge was begun, its opponents appealed to Judge Drummond, of the United States District Court, for an injunction, relying on the right of the General Government to keep from obstruction the navigable waters under its control. The complaint was dismissed, the learned judge holding that "the right of free navigation is not inconsistent with the right of the State to provide means of crossing the river by bridges or otherwise," when the wants of the public require them. But for a long time there was still trouble; when a favorable wind would blow the vessels would steam up the river in a line that would keep the draw open for hours. This caused great inconvenience and delay to those who happened to want to cross. This trouble is now obviated by the tunnels and by keeping the bridges open for land travel at certain times.

Thus we see Chicago well started on her way as a commercial centre; as we have seen she receives the products of the prairies and ships them East, she receives merchandise from the East and supplies the prairies, but here she is confronted by a new problem—that of economy in transportation. When "prairie schooners" conveyed the grain and the cattle came afoot, when it took a month, under favorable circumstances, to reach the Atlantic Coast, she never gave the matter a thought, but as her facilities increased it did not take her long to see the vast importance of the question; and how thoroughly she has mastered it. The first step was by sending away a great part of wheat in the shape of flour. The output in 1867 wa 30,000 barrels; in 1891 it was nearly 5,000,000. But it is in th transportation of corn that the most surprising economy is effected "A way has been discovered of packing fifteen or twenty bushels o Indian corn in a single barrel. The 'corn crop,' as Mr. S. B. Rug gle once remarked in Chicago, 'is condensed and reduced in bulk b feeding it into an animal form—more portable. The hog eats corn and Europe eats the hog. Corn thus becomes incarnate; for what i the hog but fifteen or twenty bushels of corn on four legs?'"

The business of pork-packing, as it is called, which can only b done to advantage on a large scale, has attained enormous proportion in Chicago, started in 1840, and there were nearly nine million hog received into Chicago in 1891, about one-third of the entire produc of the west. Some of these establishments do a business of one mil lion dollars a week. Chicago not only largely supplies this countr but sends a great deal abroad. Her dealings in beef are even large than in pork; for a number of years the larger part of the fresh bee consumed in our Eastern cities is Chicago dressed.

The western steer is an awkward piece of "raw material" tc handle. In will he is perverse, and his power of resistance is not to be despised, and despite his ugliness he must be shown the greatest consideration; he must not be injured or bruised in any way; he must have two pails of water every twelve hours and he cannot go long without a large bundle of hay. Chicago has reduced the handling of these millions of live animals to a science. That is, they are handled with the greatest possible convenience to man and the least possible inconvenience to the animal. Her methods cannot but be admired and approved. (See Stock-yards later.)

In the "Standard Guide to Chicago," the following very funny description of one of the "guides" at the stock-yards is given. "There is one particular guide at the stock-yards frequently pointed out as an extremely interesting fellow. This is 'Old Bill,' the bunko steer. He is perhaps the most depraved animal in existence. There is no element of brotherly love or patriotism in his nature.

THE CITY HALL.

His duty at the yards is to guide droves of cattle to the slaughter houses. He has mastered his little act ; reduced steering steers to science. Every day he takes his post near one of Armour's packing houses and waits until it is necessary to drive a herd of cattle up t[he] viaduct to the killing rooms. He then joins the drove, ingratia[tes] himself into their good will, and tells them that he knows a good p[as] ture not far away. At his suggestion the cattle think about it a[nd] finally resolve to let him lead them there. Bill, the bunko ste[er] laughs softly and a cruel look lights his eyes. He lopes off throu[gh] the mud towards a large gate not far away. Following after him [is] a hundred or more cattle, every one entertaining a vision of gen[tly] swelling hills covered with long wavy blue-grass and sweet clo[ver] blossoms. Bill leads them to this gate and allows the herd to [pass] through it, while he steps aside and avoids the rush. As the dust [of] the rush clears off a little a familiar figure is observed slowly strolli[ng] away from the gate. It is 'Bill.' On his face is no remorse as [he] saunters back to his post of duty near a tall fence. He is then rea[dy] to betray a couple hundred more of his unsuspecting relations."

Many people rank the packing business the first of Chicag[o] industries; this is a great mistake, because her trade in lumber [is] equally as important and her manufactories are more valuable th[an] the two put together.

The prairies are without timber. Chicago brings lumber fr[om] the upper lakes and sends it all over the prairies. In 1890, she c[om] posed of 2,000,000,000 feet of pine lumber and 3,000,000,000 shingl[es.] Think of the houses that much lumber would build ! To econom[ize] transportation there are firms that sell ready-made houses, sto[res,] churches, etc., and villages for that matter, and will send th[em] securely packed to any part of the country, express paid, on receipt of price. What more can any one ask?

When we left Chicago itself, some pages back, to describe [her] industries, she was nothing more than a thriving country villa[ge.] Great changes have taken place. Her population has increased f[rom] thirty thousand in 1850, to one million three hundred thousan[d]

1891. From 1876 to 1891 there were sixty thousand buildings erected, at a cost of three hundred and ten million dollars, with a street frontage of two hundred and eighty-six miles. Her area in 1835 was nearly three square miles, now it is nearly eighteen square miles. The city frontage on the lake is twenty-two miles and on the river fifty-eight. The distance between North Seventy-first street, being the northern city limit, and One Hundred and Thirty-ninth street, being its southern limit, is twenty-four miles. The city at its broadest point is ten and one-half miles wide. State street has the greatest extension north and south, running from North avenue to the south city limits, eighteen miles; Eighty-seventh, the greatest western extension, running the entire width of the city. Her entire mileage of streets is two thousand two hundred and thirty-five.

The city is no longer a quagmire. For many years, after Chicago had become a flourishing town, the "one unequaled, universal, inevitable, invincible thing about the place was—mud." Mired wagons were an every day sight in the streets. A stage-coach stuck fast and immovable for days has a sign near it "no bottom here." One gentleman says he saw a lady who was trying to cross Randolph Street at La Salle, leave both shoes in the mire and only reach the sidewalk in her stockings. He does not say, however, that he swam out and rescued those dirty pedal appendages; he must have been a very modest or a very ungallant man.

The people were in despair, since water will only run down hill, and part of the town was below the level of the lake. "The first effort at drainage was a curious experiment. Lake Street was excavated to the depth of three feet, deepest in the middle, and planks laid from sidewalk to centre. This did admirably in dry weather. In 'wet spells' the planks were unfortunately not submerged; they were afloat, and under the impact of the wheels and hoofs sent up streaks and shoots of vileness indescribable." Then they tried open ditches, but this was as great a failure as the other. Many were the experiments and many the failures. They could not help it; the

whole prairie was at fault. At last they awoke to the fact tha
nothing could be of any permanent good short of raising the whol
town. At once a higher grade was established, to which all ne·
buildings were required to conform; this was not high enough,
higher one was ordered; even this did not answer, and a third rais
was made. So that now the city stands nearly sixteen feet above tl
original prairie. Think of this task of lifting a city like this out ‹
the mud and water high enough, not only, to make drainage *possib
but perfect*, and to give cellars—they had none before—in whic
books and merchandise can be stored with safety. To us it seems in
credible.

"During the term of years, while Chicago was going up out of tl
mud of the prairie to its present elevation, it was the best place in tl
world in which to develop the muscles of the lower half of the body.
A street would be raised say six feet; then the old houses would l
in the ditch; the new ones of course on the same grade as the stree
so, if a man wanted to be neighborly steps had to be built. "Tl
ups and downs of life in Chicago" was long a standing joke.

This state of affairs did not last long with the better class
people and buildings. The people are too energetic and have to
much public spirit. One of the greatest undertakings along this lii
was the raising bodily, of the huge Tremont House, a solid hotel
large as the Astor, from its foundations to the proper level. Speakii
of this gigantic task, Mr. Kirkland, in his story of Chicago say
"With the trouble came (once more!) the remedy. A contractor w
found willing to raise the whole great high building (the Tremo
House) to its new grade, without even interrupting its business. Tl
cellar was vacated, huge timbers were introduced and placed so as
take upon themselves the weight of sustaining walls, five thousai
jack-screws were placed under the timbers, and a small army of m‹
detailed to work by word of command, one man to four screw
Then, at a signal by the whistle of the foreman, each man gave ea
jack-screw one-half turn; and the whole structure, by imperceptil
steps, rose in the air, the bricklayers building up the walls as fast

there came spare space wherein to lay a course of brick. It was sai
the guests did not know they were mounting toward the sky. How
ever that may be, not a wall was cracked, not the slightest accider
or untoward event took place to interfere with the entire and perfec
success of the novel experiment."

To quote still farther the same author : "Soon after, the entir
brick block of stores facing south on Lake street, and reachin,
from Clark to La Salle street, was similarly treated, and these wer
only specimen instances of a great undertaking ; the lifting of
whole city out of the slough of Despond on to dry ground.

"This enterprise benefited Chicago indirectly, thus: A youn;
man, born in central New York in 1831, grown up without wealth an
educated without help, having a widowed mother dependent on hir
for support, had bravely undertaken a large contract for the raising c
buildings along Erie Canal to the new plane made necessary by th
canal enlargement then recently effected. The knowledge of th
great task to be done in Chicago in the direct line of his experienc
brought him out to the West, and he became the leading house raise
in Chicago. That man was George M. Pullman. After making
much reputation and a little money in his original business, he turne
his attention to the greater job of improving the system of long-dis
tance travel, and began, in a small way, the enterprise which ha
revolutionized the passenger-carrying of the country, and, to som
extent, of the whole world."

Another problem closely allied to this is the question of sew
age. This is a continual source of worry and menace. It ha:
confronted them for years and confronts them yet, but their indomit
able energy and resolution will win here as it has in every other case

"In the remote past, the overflow of the waters of Lake Superio:
and Lake Michigan ran through the Mississippi south to the Gulf o
Mexico, instead of as now—northeast through the Gulf of St. Law
rence to the Atlantic. At the same time Lake Erie was emptying
into the Atlantic through Lake Ontario and the St. Lawrence ; no
by the Niagara, but by the Dundas valley, a channel not far from th

line of the present Welland canal. Then, at some epoch unknown and for some cause unguessed, the Detroit strait and the Niagara strait were opened, Lake Michigan slowly fell about thirty feet, and its outlet (now 'the Divide,' at Summit, close to the city limits, twelve miles southwest of the court-house) gradually filled up with mixed deposit; so that to-day the dry bed of Mud Lake is the sole remaining representative of the once great southward waterway. Within a few years, long before the close of the nineteenth century, the old order of things must be re-established and mighty Michigan once more find its waters flowing southward. The hand of man will compel it again to turn in its bed, and lie with its head to the north and its foot to the south as of old. The canal which is to be built as an outlet will carry a stream of water 160 feet wide, 18 feet deep, flowing 2½ miles an hour. Through this canal the largest steamers might float, but it is not intended that passage through shall be provided for them, because the locks by which they would have to descend (151½ feet) to reach the Illinois river are too small and the river itself is far too shallow for their accommodation. Some Mississippi boats can come to us, but our stately ships cannot go to them. Each must break bulk in Chicago. Also—an important consideration—light draft gunboats may pass and repass freely between the great lakes and the great river. As we stand now, any nation having control of the St. Lawrence and the Welland canal has at least the highway necessary to command Lake Erie, St. Clair, Huron and Michigan with all that lies on their shores. To accomplish the ends desired will cost the Sanitary District (practically the city of Chicago) about $20,000,000.

"The one great object of this ship canal, however, is to dispose of Chicago sewage. When the population was small, the city was drained by the Chicago river and the lake. Years ago it became apparent that a change would have to be made in this respect. The course of the Chicago river is naturally into Lake Michigan, but pumping works were erected at Bridgeport, in the southwestern part of the city, which lift an average of 40,000 cubic feet per minute into the Illinois and Michigan Canal, causing, under ordinary conditions a perceptible current away from the lake. The water thus pumpe into the canal flows south to the Illinois river and thence to th Mississippi. Pumping works at Fullerton Ave., on the north branc of the Chicago river, force water from the lake into that strean diluting its contents, and furnishing the head needed for a flow towar the Bridgeport pumps. This means of disposing of the city's sewag is wholly inadequate to its needs, and the pollution of the water sup ply of the city is constantly menaced. Measures have therefore bee taken to construct a large gravity channel as an outlet for the sew age of Chicago into the Illinois river. The Chicago Sanitary Distric has been formed by act of Legislature of the State of Illinois; nin trustees have been elected to supervise the construction of a channel a corps of engineers has been set at work making preliminary sur veys, and plans are being perfected for a channel which will answe the double purpose of disposing of the city's sewage and establishin a navigable waterway for the interchange of commerce between Lak Michigan and the Mississippi River."

Thus, by one operation, the pumping is obviated, the canal i improved, the river is purified, and the city is rendered more salt brious. The Chicago River will at length be a river; only, it wi. run backwards.

The question of pure water is an important one. Previous t 1854 it was pumped out of the lake; but the increase in population the introduction of sewerage, together with the establishment c packing houses, distilleries, etc., caused such a change in the quan tity of filth flowing into the lake that complaint began to be mad of impurity and offensiveness in the supply from the pumping works Soon "it became so grave that it could no longer be neglected." A this time, be it remembered, the water was taken into the pumpin; well directly from the lake shore, a few piles being driven aroun the inlet about close enough together to exclude a young whale The small fry of the finny tribe passed freely inward, and if the were lucky, they passed out again; if unlucky, they were sucke

INTERIOR VIEW OF THE CASINO.

up by the pumps and driven into the pipes, where they made the way into the faucets of private houses,—even the hot-water faucet in which case they came out cooked, and one's bath-tub was apt t be filled with what squeamish citizens called chowder. Abou this time a most sensational article appeared in the *Times*, gravel asserting that we were all cannibals, eating our ancestors. For, said, the cemetery being on the lake shore, a half mile of the pum ing works was subject to overflow and abrasion by the waves; wher fore the fishes were fed on the dead at the cemetery, were sucke into the pumps, and were then fed to the living in the city! C course this was fun; but it had a lasting effect and made easier th bold experiment that followed. It was an experiment, because n only had no such expedient ever been tried before, it had nev been thought of. The method they employed is something to b proud of, not for its magnitude, but for the simplicity, originalit and boldness of the idea. They ran a tunnel two miles out into th lake, and pumped the water from the bottom of the lake into th mains. The distance is long enough to give them pure water b yond all doubt or accident.

For many years Chicago was only an exchange, a buyer and seller on a large scale. She depended on the East for all her manu factured merchandise, and made nothing herself. Their first effort were in the line of rough agricultural implements; now there is on firm that turned out last year 121,780 reapers and mowers. This about one machine every minute of the day, every working day o the year. Think of it! "Even in this day of gigantic achievement the manufacture and sale by a single establishment of nearly 122,00 machines for cutting grass and reaping and binding grain, durin the briefly passing period of twelve months, is a wonderful perform ance. Had this great number reference merely to such implement as the old-time hand sickle and scythe, it would still be no sma feat; but when it is remembered that these are modern machines t be drawn by horses, and that their weight is from 650 to 1300 pound each, the fact is most stupendously presented; but, being a fact must stand upon the pages of recorded history." This firm manufactures more than one-third of the world's entire output of grain and grass-cutting machines.

"One of the curiosities in the possession of the McCormick Company is a time-worn and weather-beaten specimen of the original Reaper, as invented by the late Cyrus H. McCormick,—the first practical machine that ever entered a harvest field and the admitted type and pattern after which all others are modeled. What volumes the storm-buffeted old landmark speaks to the gray-haired man of the middle West! Why, to watch the old McCormick Reaper was the delight of his earliest boyhood, and, standing in its august presence now, he lives over again the sunny days of life's June, the while the dear remembered faces of father and mother come back to him, and in fancy he feels the 'touch of a vanished hand,' hears the 'sound of a voice that is still!'"

This is only an example; at the present time there is hardly an article of any importance, for railroad construction, for farming, for house building or decoration, for clothing, necessary or ornamental, that is not made in Chicago. At present there are 3307 manufacturing firms, with an actual capital employed of \$210,302,000. These employ 180,870 people, pay \$104,904,000, and their product is valued at \$567,012,300.

"July 3, 1871, was a 'showery day,' that is to say, one and a half inches of rain fell. From that time to October 9, 1871, but two and a half inches fell in all. In other words, in the ninety-eight days there was only a total rainfall equal to a day and two-thirds of showers, about one-fourth the average supply at that season of the year. Such dryness, if perpetual, would make a desert of the grand prairie. Meanwhile, the southwest wind, the hot haze-laden, the thirsty, the grass-killer, the corn-ripener, the hay-fever-breeder, the western sirocco—in short, the prevailing prairie breeze which, even in ordinary seasons, blows strongly and steadily, perhaps four days out of five the year round, and perhaps nine days out of ten during the summer, leaving its mark on the trend of the branches of every plastic tree, from the willow to the cottonwood: this blast blew wit out ceasing.

"It turned the prairies brown and dry as old hay, so that the lighted to the touch, and burned as long as a blade or a leaf was the fire's path. The prairie fires ignited the grass in meadow a the hay in stack, the grain in rick and the corn in shock. The wi sucked all the moisture out of the forests, so that by the square mi and the township, they burned alike the grass and the crops. turned all the wood in wooden Chicago into tinder; and as soon the fittest moment came, turned the tinder into flames and ashes."

Chicago had then a population of about 334,000. The ci limits were, Fullerton avenue on the north, the lake on the ea: Thirty-first street on the south, and Western avenue on the we: about eighteen square miles, or 11,520 acres. The north side h: chiefly wooden buildings, varying from elegant homesteads, occup ing a whole square, to the miles of small, cheap tenements, ea usually standing alone, gable towards the street, and only a few fe from its neighbors on each side, from which it was separated by hu pine fences. The pavements were wooden, but not inflammabl while the sidewalks, almost entirely of pine plank, were general raised, and allowing a free circulation of air beneath, and fit to bu like a box of matches.

"The business part of the south side also contained a great nun ber of wooden buildings; and even the brick structures were, as rule, of flimsy build, with wooden floors, doors, windows, lathing ar roofs. Of the west side no account need be made, except to say th from Jefferson to De Koven streets, to the South Branch, every thir was wooden. Worst of all and most disastrous (and insane), tl water-works (at the foot of Chicago avenue) had a wooden ceiling its engine room, and a wooden roof covered with a thin layer slate.

"The fire of 1871, broke out on Sunday night, October 8t There had been on the previous evening an extensive conflagratic in the west division, involving a heavy loss of property in the lumb

DINING ROOM OF AUDITORIUM HOTEL.

district. The firemen had worked upon the blaze for many hour finally succeeding in subduing it. The department, however, w; pretty well exhausted when an alarm was sounded at nine o'clock c the following Sunday evening. The fire was caused by the upsettir of a little lamp, in a stable, in the vicinity of De Koven and Jeffersc streets, west of the river, and south of Van Buren street. Whether tl lamp was kicked over by a cow belonging to Mrs. O'Leary is question that has never been satisfactorily settled. The fire fir crossed the river at Van Buren street, and soon enveloped the old g; works on Adams street, where the Moody and Sankey Tabernac afterwards stood, and where stately wholesale houses now tow< towards the sky. From that moment the business section of the cit was doomed, for the wind blew a perfect gale, and every momer added to the heat and fury of the conflagration, which marche steadily on, devouring granite blocks with the same ease as destroyed wooden shanties. About one o'clock in the morning had reached and wiped out the Chamber of Commerce Buildinǵ shortly afterwards it had swallowed up the Court-House, whose be tolled to the last minute. Then in one column, it pursued its furiot course eastward, laying Hooley's Opera House, the Times Buildinǵ Crosby's fine Opera House and many other noble structures in ashe Then it moved toward the northeast, and then attacked the whol< sale district at the foot of Randolph street, carrying away the Cer tral Depot, the ruins of which are still standing. Then it formed junction with another branch of the main column after the latter ha demolished the Sherman House, the Tremont House and other ma; nificent buildings in its path. Then there was a general onslaugl upon the city's centre from the left column which laid low all tl buildings lying west of La Salle street, including the Oriental and tl Mercantile buildings, the Union Bank, the Merchants' Insuranc Building, where Gen. Sherman had his headquarters, the Wester Union Telegraph office, and the solid and magnificent blocks of con mercial houses that lined La Salle street in those days. By mornin there was not one stone upon another in this great business centr<

The right column of the fire is described as having started from a point near the intersection of Van Buren street and the river, where some wooden buildings were ignited by brands from the west side. This column had the advantage of a large area of wooden buildings, say Colbert and Chamberlin, 'on which to ration and arm itself for its march of destruction.' It gutted the Michigan Southern Depot and the Grand Pacific Hotel, and destroyed other handsome structures in the vicinity. Passing along the Post Office, the Bigelow House, the Honore Block, McVicker's new Theatre, the Tribune Building, Booksellers' Row, Potter Palmer's store, occupied by Field & Leiter, and all the smaller or less conspicuous structures on the road, it branched off and destroyed the handsome residences and churches on Wabash avenue, and was finally stayed in its southern course at Congress street. The fire crossed over to the north division about half past three in the morning, and among the first buildings to go down was the engine house of the water-works, which, foolishly, had been roofed with pine shingles. The fire was carried here by burning brands which must have traveled a mile and a half in advance of the conflagration. 'This was the system' say Colbert and Chamberlin, 'by which the north side was destroyed: blazing brands and scorching heat sent ahead to kindle many scattering fires, and the grand general conflagration following and finishing up.' The north side was left a mass of blackened ruins by morning. Only at the lake and the northern limits of the city was the fire stayed. The district burned over was bounded on the north by Fullerton avenue, on the west by Halsted street to Chicago avenue and from that point south on Clinton street, on the south by Twelfth street and on the east by Lake Michigan. The total area burned over was nearly three and a third square miles; number of buildings destroyed, 17,450; persons rendered homeless, 98,500; persons killed, about 200; loss, not including the depreciation of real estate or loss of business, estimated at $190,000,000; recovered by insurance, $44,000,000. One year after the fire many of the best business blocks were rebuilt; five years after the fire the city was handsomer and more prosperous than ever; ten years after the fire nearly all traces of the calamity had disappeared.

The finding of a large mass of molten iron by workmen excavating for the new Masonic temple in 1890, called attention to the fact that there were a number of interesting collections of relics of the great fire in Chicago. The most interesting and ornamental monument of the fire is the "Relic House," well-known to North Side and Lincoln Park visitors. In 1872, when the "leavings" of the fire could be had for the asking or the trouble of picking them up, a man named Rettig conceived the idea of building a small cottage out of such material as a melted mixture of stone, iron and other metals. The queer structure was built at North Park Avenue and Central street. Ten years ago it was removed to its present site, near the junction of Clark Street and North Park Avenue, (take North Clark Street cable line), Philip Vinter, becoming the proprietor. Four years afterwards the "Relic House" passed into the hands of its present owner, William Lindemann, who has added a refreshment parlor to the saloon, and made quite a rustic spot out of the relic. The only ruin of the '71 fire, which remains standing, is on a large vacant lot between Nos. 907 and 915 North Clark Street, a few doors north of the "Relic House," on the opposite side of the street. The ruin consists of three sections of red brick wall with stone foundations showing where the chimneys, doors and windows, formerly were. The lot is owned by Hugh H. White, a lawyer, who lives in Evanston. The Chicago Historical Society has a large collection of fine relics, some from the ruins of the society's building, which was the near the corner of Ontario Street and Dearborn Avenue, but most of the relics are donations from Maria G. Carr, Mrs. E. E. Atwater, and various business firms who were burnt out. The Historical Society also has the key to the vault door in the office of the Assistant Treasurer of the United States at Chicago, which was destroyed, together with $1,500,000 in currency, and the books and the vouchers in the office. The key was presented to Henry H. Nash, Cashier. Large oil paintings of Gen. Grant, J. Young Scammon, and Miss Sneed (the

INTERIOR OF BOARD OF TRADE.

woman who Napoleon thought, was the most beautiful in the world, which were saved from the fire, adorn the walls of the society's rooms Mrs. Carr's collection is a curious one, among the burned, melted scorched and twisted things, being a bunch of forks, a mass of type bunch of tacks, pack of cards, a lot of knitting needles, a spool c thread from Field, Leiter & Co.'s dry goods house at Madison an Franklin Streets, hooks and eyes, a package of buttons, three jew' harps, thimbles, marbles, a bundle of melted glass, a piece of glas from Bowen Bros., Lake Street; an old fashioned clay pipe, chin doll's head, three crucibles, a door bell, pen-knives, one being foun under the site of a pulpit; a package of glass beads from Schweitze & Beer's store, a bundle of screws, a walking cane without head o ferrule, necks of glass bottles from Jasger's place, and a package c slate pencils from the Western News Co.'s place. In Mrs. Atwater' collection is a lump of black stuff, which was coffee once upon a time labeled, "Browned too Much," remnants of the stock of a toy house china dolls and playthings, bundle of hair pins, scissors, rosarie without the crucifix, glass beads, and a jet necklace well preserved, box of charred biscuits from the ruins of Dr. Rice's church, a lot c stained and plain window glass from various city churches, and variety of blackened cups and saucers from the ruins of crocker houses.

The city records were burned with the Court-house. No livin; man could lay claim legally to one foot of the burned district; onl the "abstracts of titles" remained, and these were held by privat parties. The narrative of the saving of these "abstracts," as give by John G. Shortall, the owner and saver of them, is of intens interest.

He had returned from church and was about to retire when h noticed the reflection of a great fire; he watched it for a short tim and, surprised at its magnitude, determined to go. So impresse was he that he took his hat and started, not even waiting to chang the house jacket he had on for a coat. He joined with the crow and hurried to the scene of the conflagration. The fire even the:

was beyond control; the crowd could do little but retreat before it; they were completely awed; the noisy stage was long since passed; they worked in silence; not a sound was heard except the roar of the flame and the crackling of the timbers. Out of curiosity he timed the burning of a house about fifty by seventy-five feet, two stories, with a sort of attic—"a very fine house, one of the best of those days." It was destroyed absolutely in eight minutes. The wind had risen to a gale; the whole air was filled with movable embers and with hundreds—thousands—of larger pieces of burning material that had been wrenched away by the wind, and were being hurled along through space, northwesterly, towards his office, one mile away. The building in which his office was situated had a wooden cornice, wooden casings, and all the front windows had awnings. The thought occurred to him that those awnings would be a likely place for embers to lodge; in that case the building was doomed. He determined to cut them down. Not being able to find the janitor he broke in the door and finally succeeded in cutting them loose, but of what use was the removal of a half dozen awnings when the whole front of the building was covered with them. Only one course was left, and that was to procure a truck and remove his valuables *in toto*. By this time the street was full with streams of people; all sorts of vehicles, trucks, wagons were flying northward before the fire. He engaged truck after truck at their own price, but they never returned. At last by force he obtained a small wagon; this was soon filled, and yet not one-fifth part of the books to be saved had been brought down; at this trying moment a friend sent him a large double team truck; at last, after hours of struggling, they had what they wanted. By this time the fire was very near; the glowing embers fell like hail; the air was fairly filled with fire. The truck was soon loaded by the help of some of his clerks who gathered around him. Then a new difficulty presented itself in the report that General Sheridan and his soldiers were about to blow up the building at the corner diagonally opposite. The driver of the truck concluded he would not stay and be blown up for all the people in

Chicago. Mr. Shortall did not blame him at all, but gave him hi choice between the explosion of the building and the explosion of the revolver he held cocked in his fingers. The driver was a very sensible man; he reconsidered the matter and reversed his decision When they started the building was on fire. During the last hour o their stay the court-house and all its contents was burned down.

Only once during this terrible ordeal was the judgment of thi: gentleman at fault; we will give it in his own words: "At one time during these moments (while waiting for the return of the trucks that seemed as years, a most providential thing occurred, well worth considering. I tried to get into the court-house at its eastern door with the intention of carrying our books in for safety, never dream ing of the possibility of *its* destruction—a large stone building, iso lated as it was. I found that east door locked, and I could not ge the key. Had I found it all our books would have shared the fate o the Public Records they duplicated." . . . "Then we started, al being safely stored on the truck. There were two prisoners who hac been allowed to escape from the jail (then in the court-house) and : had one of these two on each side of my overladen truck to hold the books on. I formed the apex of the group, with my pistol, cockec still in my pocket, and directed the truckman to drive forwarc through the rain of fire, so as soon as possible to get to windward o it; and we worked to eastward and southward, through the dense crowds of people who were fleeing towards the north, until we go finally through the fire and brought our precious books down to my house and gratefully stowed them away in safety—in safety if the wind should continue southwest, and not change, of which there was much and natural fear.

"When we arrived at home, my jail-birds, the truckman and I carried the books in, piling them up in the hall library and parlor— got them in any way. There must have been two hundred record volumes—and this I may say, in parenthesis, that it took three trucks to carry those books back again, to where we lodged after the fire. when we built our vault for them in a basement on Wabash Ave

HAVLIN'S THEATRE.

We lost nothing from the truck in that savage passage of wind and fire and insanity."

When the problem of rebuilding came up, the first question was, "Who will lend money where titles cannot be shown of records?" "This agitation was soon quelled by the passage through the legislature of what is called 'The Burnt Record Act,' which provided for the use of abstracts of titles, and other documents (though in private custody) as foundation for the new records, and as proof of ownership under certain careful restrictions. Suits brought under this act had a calendar of their own, and were tried more promptly than other cases. This was the first great step towards perfect relief; the next was the liberal and reasonable course of the 'abstract men.' Luckily for Chicago these 'abstract men' were gentlemen, and instead of taking advantage of the situation they only charged a reasonable price for reasonable service.

"Then came the question whether the city could build, and business credit be re-established by a set of ruined merchants. In answer to this doubt came a cloud of telegrams from Eastern wholesalers and manufacturers reading in this wise: 'We suppose you are burned out. Order from us what goods you want, and pay us when you can.' Many a man who, dry-eyed, had seen his property burn, felt the tears surging up, as he spelled out this message."

A law was passed forbidding the erection of wooden buildings within the city limits; there was some bitter opposition to this; the people thought their burden was heavy enough. But, find one of them to-day who will deny its wisdom. Within six weeks after the fire two hundred and twelve permanent stone and brick buildings were in course of erection in the Southern Division alone. Between Dec. 1, 1871, and Oct. 1, 1872, there were twelve hundred and fifty building permits issued. The total amount spent for building in the first year was $45,000,000, but for all this show of progress the years 1873 to 1878 were years of extreme business depression; some going so far as to call them years of disaster, but this is a great mistake, because years of economical repair and renewal cannot rightly be called disastrous. In 1873, the imports were $300,000,000 more than the exports ; indicating wild extravagance in the use of foreign luxuries. This was soon checked by the "hard times" and economy took its place. Debts were liquidated and the balance restored, so that in 1878 the exports were $300,000,000 above the imports. The process of contraction was not one of destruction, but of reconstruction. Strange it is, but true, that every check which Chicago has ever met, be it war, pestilence or (money) famine, flood, fire or scandal, has only marked a pause in her progress, a halt to gather strength for a higher leap.

A great and splendid city has risen from the prairie, in full view of all the people, who watch, criticize, compare, suggest. How narrow the man who, familiar with the facts, can give anything but commendation! But with all her greatness she stands among great cities an infant. We have tried to describe "the infant;" allow us to give an idea if possible of her maturity :

Date.	Population.	Per Cent. Increase.
1860	109,000	00
1865	178,000	65
1870	306,000	72
1880	491,000	62
1886	703,000	35
1890	1,098,000	55

If as many people come to Chicago during the next three decades as came during the last three, the business man of 1920 will see about him a population of over 10,000,000 of people. Chicago has erected since 1876, 56,240 buildings at a cost of $255,298,879; *i. e.*, the average each year has been about 4017 buildings, at an average cost of $18,235,634. At this rate, thirty years from now Chicago will have built 120,510 new buildings, at a cost of $547,069,020. But during 1889 alone 7590 buildings were put up at a cost of $31,516,000; and during 1890, 11,608 were put up at a cost of $47,322,100. The average number for the two years was 9598.

Should this average hold good for thirty years, in 1920 there would be 287,940 new buildings, which will have been erected at a cost of $1,182,571,500.

The great question respecting Chicago and all other places under heaven is, What is the quality of the human life lived in it? It is well to have an abundance of beef, pork, grain, wool and pine boards so long as these are used as a means to an end, and that end is the production and nurture of happy, intelligent, virtuous and robust human beings. This alone is success; all short of this is failure. Cheerful, healthy human life,—that is the wealth of the world; and the extreme of destitution is to have all the rest and not that. The stranger, therefore, looks about in this busy, thriving city, and endeavors to ascertain above all else how it fares there with human nature. In Chicago, as everywhere, human nature is weak and ignorant, temptable and tempted; and in considering the influences to which it is there subjected, we must only ask whether those influences are more or less favorable than elsewhere. We thoroughly believe that Chicago is learning to interpret this great question aright. Those beautiful temples dedicated to religious worship, those excellent schools of every grade, those local benevolences, those ceaseless battlings with vice, that instinct of decoration, that conscientiously conducted press, those libraries and book-stores, all attest that Chicago does not mean to laboriously cherish the shell of the nut of life and throw the kernel away. It is our impression that human nature there is subject to influences as favorable to its health and progress as in any city of the world, and that a family going to reside in Chicago from one of our older cities will be likely to find itself in a better place than that from which it came.

PART II.

DESCRIPTION OF THE IMPORTANT BUILDINGS AND POINTS OF INTEREST IN CHICAGO.

THE traveled stranger, to whom the great cities of the world are familiar, however he may become impressed with the manners and customs of our people, or with their methods of doing business, and however loth he may be to admit the justice of our claims to pre-eminence in other respects, must acknowledge that this is the best built city in the universe to-day. For nearly twenty years, or since the great fire of 1871 swept over the business center of the city, and laid it in ruins, architecture in Chicago has been steadily marching forward, until we are enabled in 1891 to point out some of the grandest achievements of the art to be found on the face of the earth.

CHARACTER OF CHICAGO BUILDINGS.—The character of the great buildings erected during recent years in Chicago demonstrates that architects have risen to the plane of the highest constructive knowledge in structures. It is not enough to use a material guaranteed by the maker, but Chicago architects themselves now employ engineers for the special purpose of examining and testing each and every piece and passing their individual opinion upon it in a written report, and only such as is accepted by these engineers is used in the buildings. So essential and necessary is this department of architectural engineering considered, that specialists are sent to the mills which furnish the iron and steel structural shapes and beams for buildings, and the metal is not only tested in the ingot, but the strength of resistance is ascertained for every finished beam. The result of all this gives to Chicago buildings which are not only theoretically safe, but known to absolute certainty to be safe down to

the last cubic foot of masonry and the last cubic inch of steel. In
this respect Chicago is unique, and it is a common remark in Eastern
and foreign cities, among those actively engaged in building, that
Chicago to-day erects the best-built structures ever known, and with
the notable distinction that she does it with the closest economy in
material and time. That is to say, that it is a fact that in Chicago

INDIAN MONUMENT (Lincoln Park).

buildings the quality is better, the distribution of material is more
skillful and the buildings are naturally more reliable. The buildings
have all been constructed fire-proof to a degree surpassing those
erected under old methods. Not only are steel and iron used for sup-
ports for girders and for joists, but they are covered with fire clay,
which is so disposed that air chambers are left next to the iron or
steel in every case, making it impossible for the metal to be over-
heated, even by the hottest fires.

AUDITORIUM BUILDING.—Among the many magnificen[t] structures of Chicago, the Auditorium is the greatest. It is the mos[t] famous building on the American continent. At once a grand oper[a] house, a superb hotel and a mammoth office building, there is not t[o] be found on the face of the earth a pile that will compare with it. I[t] represents the modern idea, as the Coliseum at Rome represented th[e] ancient. It is in construction representative of Chicago as a city where art, beauty and utility are so strongly defined though nearl[y] always blended on every side. Cost of building, $3,500,000; wit[h] ground, $5,000,000.

AUDITORIUM THEATRE.—The theatre of the auditoriu[m] building is justly entitled to the distinction of being the best equippe[d] for stage purposes, the handsomest in interior decorative work, th[e] most perfect in acoustics and the most convenient and comfortable fo[r] audiences in this or any other country. Architects and artists of in[-] ternational fame have lauded its merits and its beauties. Thousand[s] from foreign shores, who have visited it during the various notabl[e] performances which have been given within its walls, have been sur[-] prised at its size and magnificence, and gave willing testimony to it[s] superiority over their own famous places of amusement.

CENTRAL MUSIC HALL.—The Central Music Hall Block wa[s] erected in 1879 by a stock company, its list of stockholders compris[-] ing many of the wealthiest and best known citizens of Chicago. It[s] object was "to promote religious, educational and musical purposes[,] the culture of the arts, and to provide for public amusements and en[-] tertainments." The leader in this enterprise was its first manager[,] the late George B. Carpenter, whose experience and success as a man[-] ager, well qualified him for the task. The architect chosen for th[e] building was Mr. D. Adler, of the firm of Adler & Sullivan. It ha[s] a frontage of 125 feet on State street, and 150 feet on Randolph street[,] its central location rendering it easily accessible from all parts of th[e] city. It is built of gray cut stone, has a wide and massive entranc[e] of white marble, is six stories in height, and contains, besides th[e] large auditorium from which the building derives its name, a smal[l]

AUDITORIUM HOTEL.

recital hall, known as Apollo Hall, twelve stores, seventy offices, a[nd] a perfectly appointed photograph studio.

CASINO.—Located on Wabash avenue, near Adams street. Th[is] is conducted after the manner of the Berlin Panopticon, and is pri[n]cipally an exhibition of wax works. Delightful place to spend [a] hour. There is a stage performance every afternoon and evenin[g.] Lyman B. Glover, business manager. Admission to all parts of t[he] house 25 and 50 cents; children 25 cents.

INTERIOR VIEW (Auditorium Hotel).

AUDITORIUM HOTEL.—Situated on Michigan avenue a[nd] Congress street; occupies entire eastern half of the great Auditori[um] structure. It is under the management of the Auditorium Ho[tel] Company, J. H. Breslin, of New York, president; R. H. Southga[te,] vice-president and manager. The building which it occupies is t[he] grandest on the continent, and was prepared to meet the requirements of a great high-class hotel without regard to labor or expense.

GRAND PACIFIC HOTEL.—Located on La Salle, Jackson and Clark streets. The Jackson street front almost faces the Board of Trade. The Clark street front faces the general post-office. The La Salle street front faces some of the immense office buildings in the Board of Trade center. The main entrances are on La Salle and Clark streets. The ladies' entrance is on Jackson street. This building was scarcely completed in 1871 when the great fire swept it out of existence in a single night, although its construction was almost wholly of iron, stone and glass. It was immediately rebuilt and opened to guests in June, 1873. Although acknowledged to be one of the finest hotels in the world when completed, it has undergone many improvements since then.

PALMER HOUSE.—Located on the southeast corner of State and Monroe streets, in the heart of the city, with a frontage on State street, Monroe street and Wabash avenue. Main entrance on State street; ladies' entrance on Monroe street. The building occupies about one-half of the entire block. It covers an area of 76,550 square feet; is nine stories in height, has 708 rooms and accommodates usually from 1,000 to 2,400 guests. The grand rotunda of the hotel is 64 feet wide, 106 feet long and 36 feet in height. The dining room is one of the most elegant in Chicago. The parlors and waiting rooms are superbly furnished. The entire furnishings and fittings of the house are of the first order.

PERMANENT ART BUILDING.—Now in course of construction, on the Lake Front, site of the old Inter-State Exposition Building, main entrance to face Adams street. Within easy walking distance of all railroad depots, street car terminals, hotels, etc., in the heart of the business center. This magnificent structure takes the place of the present Art Institute, Michigan avenue and Van Buren street, which passes into the possession of the Chicago Club. The design of the new institute was prepared by Architects Shepley, Rutan and Coolidge, and was subjected to changes at the hands of the Committee on Buildings. The structure has a frontage of 320 feet on Mich igan avenue; the main depth is 175 feet, with projections makir an arc 208 feet in depth. The plan is that of a parallelogram. consists of two galleries, the first being devoted to plaster cast sculptures, busts, models, etc. ; the second to pictures, being lighte by sky-lights from above.

ART COLLECTIONS.—Private art collections in Chicago a: very numerous and very extensive. This is strikingly evident ; each recurring exhibit of loaned pictures at the Art Institute or els where. The annual exhibits at the Inter-State Exposition, now thing of the past, by reason of the changes necessarily pending th World's Columbian Exposition, have grown from year to year, unt they promise to rank among the best in the country. Steps hav been taken to erect a permanent Art Hall on the Lake Front, i which these annual exhibitions will be continued. This buildin will be erected for the Columbian Exposition, but will be constructe in such a manner as to be acceptable to the city as a permaner building after the exposition closes.

GRAND OPERA HOUSE.—Centrally located on the east side (Clark, between Randolph and Washington streets, opposite the Cour house, close to all the leading hotels and convenient to railroad d pots and street-car terminals. Harry L. Hamlin, manager.

HAVELIN'S THEATRE.—Located on the west side of Wabas Avenue, between Eighteenth and Twentieth streets. John A. Hav lin, lessee; J. S. Hutton, manager. This was originally Baker Theatre. It is a popular resort and deservedly so. The theat building is quite an ornament to the section of the city in which it located ; and the theatre is conducted as a high-class place of amus ment. Seating capacity, 2,000; stage, 50 x 65; proscenium opening 36, to loft, 67. The building is fire-proof and was constructed at cost of $300,000.

BOARD OF TRADE BUILDING.—Situated at the foot of L Salle, on Jackson street, between Sherman street and Pacific avenu in the heart of the business center, and only a short walk from th

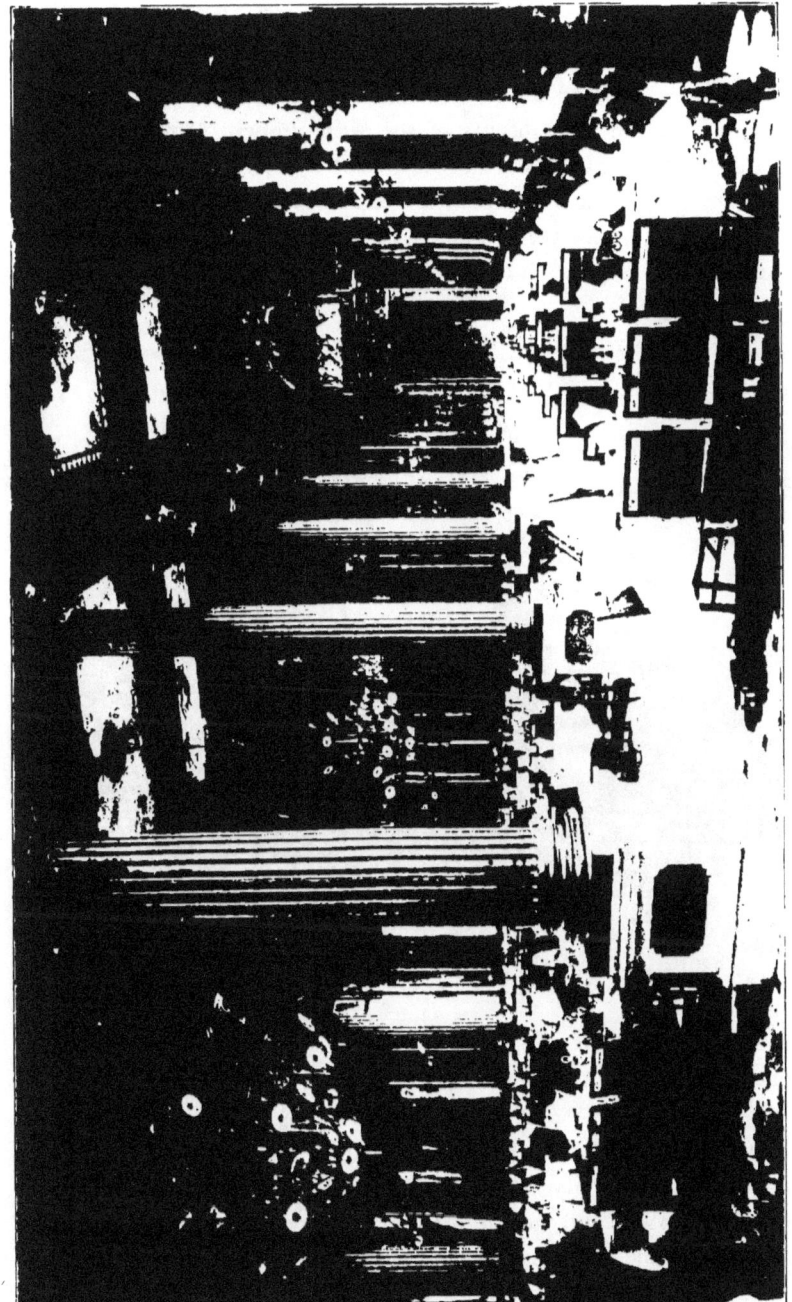

DINING ROOM OF THE PALMER HOUSE.

great hotels, railroad depots and street car terminals. The immens size and architectural beauty of the structure will attract the strai ger's attention. It covers an area of 200 by 174 feet; and is built (gray granite. The beautiful front is surmounted by a tower whic tapers to a pinnacle 322 feet above the pavement. On the top of th tower is the largest weather-vane in the world, a lake schooner 1

LIBBY PRISON MUSEUM.

feet in length, with rigging in proportion. From the street below does not appear to be a fifth of this size.

LIBBY PRISON MUSEUM.—Located on Wabash Ave., betwee Fourteenth and Sixteenth streets. One of the principal permaner attractions of the city. The original Libby prison (transported fror Richmond, Va., and put up, brick after brick, just as it stood durin the War of the Rebellion, when used as a prison for Union soldier is enclosed within massive walls, built after the manner of the middle ages (see illustration). Among the attractions offered in Libby Prison are the following: Portraits in oil of all the leading Northern and Southern generals and statesmen; all kinds of firearms used in America, from colonial times to the present period; the finest collection of shot and shell used in American warfare; the original first dispatches of war from Generals McClellan, Grant, Hooker, Sherman, etc.; the original acceptance of the command of the Confederate Army by Generals Lee and Stonewall Jackson; original portraits of Abraham Lincoln and Mrs. Lincoln, with relics and mementos; the stove, goose and shears used by Andrew Johnson when working as a tailor in Tennessee; the original will made by John Brown an hour before his execution; the very rare curiosity of two bullets that met in mid-air in battle at Petersburg; the finest collection of historic chairs in America; the original photographs of scenes in Sherman's march from Atlanta to the sea; the original commission of Jeff. Davis to Congress in 1845; also his commission in the war with Mexico; the wheel of Commodore Perry's flag-ship, "Powhatan," that opened the ports of Japan to the world; the original Arctic clothing used in the Greely relief expedition. Admission, 50 cents; children half-price; open day and evening.

CITY HALL is one of the most central, as well as one of the most prominent, structures in the city. This building and the Cook County Court-house, adjoining, stand upon the site of the first Court-house erected in Chicago, and also upon the site of the Court-house destroyed in the great fire of 1871. The old Court-house stood in the center of the block, and was surrounded by a green lawn in the nature of a park. It was a handsome building as buildings went in those days, and had a tower in which there was a clock and a great bell. This bell rang out in doleful peals on the fatal Sunday night in October, 1871, almost up to the moment the tower became enveloped in flames. After the fire the bruised and battered bell was taken from the ruins by an enterprising firm and worked up into souvenirs.

COOK COUNTY COURT-HOUSE.—Occupies the entire east half

of the block bounded by Washington, Dearborn, La Salle and Clark Sts., in the center of the business district of the South Side, the west half being occupied by the City Hall. This magnificent pile was erected in 1876-77 at a cost of about $3,000,000, and is one of th

RELIC OF OLD COURT-HOUSE AFTER THE FIRE.

handsomest public buildings in the county. It is at present for stories in height, and two additional stories are to be added durir the present year at a cost of $275,000. In this building are locate the County, Probate and various Circuit and Superior courts, the La Library, and all the County offices, except that of the State's (prosecuting) attorney, which is located in the Criminal Court buil ing, North Side.

FIRST NATIONAL BANK.—At the date of incorporatio the First National Bank had a capital of $100,000. Its office

THE TEMPLE.
Building of the Woman's Christian Temperance Publishing House.

were: president; E. Aiken; cashier, E. E. Braisted. It then stood number 8 in the order of National Banks. The capital of the bank was soon increased to $1,000,000. In 1867, President Aiken died, and was succeeded by Samuel M. Nickerson, who has held the office ever since. In 1868 Lyman J. Gage was appointed cashier. The fire of 1871 destroyed the bank's building, which stood at the southwest corner of State and Washington streets. This building was at once rebuilt, and was occupied until the bank moved into its present magnificent structure, which was erected especially for its accommodation, and with a view to the convenient transaction of its immense business.

CHAMBER OF COMMERCE BUILDING.—This structure occupies the site of the old Chamber of Commerce which was erected immediately after the fire and which was occupied by the Board of Trade until the great commercial edifice at the foot of the street was completed. The new Chamber of Commerce building is in many respect the finest commercial structure in the world and certainly one of the grandest office buildings in the United States. The property upon which it stands cost $650,000, and the building itself has cost Messrs Hannah, Lay & Company, the owners, over $1,000,000.

TACOMA BUILDING—towering above its surroundings to the dizzy height of twelve clear stories. This was among the first of the modern sky-scrapers erected in Chicago. The corner which it occupies was for years covered by a tumble-down brick building put up in haste after the fire. It was wiped out to make room for the "Tacoma." From the twelfth story we are able to obtain a splendi bird's-eye view of the city, and we can see far out on Lake Michigan if the smoke isn't too dense. This is a colony of offices.

TEMPERANCE TEMPLE.—"The Temple," is one of the sight of Chicago, and the equal of any one of the many magnificer structures that now adorn the city. In style it is a combination of the old Gothic and the more modern French. For the first tw stories the material used is gray granite with a dash of pink runnin through it. Above that is used pressed brick and terra cotta. Th harmonizes nicely with the granite, taking on a tone and color the same, with the exception that it will be a darker pink. The frontage on La Salle street is 190 feet, while on Monroe it is 90 feet. In shape the temple is somewhat novel and might be likened to the letter H. It consists of two immense wings united by a middle portion or vinculum. On La Salle street is a court seventy feet long and thirty feet wide, and on Monroe street a similar one of the same length and eighteen feet deep. Facing the grand entrance and arranged in a semi-circle are eight great elevators, and from the front court rise two grand stairways leading clear to the top of the building. A central hall extends north and south on each floor and a transverse one also extends into the wings. The lower courts and halls are resplendent with marble mosaic paving, while plain marble is used in the upper halls. In height the temple is a "sky-scraper," extending thirteen stories toward the heavens.

BRIDGES.—The Chicago river being navigable for lake vessels, and intersecting the heart of the city, a large number of bridges have been required. No less than forty-five now span this small stream. Nearly all are swinging bridges, and many of them are operated by steam. Steel construction has been employed in the bridges most recently erected. Among these, the Adams street bridge is a notable structure. It is a four-track bridge, 259 feet long on center truss, and 57 feet in width. This bridge is two feet three inches lower at the east end than at the west end, and, at the same time is reversible, the turn-table track being set on a grade of one in 115. Some doubts were expressed as to its feasibility when the plan was proposed, but the city engineers say that no bridge in the city works better than this one. The *Rush street draw* is one of the longest in the world. The Lake, Wells and Jackson street bridges are handsome structures. The present bridge at Madison street is to be moved to Washington street, and one of the finest bridges in the city erected in its place.

VIADUCTS.—In few instances do railroads enter the city above or below the street level. Grade-crossings are the rule. Engineers have long sought to remedy this state of affairs, which will probably be accomplished in time; but, meanwhile, some relief is being provided at the most dangerous crossings by the erection of viaducts. There are thirty-five of these structures in the city, the longest and finest of which is on Twelfth street, extending from Clark street to Wabash avenue, crossing the tracks of the Atchison, Topeka and Santa Fe Railroad Company, and costing $209,736.

INTERIOR OF PRESENT ROOKERY BUILDING.

"ROOKERY."—After the great fire of 1871 the municipality erected for temporary use a two-story brick building on the half block bounded by La Salle, Adams and Quincy streets, and the alley between La Salle and Clark streets and called it the City Hall. It was also occupied by the Courts. The structure was put up in great haste and without regard to architectural beauty. It is stated that pigeons used to flock to the building, induced thither by a glass roof

THE ROOKERY BUILDING.

which surmounted a disused water tank which occupied the center of the structure and by the oats which fell from the feed-bags which the fire marshals used for their horses on the Quincy street side. The story goes that one day a gentleman marched into Mayor Medill's office to complain of the pigeon nuisance and spoke of the building as a "rookery." Whether this was the real origin of the term or not, the newspaper reporters got into the habit of calling the building the "rookery," and it was generally understood that they alluded to the dilapidated condition of the structure, which from the day it was finished began to fall to pieces. At any rate the name clung to it as long as the building stood, and when the present magnificent structure took its place its owners decided to retain it.

LAKE AND RIVER FRONTAGE.—The city has a frontage on Lake Michigan of twenty-two miles and a river frontage of about fifty-eight miles, twenty-two and one-half miles of which are navigable.

LAKES AND RIVERS.—There are three lakes within the present city limits containing an area of 4,095.6 acres, as follows: Calumet Lake 3,122 acres, Hyde Lake 330.8 acres, the portion of Wolf Lake lying within the city limits 642.8 acres. Of these Calumet and Wolf are navigable. There are two rivers within the corporate limits; the Chicago river, with north and south branches, which divide the city into districts known, respectively, as the North, South and West "Divisions" or "Sides"—and the Calumet river, with Big and Little Calumet rivers, which penetrate the extreme southern part of the city.

MASONIC TEMPLE.—This most marvellous structure, taken as a whole, is in the center of the business district. The idea of a grand Masonic temple in Chicago had been encouraged by Western Masons for the last twenty years. Numerous agitations of the project were started but fell through, partly for want of some one who was willing to take the responsibility, and partly because the money could not be raised. For, though the Masons as individuals are wealthy, the lodges are kept poor by their liberal charities and funeral expenses. In 1873 Norman T. Gassette, then eminent commander of the Apollo Commandery, renewed the agitation of this subject, in connection with a special effort to secure for the site of such a temple the lot at the northeast corner of Dearborn and Monroe streets, on which the Stock Exchange now stands. But there was no adhesiveness among the Masons whom he was able to interest in the scheme, and the old trouble of a lack of money killed it. The last and successful effort in behalf of this enterprise originated in December, 1889, when Gil W. Barnard and Dr. J. B. Fatrich, of

LINCOLN STATUE (Lincoln Park).

Van Rensselaer Lodge, issued a call for a meeting of prominent Masons to consider this subject. This call had several other names appended to it, among which was that of Mr. Gassette, and was addressed to sixty Masons. The meeting took place in Mr. Barnard's office in the same month. The result was that General John Corson Smith appointed a committee of ten, with Mr. Gassette as chairman, to select a location for a Masonic Temple, to devise ways and means for erecting the building and to report to a meeting of the craft to be held subsequently. The committee addressed itself to the task with great energy, and about a month later a meeting of 120 members of the craft was called at the Oriental Consistory preceptory to hear their report and consider their recommendations. The committee in the meanwhile had had several sites offered them, but had definitely selected the lots at the northeast corner of State and Randolph streets. The report was heard and approved in many particulars, and the committee was discharged. Immediately thereafter, however, the meeting appointed Norman T. Gassette, Amos Grannis and E. R. Bliss a committee to carry out the plan that had been proposed. There was no particular organization and everything devolved on this committee, with no instructions but to "go ahead." The committee took the meeting at its word and went ahead in the most approved fashion. In less than a month, without any organization or corporate authority whatever, it had purchased the site for $1,100.000 and opened books for stock. On April 4th, the Secretary of State issued articles of incorporation to the Masonic Fraternity Temple Association, with Norman T. Gassette, Amos Grannis, E. R. Bliss, John Buehler and C. H. Blakely as directors. The officers subsequently elected were: Norman T. Gassette, president; Amos Grannis, vice-president; E. R. Bliss, secretary; and Warren G. Purdy, treasurer. The company was capitalized at $2,000,000, and the price of stock was fixed at $100 per share. The building is pronounced to be one of the finest in the world.

POTTER PALMER.—While the citizens' meetings and the city council meetings were passing resolutions and enacting meaningless ordinances, Mr. Palmer was developing a plan for the widening of State street, in his own mind. This plan was a simple one. He carried it out. How? By presenting the city of Chicago with the frontage, taken from his own lots, necessary to give this section of State street a uniform width. He did it modestly. It was done so quickly and so quietly that the citizens and the city council were taken by surprise. There was no further business, so far as State

RESIDENCE OF POTTER PALMER.

street was concerned, before them, and they adjourned. The sac:
fice made by Mr. Palmer was a great one. Every foot of the pro
erty he so generously gave away for the public good represented
large sum of money. Nobody has ever heard him speak of it, ho
ever. Only old citizens remember it now. Potter Palmer's gene
osity made State street what it is to-day, for if it had not bee
widened the retail business would have long since sought anoth
avenue not far away. And while I am on this subject, I want to s;
to you, not exactly what I think about Potter Palmer, but what ;
Chicagoans who know anything about this man *feel*. To Pott
Palmer, more, perhaps, than to any living man, is due the prese
greatness of Chicago. His influence has always been a mighty, if
silent force, in the development of this city. He has never lost fai
in her future. Time and again his counsel, his judgment and I
purse have saved the credit of the community abroad. When t:
reaction which followed the civil war set in, when values becan
demoralized, when the shrinkage in prices destroyed the capital
some of the strongest houses in existence here, Potter Palmer sto
as firm as a rock between our merchants and bankruptcy, and col
pelled their creditors to make fair and honorable terms. After tl
great fire, though one of the heaviest sufferers, he was one of tl
first to step into the debris and proclaim that Chicago should n
only be rebuilt, but should arise from its ashes greater than eve
The story of the rebuilding of the Palmer House, which we w
see farther down the street, if properly told, would read like
fairy tale. By day and night, under the blaze of the sun and
the glare of torches and calcium lights, the work never ceas
until the magnificent structure was completed. Practically pem
less, then, and for years afterward, Potter Palmer commanded u
limited credit at home and abroad. The man's integrity was I
capital, and it secured for him the means whereby he has be
enabled, during the past twenty years, not only to retrieve t
fortune he had lost in a single night, but to build up a new and
greater one. The great retail houses which we see on either si

of the street, as far as the eye can reach, have all grown up during a remarkably brief period. The oldest of them, in comparison with European houses are merely in their infancy. We will have to stand close to the edge of the sidewalk or we will be carried along by the crowd. I don't think you ever saw so many well-dressed people anywhere. Most of them are ladies. There is a good deal of what the world calls style to be seen along here at all hours of the day.

MARSHALL FIELD & CO.—You have heard of Field's before. Everybody in this country has, and, in commercial circles at least, the house is known throughout the civilized world. It is not only the greatest dry goods establishment in this country, but greater than any in existence abroad. This is the retail store; the wholesale house we will see later on. Perhaps you remember that the style of the firm only a few years ago was Field, Leiter & Co. Mr. Leiter retired, and Mr. Field remained, forming a new partnership, and great as the house was when the dissolution took place—a dissolution, by the way, which surprised and startled the country at the time—it is three times as great to-day. The American merchant, who in point of wealth and vastness of business dealings must be ranked first among "the rich by honest brains and industry," is a man whose name is unfamiliar to most readers. His home is not in New York but in Chicago, and even there he is personally little known in comparison with the prominence to which his position in the business and social world entitles him. He is the head of the great house of Marshall Field & Co., general merchants.

GRANT STATUE, LINCOLN PARK.—Situated on the North Shore Drive, Lincoln Park. A magnificent monument to the memory of the great general of the Civil War. The sculptor was Louis T. Rebisso, an exile from his native land for the part he took in striving to establish a republic in Italy. Whilst the signs of public mourning were still visible in Chicago there was a spontaneous movement for the erection of a monument to General Grant. To suggest was to act; to act was to execute. Within a year the requisite fund was subscribed, and an award of $200 made to Rebisso of Cincinnati for presenting the most acceptable design. The result is before the public in the unique equestrian group unveiled amid the impressive ceremonies of October 7, 1891. There have been many attempts in sculpture to image General Grant, but we can recall none more suc-

GRANT STATUE (Lincoln Park).

cessful than Mr. Rebisso's. The physical proportions of the majestic figure are as faultless as the facial expression. Grant was about five feet seven inches high, with a well-knit frame, the image of conscious strength and matchless endurance. He had a square and spacious forehead, a strong lower jaw and firm-set lips. His hair and whiskers were always worn short. His habitual expression indicated repose and firmness, without assumption or severity. No more im

RESIDENCE OF MR. C. V. FARWELL.

posing and successful specimen of monumental art graces any city in the United States.

HAYMARKET MASSACRE.—Night of May 4, 1886. The title is a misnomer. The tragedy recalled to mind by the name in reality occurred on Desplaines St., between the Haymarket and the alley which runs east from Desplaines St., south of Crane Brothers' manufacturing establishment. The wagon from which the anarchist speakers addressed the mob stood directly in front of Crane Brothers'

GRANT STATUE (Lincoln Park).

steps, about eight feet north of this alley. The bomb was thrown from the mouth of the alley and exploded between the second and third companies of policemen, as the six companies were halting close to the wagon. The bomb thrower unquestionably made his escape through the alley, which connects with another opening on Randolph St., east of the Haymarket. Seven policemen were killed outright, or died shortly afterward of their wounds, as a result of the explosion. A large number of policemen were badly and permanently injured. How many of those in the mob were killed or died afterward of the injuries they received in the police fusillade which followed the explosion has never been known, for their bodies were quietly buried and their wounds concealed by their friends whenever possible. The arrest of the leaders, Fielden, Spies, Engel, Lingg, Neebe, Schwab, Fischer, the searching of the *Arbeiter Zeitung* office, on the east side of Fifth Ave., near Washington street, and the dis-

POLICEMAN'S MONUMENT (Haymarket Square).

covery there of a vast supply of dynamite, arms, bombs and infernal machines; the discovery of bombs in different parts of the city, under sidewalks, in lumber yards and at the homes of the anarchists; the sensational surrender of Parsons, who had taken flight on the night of the massacre; the long trial, the speeches, the sentence, the appeal; the refusal of the Supreme Court of the United States to interfere; the efforts made to have the death sentence commuted; the day of execution, the 11th of November, 1887; the shocking suicide of the "tiger anarchist," Lingg, in his cell at the jail; the hanging of Parsons, Spies, Engel and Fischer, the commutation of the death sentences of Fielden and Schwab to life imprisonment, all contributed toward the popular excitement which followed the fatal 4th of May and continued until the gallows and the prison had performed the parts assigned them by the law. The executed anarchists are buried at Waldheim Cemetery. The cell in which Lingg committed suicide is directly in front of the "cage" in the county jail. The other anarchists occupied cells in the same row. The police monument at the intersection of Randolph and Desplaines Streets, (Haymarket Square) was erected by the citizens of Chicago in honor of the brave officers who risked or sacrificed their lives in defense of the law, and in commemoration of the death of anarchy in this city.

HAYMARKET SQUARE.—That portion of West Randolph street between Desplaines and Halsted streets, West Side. Near the east end of the square for many years stood the West Side Market House, a part of which was occupied as a police station. The square is now entirely open, the police monument being the only obstruction in the broad thoroughfare. To the north of the monument, on Desplaines street, the bomb was thrown on the night of May 4, 1886.

J. V. FARWELL COMPANY.—The great dry goods house of J. V. Farwell & Co., one of the largest in the world, and doing a business of over $40,000,000 per annum, was incorporated as a stock company on December 13, 1890; the board of directors are: C. B. Farwell, J. K. Harmon, J. V. Farwell, Jr., J. T. Chumasero, F. P. Potter, J. E. Downs and S. Farwell. The officers are: C. B. Farwell, president; J. K. Harmon, vice-president; J. V. Farwell, Jr., treasurer; J. T. Chumasero, secretary.

LOGAN STATUE.—To be erected to the memory of the late General and Senator, John A. Logan. Soon after the death of Gen. Logan, in 1887, the Illinois Legislature passed an act appropriating $50,000 for a monument of John A. Logan and for the appointment of commissioners therefor. The monument was to be erected "at such point in the City of Chicago or elsewhere in the State of Illinois

as may be selected by his widow," and the commissioners were authorized and empowered to receive proposals and to contract for the completion of such monument and to receive subscriptions therefor. It was further provided, that if the place selected for the monument should be a public park, the commissioners in charge of such park should be "authorized, empowered, and directed to place the

THE LAFAYETTE STATUE.

monument upon a site so selected by said widow, and to provide tha such monument shall be made the permanent resting place of the re mains of said John A. Logan and of his widow after her death When the bill was passed in 1887 it was the intention to erect th monument some place in the South Parks. The commissioners, o a majority of them, expressed an intention to erect the pedestal, an it was proposed to enlarge the appropriation for the monument b popular subscription; by subscription among the veteran soldiers and among the friends and admirers of the dead soldier-statesman. But, as time passed on, there were no subscriptions from any source, and the promoters of the project came to the conclusion that the $50,000 appropriated by the State would be the only available fund.

MICHIGAN AVENUE.—Formerly a residence street along the Lake Park, has changed materially within a few years. It is now Michigan Boulevard. It will probably become the great hotel avenue of the city. At present some of the grandest structures in Chicago are located along its west side. At Adams street is the Brunswick, and on the opposite corner is the Pullman building, which is more or less of a hotel. On the northeast corner of Jackson street is located the Argyle apartment building, which is really a large family hotel. North of it, on the ground owned by the Jennings estate, and occupied by Leroy Payne's stables, there will be a hotel. On the southwest corner is the Leland, and then the Richelieu. Next comes the Beaurivage, which has been remodeled into a hotel by the owner, L. J. McCormick, who will call it the Victoria. These three hotels occupy the entire block between Jackson and Van Buren streets. At the northeast corner of Congress street is the greatest of all, the Auditorium. Within three or four years the Auditorium Hotel Company will acquire possession of the Studebaker building, which adjoins it on the north, and which will be re-arranged so as to be suitable for hotel purposes. Between Harrison and Twelfth streets there are several large apartment buildings which answer the same purpose as family hotels. At Park Row and Twelfth street is the site selected for the new hotel, which will rival the Auditorium. The Batchelder interests will build at Twenty-second street, and at Twenty-third street the magnificent Hotel Metropole is being builded. There will be at the southeast corner of Thirty-fifth street a large apartment building. These different enterprises are gradually changing Michigan avenue from a thoroughfare of fine residences to a semi-business street which has no parallel in Chicago.

GRAND BOULEVARD.—This is one of the fashionable drives

of the South Side. Commencing at the southern extremity, where it joins Washington Park, we will walk up. Among the handsome residences we pass to the right and left are those of Judge H. M. Shepard, Mr. Charles H. Aldrich, Brice Worley, John W. Conley, Mark Webster, William W. Peck, H. E. Henderson, Patrick McManus, S. J. Gorman, Norman T. Gassette, J. H. Campbell, S. P. Parmly, E. Frankenthal, J. McMahon, Judge Gwyne Garnett, John

GRAND BOULEVARD.

F. Finerty, George E. Cole, and, as the political calls say, "many others." I have not asked you to go through the south parks with me, because you have all the information I can give you regarding those beautiful places in your possession already. I will let you take the parks in yourself later in the evening, and we will wind up our day's trip now by walking west on Thirty-ninth street, and north on

MICHIGAN AVENUE BOULEVARD.

Michigan boulevard. All of the streets running north and south and east and west in this neighborhood are interesting to the visitor, for they are beautifully built up and inhabited by people of means and culture. We can only notice them casually as we pass, however. From Thirty-ninth street, north to Twenty-second street, the east and west streets, with one or two exceptions, are considered desirable residence avenues. Especially is this the case with Thirty-third, Thirty-seventh and Thirty-ninth streets. The latter is a boulevard connecting Grand and Michigan boulevards. Passing west on Thirty-ninth street, we admire the cheerful aspect of the houses and find ourselves on

MICHIGAN BOULEVARD.—Michigan avenue is the popular name; but the street is a boulevard and under the control of the park commissioners. Prairie, Calumet, Lake, Ellis, Grand, the Lake Shore Drive or Ashland,—Michigan is the finest of them all. What a magnificent stretch of perfect roadway! Stately and elegant are the residences of the boulevard, with their handsome lawns and their wide-spreading shade trees, rising on either side until the street narrows to a beautiful country lane a mile to the north! The roadway is as level as the top of a billiard table. Here are some of the finest mansions in the city,—mansions of the new and golden epoch in Chicago's history.

NEW BUILDING OF CHICAGO HERALD.—There is probably not another building devoted to the publication of a newspaper in the world equalling it in magnificence, and certainly there is none other in which so much attention has been given to completeness of detail. On entering the imposing counting-room, the visitor will at once notice the fine Italian stone mosaic with which the floor is hand inlaid, the counter of black Belgian marble, surmounted with black iron, wrought in graceful designs, and the sixteen columns of genuine Sienna marble; also the Italian marble wainscoting. They will also be interested in the working of the automatic tubes, which convey advertising matter to the composing-room and news matter to the editorial floor. Passing four long distance telephones, entrance is had to the visitor's gallery, overlooking ten Titanic presses. Next in point of interest is the composing-room, to which the visitor ascends in either of the two great elevators, framed in hand-wrought iron, and which travel up a shaft walled from top to bottom with the finest Italian marble. The walls of the composing-room are white enameled, and it is finished throughout in marble, iron and oak. Even

CHICAGO HERALD OFFICE.

the type stands are of iron, with the monogram of *The Herald* wrought in gold in each, and there are cases for 180 men on straight composition, to say nothing of those employed on advertising copy. Electric calls at each case connect with the copy-box, in the front of which is a perforated peg rack where are assorted slugs, numbered on both sides for every compositor, and by which the copy cutter tells at a glance what and how many men are working on "time" copy.

An aerial railway takes advertising copy from the copy-box to the "Ad" department, and the proof from thence to the proof-readers. Electric call speaking tubes connect the principal departments of the building. The foreman's office is on an elevated platform, from which he can survey his entire force. Every compositor has a clothes locker, and the marble closets are unsurpassed in elegance by those of any hotel. Filtered ice-water, with a solid silver, gold-lined drinking cup, a restaurant finished in marble and oak, and provided with reading tables and library, are other provisions for the compositors. Four hundred electric lights illuminate this department, adjoining which is the stereotyping-room with its two-ton metal-pot, improved mailing machine, matrix drying and matrix trimming machines. A Turkish bath and marble-walled toilet-room is one of the luxuries afforded to the workers in this room.

ASHLAND BLOCK.—Located on the northeast corner of Clark and Randolph streets. Planned by Architect D. H. Burnham. Property leased from A. G. Alexander, of Louisville, Kentucky, by R. A. Waller, of this city, and L. Broadhead, of Kentucky, for a term of years. This building is sixteen stories high, with a frontage on Clark street of 140 feet and 80 feet on Randolph street. The exterior is classical. The windows of the lower stories are recessed and end in an arch at the third story. The principal entrance is from Clark street and is twenty-one feet wide. This extends to a height of two and a half stories and is finished in terra cotta of a delicate design. The first story has eight stores on the Clark street side and three on Randolph street. The second floor contains several spacious banking rooms 17 feet high and the remaining floors are divided into about 350 offices. Seven elevators are placed in the rear hall of the building. This building was ready for occupancy in May, 1892.

COLUMBUS BUILDING.—To be erected on the southeast corner of State and Washington streets, after plans by W. W. Boyington. The structure will be fourteen stories high, two floors being contained in the ornamental space above the cornice. It will cover

VIEW ON STATE STREET.

the lot, with its frontage of 100 feet on State street and 90 feet on Washington street. It will be constructed of stone, steel and terra cotta, after the best models. A main feature will be the two stores on the ground floor, on either side of the main entrance. Each will be forty feet wide. The decorations and fixtures will cost $175,000. At the rear of each will be a glass mosaic, one showing Columbus a the Court of Isabella and the other his landing in America. The contract for these mosaics has been placed in Venice. The ceiling beams of the stores will be of bronze, supporting Mexican onyx ceilings. Over the entrance to the building a ten-foot bronze statue of Columbus will be placed, which is now being made at Rome. The floors throughout the building are to be of mosaic.

The height of the tower from the sidewalk to the top of the glass globe will be 240 feet. The globe on top is to be of opalescent glass, with the continents marked in color, with a cut jewel locating Chicago, to be lighted with a 3000-candle-power electric lamp. The style of architecture in detail is Spanish renaissance. The various coats of arms of Spanish royalty will be shown in the cornice and elsewhere. Work will be begun May 1st, and the structure will be completed May 1, 1893. The building will cost about $800,000.

THE "CRIB."—The original crib is situated about two miles out in Lake Michigan, almost directly east of the foot of Chicago avenue. "The Man at the Crib," is Captain Charles McKee, who with his family, has spent eleven years in that desolate, wave washed and tempest-battered granite home. He has reared a family of five girls and one boy, all of whom are married, except one girl. Besides his wife and daughter, three men and a dog occupy the crib at present. The crib-keeper's quarters are comfortable. During the winter months, when ice floes threaten to clog the grated mouth of the water tunnel, his duties are as severe as they are important. There are thousands of visitors at the crib during the summer months; in the winter it is sometimes difficult to reach it with the city supply boat. The visitor can take an excursion boat, steam or sail, on the lake shore, foot of Van Buren street.

VON LINNE STATUE.—Erected to the memory of Carl von Linne, or Linnæus, as the world calls him, an illustrious native of Sweden. The statue is of bronze, of heroic size, on a white marble pedestal, and it overlooks the little common near the foot of Fullerton avenue. The spot is one of the prettiest in the park. The monument is encircled with fine trees, and it looks south over a fine expanse of landscape. It cost the Linnæan Monument Association

VON LINNE STATUE (Lincoln Park).

which built it $22,000, and is one of the handsomest monuments in the West. The statue was unveiled May 23d, 1891.

WATER-WORKS.—The water-works of Chicago are among the wonders of the city, not alone because of their magnitude, but because of the magnificent engineering features which they present to the intelligent or curious visitor. The great central pumping works of the system are as follows: Foot of Chicago Avenue, North Side. These works are at the Southern end of the Lake Shore drive. West Side works, corner of Blue Island Avenue and Twenty-second street. Central pumping station, West Harrison street; between

Desplaines and Halsted streets. To visit the different "cribs" situated in Lake Michigan, during the summer months, take excursion boats on the lake shore, foot of Van Buren street. The fare for round trip is 25 cents. The area of Chicago is about 181 square miles, the greater part of which is thickly populated, requiring good facilities for an abundant supply of water. This is drawn from Lake Michigan by a number of separate water-works, all of which are

SCHILLER MONUMENT (Lincoln Park).

operated upon the same plan. Owing to the perfectly level plain upon which Chicago is built, there is no natural elevation available for the establishment of reservoirs. The water, when drawn from the lake, is pumped directly into the mains against a stand-pipe head of about 100 feet.

WATER TOWERS—For the benefit of those who do not understand the principles of water distribution in a great city, the following

CHICAGO WATER WORKS.

explanation is given: A tunnel from the crib in the lake is built on an incline so that the water pours into a well under the water-works In getting there it has been allowed to fall several feet below the level of the lake. When the pumping is light, of course the water rises in the well to the level of its source—the lake—but in Chicago the demand is so strong that the pumps keep the water in the well several feet below that in the lake, raising the water from a distance maybe sixteen feet below lake surface. After the pumps have thus raised the water their work is just begun. They must now force it out the mains and into the houses, just as an ordinary well pump with the valve in the bottom of the well instead of up near the pump handle, brings the water to the pump spout. The use of the tower is now shown. Take away a section of the masonry and there remains an upright pipe. A description of the West Side water works tower will serve as an illustration. There the stand-pipe is five feet in diameter and about 167 feet high. It is made of plate boiler iron about five-eighths of an inch thick, and looks like an ordinary engine boiler, except in length. When the water passes the valve in the pump it passes through the main pipe close by the base of this tower, or may pass under the tower. An opening allows the water to run out of the pipe into the tower stand-pipe. At the West Side works there are four of these main pipes, all opening into the stand-pipe. Now comes the essential part, which is very simple, when understood. The pumps are started, say at a pressure of forty pounds to the square inch of surface. The water is forced out along the mains, and through the opening into the tower stand-pipe. That will raise the water about two and one-third feet in the stand-pipe for each pound of pressure, which is about ninety-three feet for the forty pounds. The weight of the water in the pipe represents that power, and stands there as an elastic spring or cushion, rising and falling, equalizing the pressure on the water faucets and pipes. If every one having faucets on the main should close them, the water pumped in the main would have an escape through this pipe, and the result can be imagined—the pipe wouldn't hold it very long if the pumps were not stopped. But there is an indicator, like the hands on the face of a clock, which shows just how much water is being drawn, or how much of the power is used, and the engineer regulates his pumping accordingly. After the above explanation it may be simply stated that the stand-pipe in the water tower furnishes an equalizer, so that when an engine is running at a given rate of speed or pressure, the turning on or off of a few more or less faucets by

SOL'S CLOCK (South Park).

consumers may not seriously and too suddenly affect the pressure and supply.

POST-OFFICE.—The limits or jurisdiction of the postmaster of the Chicago Post-office covers less than one-third of the area of the city proper, the outlying offices being entirely distinctive, and having postmasters of their own. The central or general office is located in the business portion of the city. It has eleven carrier stations and twenty sub-postal stations, distributed at various points within said jurisdiction. The force employed consists of about 769 regular carriers, 200 substitute carriers, 842 regular clerks, sixty substitute clerks, and about 90 persons in charge of sub-stations and stamp agencies, making a total of 1701 paid employes. Of this force, 105 carriers, 57 horses and 52 wagons are employed in the collection of the mail from the street letter-boxes.

JACKSON PARK BRIDGE.

UNION STOCK YARDS.—Located on South Halsted street, in the former town of Lake, now within the corporate limits, about five and one-half miles southwest of the City Hall. The Union Stock Yards were organized and opened in 1865. The Stock Yards Company at the present time own 400 acres of land—320 acres in one block and eighty acres in outlying lots. The larger tract is devoted to the stock yards; some 200 acres being devoted to yards, etc., while the balance is occupied by railroad tracks and car sidings. Before you, as you enter the main archway, is a town with twenty miles of streets, twenty miles of water-troughs, fifty miles of feeding-troughs

STOCK YARDS.

and about seventy-five miles of water and drainage pipes. Besides the regular water-works supply there are a number of artesian wells, having an average depth of 1230 feet. The plant of the Union Stock Yards Company proper costs about $4,000,000. Present capital about $23,000,000. The plants of the various packing companies cost, it is estimated, in the neighborhood of $10,000,000. During the year 1891, 3,250,359 cattle, 205,383 calves, 8,600,805 hogs, 2,153,537 sheep, and 94,396 horses were received at the yards, the total value of which was $39,434,777. There were slaughtered 2,184,095 head of cattle, 157,052 calves, 5,638,291 of hogs, and 1,465,332 sheep. The shipments of live stock from the yards were 1,066,264 cattle, 48,331 calves, 2,962,514 hogs, 688,205 sheep, 87,273 horses. The Stock Yards to-day are one of the wonders of the world. Twenty great trunk railroads, fed by hundreds of branches which stretch like a mighty octopus over the land, deliver and carry away the raw and manufactured articles which arrive at and depart from this spot. During the early morning the Western roads are busy unloading their freight of cattle, hogs and sheep, while in the afternoon the Eastern roads are equally busy taking delivery and loading up the stock that is going to Boston, New York and countless other points. At the packing-houses the work goes on all day—one train following another carrying away the finished product of the butcher and packer. The Stock Yards Company own all the railroad tracks (over 150 miles in all), and do all the switching or shunting connected with the business of the Yards. Every railroad company has a direct communication with the Yards, either through its own tracks or by the Belt line; at any rate, they can all get there without trouble, and no delays take place. The yards can accommodate, at their fullest capacity, over 30,000 cattle, 200,000 hogs, 30,000 sheep and 4,000 horses, and while at times they are taxed to their fullest limit, yet as a rule the stock is well and carefully looked after. As the trains come rolling in, the Company take charge of the stock; and its location, name of firm to whom consigned, description, etc., are detailed in the office of the Company.

Some idea of the magnitude of operations at the stock-yards may be formed from the following figures with reference to the great house of Armour & Co. The firm did a business amounting to $66,000,000 during the year ending April 1, 1891. The hogs killed by the house numbered 1,714,000; cattle, 712,000; sheep, 413,000. Armour & Co.'s employes numbered during this period 7,900, and the aggregate wages paid was $3,800,000. The firm had 2,250 refrigerator cars. The total area covered by the buildings of the firm was fifty acres; total floor area of buildings, 140 acres; chill room and

SCENE IN LINCOLN PARK.

cold storage area, forty acres; storage capacity of buildings, 130,000 tons. The Armour Glue Works made 7,000,000 pounds of glue within the same period, 9,500 tons of fertilizers, grease, etc. The ground covered by the buildings of this department cover fifteen acres, and the number of employes is 600.

GRAIN ELEVATORS.—The visitor to Chicago will be surprised and interested by a visit to some of the great grain elevators of the city. The greatest elevators in the world are to be found here, and they are more numerous than in any other city on earth. A few figures in relation to one of them will serve as a description for all.

A grain elevator of the first class costs about $500,000; 12,000,000 feet of lumber is consumed in its construction; the outside brick wall is sixteen inches thick; a fire wall, two feet thick, usually divides the building in the middle; the height is about 155 feet; length, 155 feet; as a protection against fire iron ladders run this entire height and on all floors there are electric push buttons communicating with annunciators in engine room, and in the latter department there is also a fire pump with a capacity equaling that of four steam fire engines. Two hundred bar-

SCENE IN GARFIELD PARK.

rels of water, each accompanied by a couple of iron pails, are scattered about over different floors, and twenty-two chemical fire extinguishers are placed at convenient stations throughout the structure; forty-five fire plugs, to each of which is attached 1,000 feet of two and one-half-inch rubber hose, together with fourteen fire alarm boxes, about complete the precautionary measures for combating the devouring element; the superintendent and chief engineer are located at opposite extremities of the bulky framework, the one in a separate brick office building, with an electric instrument within

ARMOUR ELEVATOR.

reach, by which he is enabled to converse with the heads of departments, and the other in a large two-story, fire-proof brick building, where he takes pleasure in showing visitors a little bottle of river water after it had been transmogrified in passing through the granite filter. Once every week a fire drill is ordered, the time of turning in an alarm for which is known only to the watchman in charge. When the alarm is sounded every man takes his place, but no water is thrown. These drills demonstrate that the structure may be deluged with water in exactly seven seconds. It requires 100 employes

INDIAN MONUMENT (Lincoln Park).

to run a grain elevator; to move the ponderous machinery a 1,000 horse-power compound Corliss engine is required, making fifty-six revolutions per minute without varying one revolution in a day's run. This is one of the most elaborately finished pieces of mechanism in existence, and was constructed at a cost of $50,000. The diameter of the drive-wheel is twenty feet, and that of the shaft eighteen inches. Crank pins fourteen inches in diameter and fourteen-inch steel pins are provided, the momentum of which adds impetus to the work of the engine. The main belt is of rubber, 200 feet in length and five feet in width. It is the largest bit of rubber ever manufactured from any material by any firm for any purpose, requiring special machinery in its construction. The chimney of the elevator has a 14-foot base and an altitude of 154 feet.

WASHINGTON PARK CLUB.—Situated at South Park avenue and Sixty-first street. Take Cottage Grove avenue cable line. Organized 1883. Occupies an unpretentious though commodious club

WASHINGTON PARK FOUNTAIN.

house, within easy access of the Washington club racing park, south of Washington park. It is a combination of the higher class of sporting, country and city clubs, members of nearly all the other leading clubs being connected with it. The club house is more in the nature of a rendezvous than a resort, and is handsomely fitted up for the comfort of the members and the ladies of members' families. The racing meetings of the Club are of national celebrity.

ARMOUR MISSION.—Located at Butterfield and Thirty-third streets. Take State street cable line. Directors—Philip D. Armour, J. O. Armour, William J. Campbell, John C. Black, P. D. Armour Jr., Edwin Barritt Smith; Rev. Howard H. Russell, pastor; established in November, 1886. This magnificent charity owes its origin to a provision in the will of the late Joseph F. Armour, bequeathing $100,000 for the founding of such an institution. He directed that the carrying out of his benevolent design should be chiefly intrusted to his brother, Mr. Philip D. Armour, who, accepting the trust so imposed, has given to it the same energetic and critical attention that he has given to his private affairs. He has greatly enlarged upon the original design and in consequence has added enough from his own resources to his brother's bequest of $100,000 to make the present investment about $1,000,000. Armour Mission is incorporated under the laws of Illinois. In addition to the Mission building proper, the Armour Mission corporation owns the Armour Mission Flats, consisting of 194 separate flats. The entire revenue derived from the rents of these flats is used for the maintenance of the Mission and its departments. The corporation also owns adjoining ground upon which Mr. Armour has recently erected a manual training school, not yet ready for occupancy. The Mission is a broad and wholly non-sectarian institution. It is free and open to all, to the full extent of its capacity, without any condition as to race, creed or otherwise.

UNIVERSITY OF CHICAGO.—The *newest* thing in the city is the new University of Chicago. The old institution of that name after a struggle for existence for nearly thirty years, succumbed to financial difficulties in 1886, and suspended its educational work. So profound, however, was the conviction that Chicago was the ideal location for a great institution of learning, that efforts began to be made almost immediately looking to the establishment of a new university. It was soon found that John D. Rockefeller was interested in the project. In 1888 the Baptists of the United States organized the American Baptist Educational Society, and elected Fred. T. Gates its corresponding secretary. Mr. Gates soon became persuaded that

A SCENE ON THE RIVER.

the first great work for the new society to undertake was the establishment of a new university in Chicago. He and Mr. Rockefeller entered into correspondence, and to their conferences with each other Chicago owes its university. In May, 1889, the Education Society resolved to undertake the raising of $1,000,000 to found a well-equipped college in this city. Mr. Rockefeller at once made a sub-

OAKWOOD DRIVE.

scription of $600,000, conditioned on the subscription being increased to a full $1,000,000 within one year. T. W. Goodspeed was associated with Mr. Gates in the effort to raise the $400,000 required by this condition. Not only was this done within the time specified, but $150,000 more than was required was secured.

Marshall Field gave a site of a block and a half valued at $125,000, but now worth much more than that sum. To this gift from Mr. Field there has since been added two and a half blocks, making the present site four blocks. The intersecting streets have been vacated by the city council so that the site consists of a solid block 802 by 1,261 feet, or nearly twenty-four acres.

CHICAGO LIGHT.—Chicago light is located on the inner pier, north side of Chicago river; was established in 1859; is a third order fixed white light, in a black skeleton iron tower; visible sixteen miles. This is the principal one of seven lights maintained by the government as aids to navigation near the mouth of the Chicago

DREXEL MONUMENT (Drexel Boulevard).

river. The harbor here is the most important on the lakes, with a greater average number of daily arrivals and departures during the season of navigation than any other in the United States. This city is in the ninth light-house district, with Commander Charles E. Clark, United States Navy, as inspector, and Major William Ludlow, of the Corps of Engineers, United States Army, as engineer. The eleventh district formerly embraced the three great lakes—Michigan, Huron, and up to the national line of Superior. The ninth is a division of the eleventh district. It includes all aids to navigation on

Lake Michigan, Green Bay and tributary waters lying west of a line drawn across the Straits of Mackinac at the narrowest part east of McGulpin's Point light station. Since the boundary of the district was established a fog signal has been placed at Old Mackinac Point, in the Straits, which is also included in the ninth district.

CRIB AND BREAKWATER LIGHTS.—There are two lights on the old breakwater, both established in 1876; one of these, the south light, is a fifth order light, and the north is a lens lantern. At the new breakwater there are three lights, tubular lanterns, tended by two laborers. The light on the old north pier is a sixth order light, and has a fog bell struck by machinery. Calumet light, at South Chicago, is on the outer end of the pier north of Calumet river, eleven miles southeast of Chicago breakwater. It is a fourth order light, red, thirty-three feet above lake level, and is visible about twelve miles. It was established in 1873. Formerly it was in a tower rising above a structure on shore, but was in 1876 removed to its present quarters, which is fully a mile out on the pier. A beacon light is established at the old Crib. This light-house is provided and maintained by the city of Chicago.

GROSSE POINT LIGHT.—The best light and light-house near Chicago is that at Grossé Point, just north of Evanston. It was established in 1873, and as it now stands complete has probably cost the Government more than $100,000, in addition to the expense of maintenance. Grosse Point light is a second order, fixed white coast light, varied by a red flash every three minutes, the regularity of the flashes being controlled by clock-work. The "lantern" is a prismatic lens, equaling in power 163 candles, and this feature of the outfit alone cost $15,000. The tower, from the water's level to the centre of the lens, is 120 feet, being built of brick and having ninety-nine piles placed beneath the stone foundation.

THE PUBLIC LIBRARY.—The Public Library occupies the entire fourth floor of the City Hall (excepting council chamber). Was founded in 1872. The library contained on January 1st, 1892, 171,709 volumes, and the collection is increasing by purchase and

THE METROPOLE HOTEL.

donation at the rate of somewhat over 10,000 volumes annually. I
literary treasures, many of which can not be duplicated at any cos
are at the lowest estimate valued at $275,000. With an annual ci
culation and consultation of over 1,500,000 volumes, it leads the ci
culation of the free public libraries of the country. At the Paris E:
position of 1889 it received the distinguished honor of an award of
gold medal, on an exhibit consisting of the annual report, findin
lists and a volume showing in detail the administration of the librai
in every department. A reading-room is maintained, which la
year was patronized by 500,000 visitors, 450,000 periodicals bein
given out across the counter. There are also reference department
including general, patent and medical, which are consulted by thoi
sands of people in search of special knowledge, annually.

HOTELS.—There are at present between fourteen and fifteen hui
dred hotels in the city of Chicago, including small and large, and house
of all grades, but excluding lodging houses, boarding houses an
distinctively family hotels, where no transients are received. Th
united capacity of these hotels is estimated at 175,000. It is believe
that they could, if pressed, accommodate 100,000 additional guest
But this will not be necessary. Numerous immense hotels are eithe
projected or being constructed at the present time. The spring of 18c
will find Chicago ready with ample hotel accommodations for 500
000 guests. Neither the boarding houses, nor houses where furnishe
rooms may be rented, nor lodging houses, are considered here
Outside of the hotels there are eating houses or restaurants and café:
with an estimated feeding capacity at the present time of 25,000 pe
sons daily.

CHICAGO ATHENÆUM.—In the summer of 1890 this honore
institution, which has justly been called "The People's College,
entered upon the most promising period of its history, at the openin
of its twentieth year. At that time the Board of Directors, compose
of some of the best known and most influential citizens, with Ferc
W. Peck, Esq., as president, secured a valuable property 91 x 97 fee
at 18 to 26 Van Buren street, one of the choicest locations in the city

which has been enlarged to a seven-story building and fitted up in the
most attractive style, with all desirable conveniences. The property
was purchased for $200,000, besides which $90,000 have been expended in the improvements. Situated in the very heart of the city,
close to the Art Institute, and in the same grand square on which the
Auditorium stands, it is destined to become a recognized educational
center, and one of Chicago's most beneficent institutions. The Athe-

JACKSON PARK PAVILION.

næum entered its new home in March, 1891. From the date of its
organization in October, 1871, its animating spirit has been philanthropic. Though a private corporation, it has always maintained the
Athenæum solely for the public good, having been chartered as an
institution not for pecuniary profit. The benefits that it has bestowed
upon this city cannot be over-estimated. Open daily throughout the
year, and five evenings a week for nine months of the year, with an

able corps of twenty-nine teachers and a large list of studies—all elective—young men and women may enter at any time, without examination, and receive the desired instruction at moderate cost.

COOK COUNTY HOSPITAL.—Situated between Wood, Harrison, Lincoln and Polk streets, West Side. Take Ogden Avenue, Taylor street, or Van Buren street car. One of the largest public hospitals in the world. It is conducted under the management of a

WORLD'S FAIR GLOBE.

Warden, appointed by the County Commissioners. The visitors will be much interested by a walk through the spacious wards and corridors of this immense institution. The Cook County Hospital was established in 1865, though it did not begin its work until January, 1866. Previous to that time the city had been accustomed to board its sick at Mercy Hospital. But in January, 1866, it fitted up two wards in the old City Hospital, at the corner of Eighteenth and

THE SEA WALL.

Arnold streets, and moved to them twelve patients from Mercy Hos
pital. These wards were soon filled and additions to the building wer
erected. But very soon these also were overcrowded, and in 1876 th
institution was removed to its present location, at the corner of Wes
Harrison and Wood streets. The new buildings, which were not al
erected at the same time, consist now of a long administration build
ing of imposing appearance, and a pavilion of four wards, and a win;
of three wards on each side of it, with generous spaces between al
these buildings, conducing greatly not only to their appearance, bu
to the light, ventilation and comfort of the wards. They are situate
on a lot containing twelve acres of ground. During the six month
ending January 1, 1889, there were received and treated 3,25
cases, and during the six months ending July 1, 1889, 3,903 case:
showing an increase of 648. As there were 435 patients present o
January 1, 1889, and 488 on July 1, 1889, the number in the hospit
during the two periods respectively was 3,690 and 4,391. So that, ɛ
large as the institution is, it is only a matter of time when its va:
accommodations will have to be increased to keep pace with th
growing wants of the city.

FIRST REGIMENT I. N. G.—Organized in August, 1874. A
the first meeting held in behalf of the undertaking forty-eight me
enrolled themselves. In January, 1875, having grown into seve
companies, the regiment took quarters on Lake street, adopted i
uniform—the same it wears to-day—and received its equipment
arms from Springfield. In February of that year the regiment wɛ
assembled and bivouacked in the armory during the Relief and Ai
Society riotous demonstration. On May 13th it made its first publ
appearance with 520 men in line. Since that day its popularity hɛ
never waned. In 1877, during the railroad riots, the regiment twic
dispersed mobs at the point of the bayonet without firing a sho
In 1878 the First removed to its armory on Jackson street. Durin
the riots of November, 1886, at the Union Stock Yards and oth
points in the city, the regiment was called into service to quell di
order. Since then its history has been one of peace and continue

prosperity. The enrollment at present is 650 men. Upon the rolls of the regiment is no small number of names which have won renown on bloody fields.

PRAIRIE AVENUE.—Prairie avenue is the avenue of avenues in Chicago. There are people, and very nice people, and very wealthy people, and I might add very exclusive people, living on other avenues, but on no avenue in the city are there to be found

SCENE IN LINCOLN PARK.

the homes of as many people whose names are so closely allied to the enterprise, the progress and the culture of Chicago. The Sweenie residence is on our left as we move south, and we pass the homes of Josiah H. Boyer, Joseph L. McBirney, Walter H. Wilson and John H. Hamline, on the same side of the avenue. On the other side are the handsome residences of John G. Shortall, Henry L. Frank and of P. E. Studebaker, the wagon and carriage manufacturer. Next

door to him lives William R. Sterling. A little further down is
Mr. Granger Farwell's place, and opposite is the home of the great
coal merchant, Robert A. Law. South of Mr. Farwell's are the
homes of Hugh J. McBirney and Isaac M. Linville, and the residence
of George M. Pullman is a noble mansion, but far from being the
home which you supposed Pullman lived in. Mr. Marshall Field's
is an elegant, but unostentatious mansion. Like the homes of the

SOL'S CLOCK (Lincoln Park).

neighboring millionaires, there is nothing about P. D. Armour's
residence suggestive of the great wealth of its owner. It is a handsome dwelling as to exterior; as to interior, it is fitted up with a
regard to comfort principally, but at the same time an air of genteel
refinement and elegant luxury pervades every part of it. From this
point south we pass, on either side of the avenue, the homes of many
of the leading people of Chicago. As a rule the dwellings are mod-

est. The new fads in architecture, or what Joe Gargery might have called architectitooralooralism, have not found their way into favor along here to any great extent as yet. The street is as quiet as a country lane. Even the banana man's voice is hushed. No noise breaks the dignified stillness of Prairie avenue, save the occasional whirr of an Illinois Central suburban train as it flies by the back yards of the buildings on the east side. Although close to the business center, the numerous annoyances of city life are practically left behind by the busy men who make their homes here when they enter its secluded and sedate precincts.

FARWELL HALL.—A celebrated assembly room, and the Young Men's Christian Association. Farwell Hall in its time has held many notable gatherings. It was here that P. P. Bliss, the composer of sacred music and sweet singer, delighted vast audiences day after day for months during the great Moody & Sankey revival period. Yes, he's dead. Went down with his wife and a score of others in the horrible Ashtabula railway accident. Here Moody and Sankey have held forth frequently, and here also, Francis Murphy has preached gospel temperance to multitudes. Others equally well-known have been heard from the platform, among them no less a personage than George Francis Train. It was in Farwell Hall that the bolt occurred among Republicans which resulted in the defeat of Grant and the nomination of Garfield in 1880. The Young Men's Christian Association uses this hall frequently for large gatherings, noonday prayer meetings, etc. Passing over La Salle street we come upon the fronts of two blocks of buildings which will probably be transformed during the next three years. This part of Madison street is not up with the times. Restaurants, billiard halls, saloons, second-hand book stores, news-stands, etc., monopolize it.

McCORMICK HARVESTING MACHINE COMPANY.—Cyrus H. McCormick, president; Eldridge M. Fowler, vice-president; E. K. Butler, general manager. Offices, corner Wabash avenue and Congress street; works four miles southwest, on the south branch of

JACKSON PARK BEACH.

the Chicago river, at the corner of Blue Island avenue, accessible from the business center of the city, via Blue Island avenue street-car line.

This immense establishment is of such magnitude in itself, and of such world-wide scope in its influences, as to make it the paragon of the nineteenth century business enterprise.

SOUTH PARK FLAG.

NEWSPAPERS.—There are published in Chicago 24 dailies, 260 weeklies, 36 semi-monthlies, 5 bi-monthlies, and 14 quarterlies, making a total of 531 daily and periodical newspapers. The fact was disclosed in the last report of the postmaster general that the quantity of newspapers mailed by the publishers at the Chicago post-office equalled the amount mailed at Boston, Cincinnati, New Orleans,

Buffalo and Baltimore combined, or at St. Louis, Cincinnati, San Francisco, New Orleans and Baltimore combined, and also at Philadelphia, New Orleans, Baltimore and Cincinnati combined, or in the entire thirteen Southern States, with St. Louis combined, amounting to 20,000,000 pounds of serial matter. The newspapers of Chicago have contributed wonderfully to the growth, to the prosper-

GATES AJAR (Washington Park).

ity and to the fame of the city. To her great dailies is Chicago particularly indebted for the intelligent and wide-spread publicity they have given her at home and abroad.

TRIBUNE.—Location of publication office, southeast corner of Madison and Dearborn Sts. The Chicago Tribune Company, proprietors. Joseph Medill, editor-in-chief. The *Chicago Tribune* is a daily newspaper, with every equipment necessary to the successful

conduct of a great journal. It has the advantages of age and experience, and the means to present to the public the fullest and most reliable information of events transpiring in the world. Its building, erected after the great fire of 1871, on the site of the former structure, was planned and completed for the home of a great newspaper. There is no facility lacking. Its presses, manufactured to order, combine the very latest improvements, and have the speed necessary to supply any demand that may arise. In every department where mechanics are important, the *Tribune* is unsurpassed. In its arrangements for the collection of news the *Chicago Tribune* acknowledges no superior in its profession. Its correspondents, many of whom have a national reputation for their intimate knowledge of, and prominence in, political and social affairs, are under instruction to deliver to the *Tribune*, up to the latest hour in every morning of the year, impartial and full reports of every event, regardless of expense. Its financial reports are relied upon by bankers, capitalists and operators; its record of occurrences at home makes it a family daily; its political and literary features are among the ablest and most discriminating in the country.

COLUMBIAN ASSOCIATION.—Principal object the improvement of the home through the enlightenment of housekeeping as to scientific sanitation, relative value of various foods, and the most hygienic and economical method yet discovered of preparing them. There has been some concern lest women should, as their horizon widened, rush as a mighty, one-minded multitude out from their homes and leave the hearthside deserted. The widespread and enthusiastic interest which has been awakened by the proposition of the founders of this association to afford housekeepers reliable scientific information which will enable them to conduct their households more successfully shows that women first of all are anxious to improve their homes and that with all their gettings they greatly desire to get the understanding which will enable them to do so.

The association numbers about one hundred members and is really the outgrowth of the committee on household economics of the world's congress auxiliary, of which Mrs. John Wilkinson is chairman and Mrs. Thomas F. Gane vice-chairman. The members of the committee on household economics are elected by the general committee of the world's congress auxiliary and its meetings are open only to its members. The meetings of the Columbian Housekeepers Association are open to any one interested in their work.

SOUTH PARK LAKE.

GERMAN SOCIETY OF CHICAGO.—The German Society of Chicago (Deutsche Gesellschaft von Chicago, Ill.) was established in the month of May, 1854, under the name of Society for the Protection and aid of German Immigrants (Huelfs-Verein fuer Deutsche Einwanderer), and owed its origin to the fact that both the vast increase and the growing importance of German immigration to this country called for some means of protection to those immigrants who

SCENE IN THE DOCK.

were ignorant of our language and the peculiar conditions of this country, and who, on that account, might easily be taken advantage of by the dishonest and unscrupulous in our community.

OGONTZ ASSOCIATION.—Founded by the Chicago Alumnæ of the Ogontz School in 1891, who conceived the idea, in the name of their alma mater, of a lunch room for self-supporting women. The following plan was adopted: each active member subscribed $10 in annual dues, and each associate member subscribed $15, while many added their gifts of furniture, table furnishings and books. In addition friends and well-wishers added greatly to their contributions by placing their names upon the guarantee fund. In February, 1891, all arrangements were finally completed. Two sunny rooms were selected on the thirteenth floor of the new Pontiac building, which stands in the midst of the printing district, on the corner of Dearborn and Harrison Streets. One room was tastefully fitted for a reading and reception room, and provided with an excellent assortment of books, magazines and games; also tables, comfortable chairs and a piano. Over this room three or more members of the Ogontz Association preside daily; one to attend to the books, which may be taken from the library if returned within two weeks, and one to act as cashier. Others play, sing, or assist in making the lunch hour pleasant, and become acquainted with the members of the Lunch Club.

A monthly payment of ten cents entitles any wage-earning girl or woman to full membership, and enables her to obtain a wholesome lunch at small expense. Tea, coffee or milk is sold for two cents, homemade sandwiches or rolls or cake for five cents. During the summer ice cream and iced tea are served, and through the winter hot bouillon is furnished.

The light and pleasant lunch-room, which opens from the reading room, is well supplied with neat tables and chairs, muslin curtains and a cupboard for china. At one end stands the lunch-counter, behind which gleam tea and coffee urns. Here each member receives from the matron, assisted by one of the members of the Ogontz

Association, her order, accompanied by a check, and is at liberty to seat herself at any table. Many prefer to bring their own luncheon, and desire only a cup of tea or coffee.

BAPTIST MISSIONARY TRAINING SCHOOL.—Located at 2411 Indiana Ave. The first school established in this country devoted to the training of young women for missionary work is the one located in Chicago, conducted by the Women's Baptist Home Mission Society. The society itself is exceptional in being the first organization of the kind composed wholly of women, and was the result of a pressing demand from all parts of the country for missionary work, which only women could do, among women and children. Thirteen years ago so urgently was this need set forth by Miss Joanna P. Moore, who had been a nurse during the war, and remained in New Orleans on her own responsibility to work among the colored people; also by Mrs. C. R. Blackall, who had spent some time in the Indian Territory, and who declared that the need there was epitomized by an Indian woman, who said to her, "We want to live like Christian women, but we don't know how:" and others, who saw in different parts of the country the necessity of work among the women and children of the foreigners, who were then, as now, pouring into this country at the rate of seven and eight hundred thousand per annum, that the ladies of the several Baptist churches in the city decided to organize a society for this work. The representatives of the different churches throughout the country, excepting those from Boston, were in favor of making Chicago the headquarters of the organization, not only because it had its inception here, but because of the central location. The New England women, however, decided to organize a separate society. The society organized here now has between thirty and forty thousand regular members, and was last year in receipt, from all sources, of between $60,000 and $70,000.

WATER TRANSPORTATION.—A large number of steamers ply between this city and points on all of the lakes, and on the St. Lawrence river during the summer season. These in many instances carry passengers.

DEARBORN AVENUE CHURCH.

Although Chicago is termed an inland city, because it is nearly a thousand miles from the ocean, it possesses vast marine interest through its location on Lake Michigan, one of the chain of great lakes stretching along our northern frontier. The magnitude of the lake traffic is shown by the statistics collected by the government. A limited means of water communication in a southern direction is enjoyed in the Illinois and Michigan canal, extending from Chicago

FLORAL DESIGN IN SOUTH PARK.

to the Illinois river, navigable for light craft thence to the Mississippi river. The freight transported over this route in 1889 aggregated 917,047 tons. An ambitious scheme in this direction, which has been undertaken by the city of Chicago, contemplates the construction of a grand water-way not less than 160 feet wide and not less than eighteen feet deep from Lake Michigan to Lockport, Ill., for the improvement of low-water navigation of the Illinois and Mississippi rivers as well as to afford sanitary relief to Chicago. It is expecte[d] that the United States government will co-operate in making t[he] connecting rivers navigable for large vessels, so that the lake and t[he] Mississippi river traffic may interchange. Another water-way, calle[d] the Hennepin canal, is projected across the upper part of the State [of] Illinois, also to connect with the Mississippi river.

The Goodrich Line is the pioneer and leading line of the lal[e] steamers, comprising the most elegant, most modern, as well as t[he] safest steamships which ply Lake Michigan. Founded in 1856 [by] Capt. A. E. Goodrich, and ten years later incorporated under the la[ws] of Wisconsin. Docks foot of Michigan Avenue. The steamers [of] the Goodrich Transportation Company ply between Chicago and [all] ports on Lake Michigan and Green Bay, forming regular lines duri[ng] the navigation season.

RAILROAD TRANSPORTATION.—The railroads, howev[er,] are the chief factor in conducting the trade and commerce of Chica[go.] No other city in the world is so well supplied with railroad lin[es.] Twenty-six independent roads run out of the city, diverging to [all] parts of the United States, Canada and Mexico. These railroa[ds] with their branches and immediate connections, have a total leng[th] of over half of the total mileage of the railroads of the country. [A] belt railroad encircling the city connects with all- lines, enabli[ng] freight to be easily transferred from one to another without breaki[ng] bulk. The immense traffic of this character, however, has so [far] outgrown the facilities afforded by the belt road referred to that t[wo] other intercepting lines have sprung into existence, one of which [en-] circles the city at a distance of twenty-five to forty miles from [it.] This line is known as the "Joliet Cut-Off." The third belt ro[ad,] which is known as the Chicago and Calumet Terminal, traverses p[art] of the intermediate territory, intersects a number of important r[ail-] roads, and will ultimately connect with all lines. To still furt[her] facilitate the interchange of freight cars among the various railr[oad] lines, a great union transfer yard is being constructed on the w[est] side of the city. These railroads and their belt-line connections h[ave]

established a multitude of junction points in the immediate vicinity of Chicago, possessing transportation facilities of the most complete character for industrial enterprises. Raw materials originating on the route of any railroad are thus easily delivered to a factory on any other line by a short transfer, practically taking every Chicago railroad to the doors of every Chicago factory. Manufacturing products are likewise distributed without difficulty over the region traversed by every railroad line. These facilities have stimulated the growth of an unusually large number of manufacturing towns as suburbs of Chicago. Among such suburbs the town of Pullman has become famous by reason of its having been built with a special view to providing workmen with comfortable homes, pleasant surroundings, and everything necessary for their convenience and social enjoyment.

RAILROADS.—Chicago is practically the terminal point of all the great trunk lines of railway, North, South, East and West, in the United States, the Dominion of Canada and the Republic of Mexico. Nearly all the railway systems of the continent have, either directly or by proprietary connections, sought and obtained an entrance to this city and a share in the immense traffic which centers here. Over ninety thousand miles of railway center in Chicago at the present time, and it is conceded to be the greatest railway *depot* in the universe; more passengers arrive and depart; more merchandise is received and shipped here daily than in any other city on the globe. Illinois, of which Chicago is the metropolis, has the greatest railway mileage of any State in the Union—14,017 miles.

ST. CLAIR TUNNEL.—This is the greatest submarine tunnel in the world. It extends from Port Huron, Michigan, under the St. Clair river to Sarnia, in the Canadian Province of Ontario, and connects the Grand Trunk Railway system of Canada with the Chicago & Grand Trunk Railway and its connecting and associate lines. The tunnel proper is a continuous iron tube, nineteen feet and ten inches in diameter, and 6025 feet in length (or a trifle over one mile). The approaches, in addition to the tunnel proper, are 5,603 feet in length, making all told a little over two miles. This great international undertaking was completed at a cost of $2,700,000, and opened for freight traffic October 27th, and for passenger traffic December 7, 1891. The tunnel is lighted by incandescent electric lamps, placed at suitable intervals. By reason of the method of construction employed, and the material (iron) used therein, the tunnel is absolutely water-tight. As illustrating the accuracy of engineering

SCENE IN LINCOLN PARK.

skill, and without entering into lengthy details, suffice it to say that the construction of the tunnel was begun and carried on from both the American and Canadian sides of the river simultaneously, and when the edges of the tunnel shields met midway under the river bed, the total errors in lines were found to be too small for measurement. Trains of the Chicago & Grand Trunk Railway are hauled through the tunnel by coke-burning engines especially constructed for the purpose. They are said to be the largest engines in the world. The entire weight of the engine and tender rests upon ten drive-wheels. The weight of one of these monster engines in actual service is found to be approximately one hundred tons.

ILLINOIS CENTRAL RAILROAD.—The great and only rail artery connecting Lake Michigan with the Gulf of Mexico; one of the principal and one of the most ably managed lines in the United States. Miles of railroad operated during the year ending June 30, 1891, 2,875; cost of operation, $11,890,366.21; gross earnings, $17,-881,554.77; net earnings, without deducting rentals or taxes, $5,-991,188.56. The history of this road is identical with that of the State of Illinois, to the prosperity of whose people it has contributed in a very large measure. The charter under which the corporation was organized exempts the company's property from taxation in this State, but requires a payment to the State, in lieu thereof, of 7 per cent. of the gross receipts of the original railroad, 705.53 miles in length, or the lines from Chicago to Cairo (364.90 miles and from Centralia, Ill., to Dubuque, Iowa, 340.63 miles). The sum so paid during the years from 1855 to 1890 amounted to $12,365.618. In this period the stockholders of the company received, in cash dividends, $64,782,357. The vast amount of money which the Illinois Central Railroad Company has turned into the State treasury very materially assisted the latter in liquidating the indebtedness contracted during the War of the Rebellion, and in meeting the regular annual expenditures of the commonwealth for educational, charitable and other purposes. The Governor of the State of Illinois is, *ex officio*, one of its directors.

WISCONSIN CENTRAL LINES.—Although forming the connecting link between the Northern Pacific railroad system and Chicago, and although operated by the latter company as lessee, the Wisconsin Central lines, familiarly but incorrectly regarded by the public as the Wisconsin Central Railroad, must be referred to separately. In April, 1890, a contract lease was made by and between the Wisconsin Central Company, the Wisconsin Central Railroad Com-

pany, and the Northern Pacific Railroad Company, whereby the latter company obtained a lease of all the lines of railroad owned and controlled by the Wisconsin Central lines between the cities of Chicago and St. Paul and Ashland, including the lines of railroad, real estate and terminal facilities of the Chicago & Northern Pacific Railroad Company in the city of Chicago, thus giving to the Northern Pacific Company a complete line from St. Paul to Chicago, with ample terminal facilities in the latter city. This combination of interests was deemed by the directors of the Northern Pacific of the utmost importance, as giving access to the city of Chicago by a line of its own ownership and possession, with unsurpassed terminal facilities. While the terms of the lease relieve the Wisconsin Central from operating details, it leaves the building of branches, feeders, and all extensions of, and permanent improvements upon, the Wisconsin Central lines, to be jointly agreed upon by the lessor and lessee, and to be actually constructed by the Wisconsin Central companies. The development of the land grant and management of the iron properties remain in the exclusive control of the Wisconsin Central Railroad Company. The Wisconsin Central, from its inception, has been peculiarly identified with Wisconsin, its growth and progress. Almost nine-tenths of the mileage of the system is within the borders of that State, and its principal offices are located at Milwaukee.

GRAND CENTRAL DEPOT.—No visitor to Chicago can escape having pointed out to him among the greatest attractions of the city, the magnificent Grand Central Depot, located at the corner of Fifth avenue and Harrison street. It is one of the best specimens of the highest type of modern architecture to be found in the world. Where this grand pile rises to-day the Bridewell or City Prison stood years ago. The site was long given up to stone and coal yards; it was for years one of the most uninviting spots in the city. The erection of the Grand Central Depot has made it one of the most attractive, and gradually the old buildings, which still stand in the vicinity, are giving place to structures which comport with the dignity and grandeur of the great railroad station. It is more familiarly known as the Wisconsin Central Depot than by any other name.

THE UNION DEPOT.—The ground covered by this railway station extends from Madison street on the north to Van Buren street on the south, and covers about a block in width along the river front. This depot has been frequently referred to before, and it only remains to be said here that it is one of the handsomest in the coun-

SOUTH PARK SCENERY.

try, and that its train shed is the largest in existence. On the west side of Canal street, and particularly in the vicinity of Madison, is a block of buildings which has long been not only a disgrace to the west division of the city, but to all Chicago. It is covered in part by tumble-down frame buildings, and in part by lodging houses of the lowest description, and the vicinity is the resort of idlers, thieves and vagabonds generally. The lodging houses have frequently been the scene of crimes which have shocked the community, and they have been as well a menace to the general peace of the city in times of riot and disorder. In these lodging houses, also, have been colo nized at various times men who have been hired to do disreputabl work at the polls. To our right is the old Washington Hotel, landmark which will shortly disappear to make room for an elegan block of buildings. Beyond this, at the northwest corner of Cana street, is a handsome European hotel, and further on is the Gaul House, one of the oldest and best known hotels in the city. From this point to Union street there is not much to be seen that reflect credit on the west side, or that will interest the visitor.

PULLMAN.—Pullman to-day presents the most advanced and improved example of city construction which the world has seen and it is carefully studied for its suggestive value by men of science capitalists, economists, and students of social science throughout the world.

Pullman is unquestionably one of the greatest attractions Chicago has to offer her visitors. It is situated on the west shore of Lake Calumet, fourteen miles south of the Court-house. The extreme length of the town is about two miles in a north and south direction and it is half a mile in average width. The surface of the streets around the arcade is about nine feet above the lake level, permitting good basements for building. The land rises to the north and west and the surface at the foundry is fifteen feet above the lake level All improvements in the way of draining, paving, sewerage, gas and water preceded the population, or were put in when the houses were built. Pullman has a population of 11,783, and 6,000 operatives are employed in all the industries here, and their average earnings are $: a day, or over $600 a year each. These earnings averaged $610.7: each in the Pullman industries for the fiscal year ending July 31 1891. In no other place are all workmen so well provided for as here.

This beautiful town is the "pet" of Mr. Pullman; it is his "hobby," if the complete realization of an ideal can be so termed. As long as it was merely an *idea* it received scanty approval, but now that it is a *fact* there are none to be found who ever had the slightest doubt of the ultimate success of the undertaking.

The idea was not a new one to Mr. Pullman, but it was not until 1880 that it began to take physical shape, architectural, mechanical, commercial, industrial and sociological detail. The perfect success of the plan is no doubt largely due to the fact, first, that Mr. Pullman was working out his own plan, and second, it was his privilege to work out that plan with no one to meddle and object. No doubt if some of our larger cities had been planned on a similar basis it would be better for those cities; this may not be a democratic idea, but study the history of this model village and draw your own conclusions. Mr. Pullman is a man of strong character and broad views. He welcomes knowledge from every source, but in his own affairs he proposes to be his own master. "So, having ample power, though little sympathy or encouragement, he managed every detail, and ever since success has crowned the work there is no man who disputes with him the credit of devising it, or arranging its details down to the smallest particulars."

The tract of land now "Pullman," at the beginning of 1880, was a lonely waste of low, nearly level, grassy prairie on the west shore of Lake Calumet, fourteen miles south of the center of Chicago. The principal advantage it has was that it was crossed lengthwise by the Illinois Central and Michigan Central Railways.

It has taken just ten years to change this unpromising plain into the most exquisite, best regulated manufacturing town in the world. It has nearly eight miles of paved drained streets, including a grand boulevard 100 feet wide, abutting on the lake; twenty-five blocks of brick dwellings along these streets, capable of housing 1,750 families; an arcade building 256x164 feet in size, containing all the stores of the place, the bank and post-office. The second story is used for offices, the library and theater; and the third floor holds lodge-rooms for societies; it is heated throughout by steam; a handsome and well-kept hotel, that can accommodate 100 guests; school-houses, where 1,000 pupils a day can be taught; a water-tower 195 feet high, on top of which is a large boiler iron tank which holds half a million gallons; this is always kept filled for use in case of fire, and only for fire use. A market 110x100 feet in size, with stalls for meat, vegetables, fish, poultry, etc.; and in its upper story a public hall with a capacity of 600; gas works connecting with every house in town; green-houses for furnishing the town, its parks and gardens with flowers and shrubs. Brick-yards with a capacity for turning out 30,000,000 bricks a year; the clay for them is dredged from the bottom of the lake; the bricks are all machine-made. Ice-houses, holding 24,000

LINCOLN PARK LAKE.

tons of ice; lumber yards covering eighty acres; about fifty different kinds of lumber are used here, and nearly half a million dollars' worth is always kept on hand; this lumber is obtained from South America, Central America, Mexico and from half the States of the Union. Finally, the soul of the whole and the reason of its existence, the great Pullman Car Works, the Union Foundry, the Drop Forge and Foundry, the Street Car Works, the Terra-Cotta Works, the Standard

Knitting-mills, the Columbia Screw Factory, the Allen Paper Car-wheel Works, the Calumet Paint Manufacturing Works, the Pullman Iron and Steel Works, and other enterprises.

It is perhaps too much to say that any one mind could grasp in advance each of these details; but the idea contained the plan and potentiality of them all, and laid the broad and deep foundations on which they could rise, have risen and are constantly growing. Then, too, Mr. Pullman's designing mind has seized each position and made it a stepping-stone for each further advance. It has been his daily thought and nightly dream, and nothing has seemed to him too good and great for his model town.

The car shops furnish cars of every description, and have a capacity of turning out each week 3 sleepers, 12 passenger cars, 240 freight cars and several street cars, the number depending upon the value of the cars (making about 4 cars an hour during working hours). The other industries furnish, with the exception of glass, blankets, car springs and plushes used in upholstery, everything used in the construction of the best cars; all marble work, glass embossing, mirror-making and electro-plating are done here. The total value of the finished product from all the manufactories at Pullman is about $15,000,000 a year. This comes by the labor of about 5250 operators, whose average earnings are $2 a day. Of these only a few are children (perhaps 200 in all), and still fewer women, of whom only 150 are employed. Some of the latter hold clerkships; some work in the upholstering rooms, and some in the knitting-mill.

In selecting the architectural style to be followed at Pullman, it was deemed necessary to choose one that could be adapted to the great variety of buildings devoted to different uses. In general terms the style employed might be designated the round arched or Romanesque, without the Byzantine details of the great shops and principal buildings. It may be said that the buildings suggest a simplified modification of the Queen Ann style of architecture.

Turning now to the less obvious features, one finds still more to admire. The sewerage and surface drainage preceded the popula-

STOCK YARDS.

tion, being established at the same time when the dwellings were building. The surface drainage carries the rainfall into Lake Calumet. The sewerage proper is a separate system, connecting with every sink and cesspool, and taking the entire sewage from the houses and shops. Each house is supplied with sanitary plumbing. The sewage is conducted below the surface to a huge tank beneath the water tower, whence it is pumped and piped (1,800,000 gallons

WORLD'S FAIR GLOBE.

a day) to the Pullman farm, three miles away to the southwest, to be used as a fertilizer. The sewage tank is thoroughly ventilated through pipes debouching above the top of the water tower, and has, besides, a connection with the tall chimney of the boiler house, which outlets combined produce a down draught in all the sewer openings. The town has no evil odors.

The water supply does not come from the water tower, as many suppose, but from the Chicago water system. The town has fifteen miles of water mains.

The Pullman farm consists of 140 acres, thoroughly piped and underdrained for the reception, purification and utilization of the Pullman village sewage. Hydrants are so placed that the distribution can be conveniently done. All organic matter in the sewage is taken up by the soil and the growing vegetation, and the

SOL'S CLOCK (Lincoln Park).

water (which is, of course, by far the greater mass) runs off through underdrains to the ditches, and they deliver it pure and clear as spring water, into the Calumet river. In winter the sewage runs upon one field or one filter-bed, and then on another, the filtering process appearing as perfect as in summer. Thus are the waste products largely transmuted by vital chemistry into luxurious vegetable forms. The most profitable crops have been found to be

onions, cabbage, potatoes and celery. One acre takes care of th
sewage of one hundred of the population. This solution answei
one of the problems so often propounded in relation to the sewag
of Chicago, namely: "Why not utilize it for fertilization?" At or
acre to the hundred of population, it would require twelve thousan
acres to dispose of the sewage of Chicago, twenty square mil
from which settlers would have to be excluded. At some futu:
time, when lands naturally fertile and spontaneously productive sha
have grown more scarce and distant, this may be effective; but now
is a manifest impossibility. Even in old Europe, where there are
least 150 sewage farms, there is scarcely one which pays expenses
handling, instead of the large profit which might be expected fro
a free gift of unlimited manure. The difficulty seems to be in tl
impossibility of rotting or properly composting the crude elemen
of the sewage. The Pullman farm pays a reasonable profit. One
the most admirable features of the town—true it is a negative one
is that there are no saloons, no gambling houses and no almshous
and as a natural sequence I suppose, though I do not know po:
tively, no jail. They have a cemetery; but it is not a paying inves
ment. The growth of the "City of the Dead" is very, very slo
Now, some people who have no doctor friends, who are not int
ested in some cemetery company, or in a coffin or tombstone esta
lishment will think this a great advantage; but to most of us co1
mon mortals (we are a race of vampires) it is a great defect.

The absence of drinking shops is due to the fact that the Co1
pany has not parted with its realty; in fact, this policy was adopt
to prevent just such evils. Whenever and wherever public sen
ment is up to it, they can exclude any evil by popular consen
but in this case the promoters preferred to take no chances, a
"prohibition prohibits" in Pullman, however it may strugg
prevail, triumph and fail elsewhere. Do not misunderstand m
no one is prevented from drinking, only they must go elsewh(
for it.

Just outside of the town limits there are drinking places

BEACH FRONT.

the scores, with plenty of customers; so drunkenness is not unknown; but it is marked, exceptional and disgraceful. The operators know which of them are drinkers and which are not, and form their likes and dislikes accordingly; but the management leaves it all to them, taking no cognizance of the matter. Freedom is held to be the only condition for a healthy, stable growth of morals, intelligence and wealth.

FLORAL DESIGN (Lincoln Park).

At Pullman personal liberty of thought is associated with that of action. Religion is not assailed and dwarfed by patronage—certainly not by opposition. There are eight places of worship in town, representing as many shades of sectarian belief. Each is entirely sustained by the voluntary contributions of its members. The company built, at the outset, a beautiful green-stone church, but it is rented to a congregation like any other edifice or tenement.

Good order in the community is always maintained, without interfering with the freedom of the individual, so long as his freedom does not trespass on the liberty of another. There has never been any attempt (by the founders) to set up any religious denomination in the town. There was a church building constructed at the outset, but it was rented to a society which represented the majority in the town.

SCENE IN SOUTH PARK.

Within a stone's throw of the green-stone Presbyterian Church is a new building put up by the Catholics. In addition to this the Swedish Lutheran and other denominations have rooms where services are held. There is no artificial stimulus anywhere. There are no lectures given to the workmen. Neither politics nor religion has any part in the administration; that is left to the individual. Sunday is a day of relaxation; many go to church; many go to the lakeshore and take part in the out-door games. The town gave a small

Democratic majority at the last election. The men know that they are perfectly free from criticism on the part of the management, whatever result is declared at the polls.

The Pullman Loan and Savings Bank is the local financial depository of the Company, and also the custodian of the voluntary hoards of the citizens. Its savings deposits in 1891 amount to $467,981.45, in the names of 1,828 depositors. The average sum held by each savings depositor in 1884 was $145.43. In 1890 it had grown to $243.97, and in 1891 is $256. By purchases in the immediate vicinity, 885 of the operatives are freeholders in their own right. In all 2,297 live outside the town. All employed are free to live where they please, but Pullman town is always full.

No reserve or "hospital money" or "insurance fund" is exacted by the Company, nor are any store accounts collected on the wages pay-roll. (The Company is not interested in the shops except as landlord of the shop-keepers.) The only deductions from the earned wages are rents due by those who occupy Company houses or flats.

The position of the city already built is about half a mile in width, and is two miles from the north to the south end of the town. The successive blocks are unlike, giving pleasing changes to the views along any street. There are now about seven miles of paved streets and twelve miles of sidewalks. At intervals of thirty feet shade trees are planted along both sides of the streets, and on the main streets flowers are grown around the trees. Open places planted with shrubbery and flowers really constitute a long park, in the midst of which the homes of the people stand. The monumental buildings and vast shops in the long stretches of meadow, walks and shrubbery emphasize the park features of Pullman.

There is one style of flats having from two to four rooms each, which rent for from six to nine dollars a month. Of these there are now six buildings, each containing twelve families, one building containing twenty-four families, two containing thirty-six families, and one containing forty-eight families. There is not a room in these buildings which has not one or more windows, giving residents abundance of fresh air and light. These flats and their surroundings are kept in order by the Company. Blocks 14 by 27 and 30 contain 300 flats each apartment containing from two to five good rooms and its pro per proportion of basement. Still another style of flats is seen where every family has a separate entrance, and is accommodated with five good rooms and a basement. These flats rent for from $14.00 to $16.00 a month. There is now a tendency in cities to build flats

LINCOLN PARK FLOWERS.

and the advantages in them are usually set forth as follows: The tenant secures a home for a lower rent, and is brought nearer his place of work and business. In case of sickness and trouble he has help close at hand; the common hallway is lighted and the whole building cared for by a janitor, services which cannot be rendered in single houses. By accommodating many families upon a small tract of land, men are able to reduce their living expenses to a minimum while all have the advantage of living upon improved streets and in

LINCOLN MONUMENT (Lincoln Park).

close proximity to parks and gardens. Of course separate sinks, water-taps and closets, all inside the houses, are provided for every family.

There is a variety of single houses with rents ranging all the way from $16 to $50 a month. These houses are adapted to the needs of men receiving from $2 a day to $5,000 a year. The average rental of all the tenements in Pullman is only $14 a month.

"The connection of the Pullman Company with the so-called labor riots was short but full of interest for the moment, and suggestive for the future. Pullman industries were a shining mark, and the elements of destruction would score a brilliant victory if they could lay them low. Therefore the attack was expected, and it came—from the outside, of course. With a shrewdness worthy of them, the assailants chose as the weakest point in the industrial citadel, the cabinet shop, which was largely filled with foreigners, not yet imbued with the 'American Idea.'

"The foreign idea of irresponsible conflict between labor and capital, and of 'Internationalism' as the only refuge of the former from the oppression of the latter, these men had either brought over with them or readily absorbed from the plausible talkers sent among them. The mass of other workmen, not so much convinced by argument as moved by brotherly feeling, consented to join in the demand for an eight-hour day and other proposed changes, and at an appointed time a committee called on Mr. Pullman to lay that demand before him. The committee, as usual in such cases, was chosen mainly from the men known to, and respected by their employers ; but contained also some of the 'walking delegate' element, men who had entered the employment on purpose to interfere with it. Mr. Pullman, recognizing easily the 'outsiders,' invited a statement of their position. They had free scope to ask what they had determined on, and to enforce the demands by such arguments as they thought best. When they had entirely covered the ground he expressed himself thus :

"That they evidently entertained the deliberate purpose of either controlling the works or stopping them. The latter they might do, but to what purpose? When work stopped wages stopped. How would their families fare? The Company would live, doing its work elsewhere or not doing it at all. As to the former, the Company was satisfied with its present management and proposed to be as free in its actions as were its employés in theirs."

This was all. Mr. Pullman was kind, but firm. After their interview he refused to discuss the matter again. They knew his decision; it was unalterable. The men "went out," stayed two weeks and returned to their work. Since then things have gone smoothly; differences there are frequently, but they are settled in free discussion between the management and the operatives. These conferences are carried on in a friendly—not servile—spirit, and sometimes result in convincing the one party, sometimes the other; oftenest in a compromise of conflicting interests and claims.

"The historian is not the prophet, but it may be said without undue presumption that if—*if* the path in front of Pullman proves as fair to the foot as its vista appears to the eye, then the enterprise sounds the key-note for the full and final chorus of concord between labor and capital. In that case its founder has, single-handed, built the enduring monument of the passing nineteenth century; a pyramid, the broad, deep ground course whereof is human nature, while its sunlit cap-stone is peace."

PULLMAN PALACE CAR COMPANY.—Main office, Pullman building. President, George M. Pullman. Directors, George M. Pullman, Marshall Field, J. W. Doane, Norman Williams and O. S. A. Sprague, of Chicago; Henry C. Hulbert, of New York, and Henry R. Read, of Boston. One of the greatest corporations in the world.

DOUGLAS MONUMENT.

PART III.

PARK SYSTEM.

"THE splendid park system of Chicago, constituting (with its connecting boulevards), one of the most extended in the world, took its rise in the construction of Lincoln Park, and this in its turn was the offspring of the cemetery established in 1835,

IN THE ZOO (Lincoln Park).

north of and adjoining what is now North avenue. In all, this burial place included sixty acres of what was once sand hill and pine forest, but became, by the care of lot owners, a fine and well-ordered graveyard. The city also owned sixty acres north of and adjoining the burial place. In 1860 the council passed an ordinance forbidding the sale of lots and the interment of dead in the last named tract,

and in 1864, another ordinance setting apart the same for a publ
park. The latter ordinance also forbade the sale of more lots in tl
first plot, and the interment of bodies on the part not sold—tl
Potter's field. To-day in the appearance of the magnificent par
with its statues, fountains, hills, dells, lakes, streams, flower-bed
palm-house, menagerie, and miles of roads and paths, there is almo
nothing to indicate that it was once the burial place of uncount
thousands of our fellow-citizens, many of whom, no doubt, accidental

LINCOLN PARK LILY-BEDS.

omitted in the removal, still sleep beneath its surface. Nothing, e:
cept a single tomb, that of the old Couch estate, to which, for certa
reasons, the Park Commissioners never obtained title; this remai
silent and grim, as if to remind the pleasure-seekers that 'in tl
midst of life we are in death.' This park besides having the adva
tage of being the first, has also the peculiar and inestimable adva
tage of a Lake Shore drive. The Lincoln Park Commissioners we
shrewd enough to see and profit by this opportunity at once; almo
the first outlay they made was in preparing a drive-way along the Pa

front. This served a double purpose; it reconciled the people to th[e] increase in taxes, and it shut out and made forever impossible th[e] alternative of the Lake Shore for a railway entrance to the city.

"It is easy to perceive that a range of wind-swept sand hills i[s] an unpromising place for a park, but hard to conceive of the im[-] mensity of the task of subduing it to verdure and beauty. On th[e] other hand, there are some compensatory features; the sand is eas[y] to move by plow and scraper, and is a self-draining material when re[-] duced to the desired form. On the whole, one would rather attac[k] for park purposes warm sand than cold, refractory soaked clay o[r] hardpan. A design once fixed on, with a pond here and there to b[e] excavated, a hill or two or three to be brought low, a mound to b[e] raised, a slope to be graded, a ridge to be ranged, numberless flowe[r] beds to be started, a hot-house, a conservatory, a green-house, a palm-house, a boat house, a tool and machinery house, a keeper'[s] dwelling and barn to be built—all these things and a thousand other[s] being laid out for deliberate achievement, the thing goes on ste[p] by step, and the change, to an occasional visitor, seems almost mag[i-]cal. 100,000 cubic yards or more of clay make a substratum to th[e] grass plots; ten thousands of loads of black soil and the fertilizin[g] city street sweepings make the top dressing; thousands of tree[s] home grown and imported, soon stand in orderly confusion, and b[e-]hold! 'The wilderness blossoms as the rose.'"

There are 2,236 miles of streets, and some fifty miles of boule[-]vards in Chicago, the latter connecting the surrounding cordon [of] attractive parks. The city is proud of the chief streets, which are 6[0] to 100 feet wide, with State street 125 feet wide. They are straigh[t,] cross at right angles, are mathematically as nearly level as drainag[e] will permit, are generally well lighted and paved, and in the busi[-]ness section are bordered by solidly constructed buildings; while th[e] residential section displays very fine dwellings, and Michigan avenu[e] at the lake front, is one of the handsomest foliage bordered streets [of] residences in the world. The outskirts are beautified by twent[y] parks, making with the miles of connecting boulevards a semi-circ[le] around the city, having each end resting upon the shore of the lake. Nature gave to the monotonously flat prairie around Chicago no scenic charms excepting the glorious view over Lake Michigan. It has been a most admirable thing for the city that somebody has been able to pause in the universal and engrossing chase after the almighty dollar long enough to design these pleasant parks. The broad expanse of prairie was low, level, and treeless originally, but abundant foliage has been planted, and art has made little lakes and

AMONG THE LILIES.

miniature hills ornamented by attractive flower gardens and shrubbery. There are nearly 2,000 acres of these parks, the system beginning on the northern verge, with Lincoln Park on the lake front, covering 250 acres, and stretching around to the South Park, and thence down to Washington and Jackson Parks, the latter fronting for almost two miles on the lake shore in the southern part of the city. Large sums have been spent in their care and development, and about $2,000,000 additional will be spent on these parks in anticipation of the fair. The Drexel Boulevard, which is the favorite driveway to the South Park, 200 feet wide, is the most handsome of the connecting roadways, and is among the celebrated avenues of America. A magnificent fountain, surmounted by a bronze statue of the late Francis M. Drexel, the founder of the noted Drexel banking firm, adorns its entrance. This broad parkway has a fine carriage road on either side of a central walk for pedestrians, the latter winding among picturesque gardens, and the whole boulevard being well shaded, though the trees are still young. Washington Park, beyond

IN THE ZOO (Lincoln Park).

the South Park, contains 371 acres, Jackson Park 586 acres, and the broad midway plaisance, connecting them, 80 acres. These three are the grounds devoted to the World's Fair, and, combined, cover 1,037 acres, the chief buildings being located in Jackson Park.

The park system proper is under control of the commissioners, elected by the courts. The parks under the supervision of these commissioners are maintained by direct tax upon the respective divisions of the city. Under the control of the city government are a number of small parks, squares and "places" which are maintained

COMMERCIAL NATIONAL BANK, DEARBORN STREET.

at the expense of the city treasury. This chain of parks and boule
vards gives one of the finest drives in the world, and there is n
reason in the world why it should not be, for no expense wa
spared in its construction and no expense is spared in keeping it up
Besides it is as autocratic as the private park of an English noble
man; no vehicle that would injure its surface or mar its beauty i
allowed upon it.

"Under the provisions of the park acts, any street boulevard i
placed under the control of the Park Board, as to its care, govern
ment and use, and the Board can assess adjacent property for its re
imbursements. The Board thereupon forbids the use of the roadwa
for business travel, and even for funerals except so far as absolutel
necessary to the residents on the street itself. The Board must b
applied to for permission by any railway which desires to cross it
boulevards; in short, the whole length of each is treated as part o
the park. This is not looked upon with favor by the residents on th
parallel streets near by, as it not only gives the favored avenue a cer
tain glory and distinction, but also throws on the other roadway
more than their share of the public business, the traffic which i
heavy, dirty, noisy, unsightly, undesirable and pavement wearing.
Still, they submit, perforce with as good a grace as may be, 'it is fo
the city's good.'"

Only a very few years ago, complaint to the effect that the grea
parks of the city were too far removed from the people, and practically inaccessible to the very class whom they were intended to serv
was general. Now, however, they are becoming the nuclei around
which the populous districts are growing. In a few years, instead o
being on the outskirts of the city, they will be breathing places in it
interior.

"It is unquestionable that the park and boulevard system o
Chicago was planned and carried out far ahead of the city's actua
needs. In truth, even at the present time, they are beyond all proportion to the use made of them. Large expanses of park are lonel
solitudes, except on some special feast day. Long stretches of boule-

vards are as inappropriate to their respective neighborhoods as would be a cathedral in a country village. This being so when the city has long passed the million mark, how almost absurd must they have seemed when they were laid out encircling, though far away from a town of only 300,000 souls! But, all this being true, it only proves the projectors to have had the gift of second sight. If it had not been done when it was it would have been impossible ever after-

SOUTH PARK LILY PONDS.

wards. In spite of the loudly-blamed greed of the property owners, (who in general, though not invariably, got every penny they could,) land was bought at prices far below present values. The limit of permitted rates of assessment (between one and two cents on the hundred dollars of value) gave, at first, very scanty means for improvements and sinking-funds; but as surrounding lands and lots rise, (partly by aid of the parks and boulevards themselves,) the same old rates gave generous yearly sums to successive Boards, while the lessening of the debt, by calling in bonds for the sinking-funds, reduced year by year the interest charges, so that in the Columbian year the whole system will be substantially clear of incumbrance, while the available funds will authorize expenditures not less than magnificent. Not only has this generation planned for the next and its successors a princely pleasure ground, it has bought it and paid for it, and devises it to the future free of the usual purchase money mortgage."

CONSERVATORIES.—Winter visitors will find the conservatories of the different parks among the most attractive sights in the

THE CONSERVATORY.

city. These conservatories are open during all seasons, and are in charge of a skilful corps of gardeners chosen by the several park boards. The new greenhouse, propagating house, and palm house at Lincoln Park will attract the attention of the visitor. Among the curious things to be seen within its walls is a sago palm 100 years old that came from Mexico many years ago; a tree fern 15 feet high; a very large date palm, and a Carludonica palmata in bloom. Mr. Stromback, the chief gardener, gives some interesting facts in refer-

LAKE SHORE DRIVE.

ence to the water-lilies that have proven so attractive outdoors during the past summer. The large lily with the tub-like leaves, Victoria Regia, is annually raised from seeds, a single pod having been known to contain 435 seeds. It is a night bloomer, and the blossom is quite fragrant. Some of the other water lilies are also night bloomers, while some open in day-time. The water in the basins in which they are grown flows from the engine house near by, after being heated to something like 90 degrees Fahrenheit. The managers of Lincoln Park have the honor of being the first to bring these wonderful lilies to Chicago. The greenhouse at Lincoln Park is now one of the largest and most beautiful in the country. The new palm house, referred to elsewhere, is completed. The propagating departments are themselves worthy of the attention of all lovers of plants and plant culture. Some magnificent chrysanthemums, ferns, and orchids are seen here. More people visit Lincoln Park greenhouses than any of the others.

Nothing could excel the delicious sense of refined taste pervading the conservatory at Washington Park, with its bank of chrysanthemums presenting a symphony in color, its aquarium half hidden beneath the delicately traced fern fronds that spring from the margin and gracefully bend and reflect in the mirrored surface, and its giant palms forming leafy frescades suggestive of tropical luxuriance and love-making. That remarkable aquatic production, the water hyacinth, is cultivated here extensively, and the round balls are seen like Limniades, or, what are more generally known, ducks, swimming about in the basins on top of the water. Upon entering the greenhouse the large stock of diminutive variegated-leaved plants intended for next summer's lawn decorations are observed in a room by themselves, laid off systematically in designs, so as to make a pretty display, thus utilizing a hitherto neglected agent for indoor ornamentation. In the cactus-room is a great assortment of that peculiar plant. A striking novelty in the palm-room is a plant from the West Indies bearing an edible fruit. The fruit is said to be like honey, quite palatable and much sought by natives of the islands, but owing to the frailty of its rind it cannot be successfully transported to this country. The outside covering resembles that of the American custard apple or pawpaw.

One of the most popular conservatories in the public parks is that at Garfield. Here is to be found one of the largest assortments of orchids in the city. The greenhouse contains a date palm of

SCENE IN LINCOLN PARK.

extraordinary dimensions—probably the largest specimen of that particular variety of palm in all Chicago. The stock of agaves or century plants is very full, and one of these plants, the gardener asserts, is known to be thirty-two years old.

Decidedly the handsomest and costliest conservatory at any of the parks is the new $50,000 edifice recently erected by the West Chicago Board of Commissioners at Douglas Park. The new building is filled with an immense quantity of rare plants. In the east wing is a large circular basin of water, in which are grown aquatic productions, including the Victoria Regia lily. Last summer this plant flourished in the basin in a way it has never been known to do before in the city, its leaves having reached the remarkable size of 7½ feet. Above the basin and ranged in a circle around the margin

LINCOLN PARK SCENERY.

are suspended in baskets a splendid collection of that unique exotic, the pitcher plant, nearly all of them in bloom and no two alike.

A eucalyptus, growing in free ground indoors, measuring 47 feet in height, is one of the numerous attractive sights to be witnessed in the famous Humboldt Park conservatory. The greenhouses at Humboldt are among the largest and handsomest to be found anywhere. At the threshold are caught glimpses of banks of color and vistas of verdure of the most entrancing character, and the air is richly per-

JONES RESIDENCE.

fumed by heliotrope, tuberose, and orange blossoms—a veritable paradise. In the palm-room, the central plateau resembles a miniature tropical forest, and ranged around this are fern-covered and vine-clad rockeries calculated to revive memories of dense woodlands. The fernery, a separate room, is, without doubt, one of the most artistic creations of the conservatory, being arranged to show to the best advantage those lovely contrasts which are a prominent peculiarity in the foliage of this class of plants.

SOUTH PARKS.—Washington Park, Jackson Park and Midway Plaisance are known collectively and familiarly as "The South Parks." The cost to the city of the ground which they cover was $3,208,000. They are as yet in their infancy, but even now they rank among the finest parks in the world.

DOUGLAS PARK.—Area, 179.79 acres; situated four miles southwest of the Court-house; bounded on the north by West Twelfth street, on the south by West Nineteenth street, on the east by California avenue and on the west by Albany avenue. The district in the vicinity of this park was almost entirely destitute of residences ten years ago. Within a decade it has been built up, however, until those who have not visited the section for four or five years, or even two years, would hardly recognize it as the same. The popularity of the park, which has always been a beautiful piece of ground, has increased with the growth of the neighborhood and the improvement of the streets and drives in the vicinity. Douglas Park is beautifully laid out, well wooded and admirably situated. It has been cared for nicely of late years, and its lawns and flower beds bear evidence of skillful attention. Some of the avenues through this park are not surpassed by any in the city. The lake covers an area of seventeen acres. There is a handsome boat-house and refectory here. Douglas Park also has a medicinal artesian well with properties similar to those at Garfield and Humboldt Parks. The conservatories and propagating houses are among the largest of the system. Vast improvements are promised for Douglas Park within the next two years.

DREXEL BOULEVARD.—The eastern entrance to Washington Park commences at Oakwood boulevard and the junction of Cottage Grove avenue and Thirty-ninth street. It is a double driveway, 200 feet wide for its entire length, running south to Drexel avenue and southwest from that point to the park. Through the centre is a wide strip of sward, covered here and there with beautiful shrubs, rose bushes and mounds. Upon the latter, which are interspersed

LINCOLN PARK FLOWER BEDS.

with flower-beds of beautiful design appear, during the summer season, unique figures wrought from flowers and foliage, and which attract thousands of sight-seers annually. At the intersection of Drexel avenue is a magnificent bronze fountain, presented by the Messrs. Drexel of Philadelphia, in memory of their father, after whom the boulevard was named. On either side of the driveways are to be seen some of the handsomest mansions and prettiest villas of Chicago.

GARFIELD PARK.—Area 185.87 acres, situated four miles directly west of the Court-house; bounded by Madison street on the south, Lake street on the north, and running a mile and a half west from the head of Washington boulevard. This was formerly known as Central Park. The name was changed in memory of President Garfield. The lake in the centre of the park covers an area of 17 acres

IN GARFIELD PARK.

The park is extremely picturesque, the drives and promenades being laid out in the most enchanting manner. The boat-house is one of the finest to be seen in the park system. There is a handsome fountain here, the gift of Mrs. Mancel Talcott, and an artesian well which furnishes half the city with medicinal mineral water. It is 2,200 feet deep, and discharges at the rate of 150 gallons per minute. The water is recommended for anæmia, diseases of the stomach and kidneys, and rheumatic disorders. Garfield Park is beautiful as it is, bu

NICKERSON RESIDENCE.

just at present it is receiving the attention of West Side citizens, wh(
contemplate making many improvements.

JACKSON PARK.—Area 586 acres; about eight miles from th
Court-house; bounded by Lake Michigan on the east; Stony Islan(
avenue on the west; Fifty-sixth street on the north, and Sixty
seventh street on the south. This beautiful park has been brough
into great prominence of late by reason of its selection as the site fo
a portion of the Columbian Exposition. About one-third of the parl
has been improved up to the present year, although immense work
have been in progress for some time in preparing the unimprove(
portion for the public. These works include excavating and dredg
ing for the chain of lakes which are to have connection with Lak
Michigan; bridge and breakwater construction; leveling and em
banking, and landscape gardening on an extensive scale, the im
proved portion of the park at the northern end. Here there is
broad stretch of sward which has been used frequently as a parad
ground by the militia, and by large picnic parties. This is sur
rounded or hemmed in by a wooded avenue of great beauty, whic
opens upon a sea-wall and a beautiful view of Lake Michigan
There is erected here an immense shelter, of great architectur&
beauty, where thousands may, on occasion, be protected either fror
the heat of the sun or from a sudden rainfall. The trees and shrut
bery in the improved part of the park, as well as the flowers, are ver
attractive, although the variety which one finds in some of the othe
parks is lacking. The number of trees and shrubs in the unimprove
portion is comparatively small. About Sixty-first street there is on
clump of oaks and maple, shot here and there with bunches of fier
sumac. There is another and a larger grove west and north of this
Beyond there, except for a few small bunches and a fringe along th
west fence, the unimproved portion is unbroken by wood.

LAKE SHORE DRIVE.—This is the grandest boulevard driv
in Chicago. Beginning at North Side Water-Works on Pine stree1
its skirts the lake to the northern extremities of Lincoln Park, wher
it connects with Sheridan road, which is nearly completed for 2

miles along the north shore. Before reaching the park some of the most magnificent mansions in the city are passed on the left. On the right is a fringe of sward, dotted with flower-beds and covered with beautiful foliage in the summer months. The lake beats against an embankment to the right, and frequently the spray is dashed across the flower-beds when the sea is high. Reaching the park you pass through beautiful avenues until you strike the drive again. Here vast improvements are being made. Some years ago the State Legislature gave the Lincoln Park Commissioners the right to issue bonds for $300,000 with which to defend the shore line against the encroachments of storm-tossed Lake Michigan. With that sum as a nucleus the commissioners designed and began work on a system of improvements which, when completed, will have cost a sum many times that raised from the original issue of bonds. Enough has now been finished to give a general idea of the work as it will appear when a continuous sea-wall will extend from Ohio street to almost the extreme northern limit of the city. The work was commenced in the Spring of 1888 at the foot of North avenue. Several hundred feet out in the lake a line of piles was driven. Powerful dredging-machines were placed in position and slowly but surely acre after acre was reclaimed from the lake. It is at this point that the Lake Shore Drive joins the boulevard now in course of construction. It will be finished this year. The breakwater proper rests on piles driven thirty-five feet into the sand. On this foundation granite blocks are laid and securely cemented. Back of this starts the paved beach, forty feet in width, slanting at an angle of about twenty degrees until it meets the granilethic promenade. This promenade is the most attractive feature of the improvement and is destined to become famous. Imagine a twenty-foot promenade, smooth as glass, three miles in length, with Lake Michigan vainly striving to scale the paved beach to the east of it, and a grand boulevard lined with carriages to the west of it; a promenade commanding on one side a magnificent view of the lake, and on the other a prospective of Lincoln Park with all its natural and acquired beauties. There is nothing rigid in the lines of the promenade or boulevard. Without detracting from the attractiveness of the sweeping crescent described by the sea-wall at Jackson Park, it must be said that the sinuous curves marking the contour of the Lincoln Park beach, promenade, boulevard and canal, are more artistic and pleasing. The old shore-line has been followed as nearly as possible. It is hard to improve on nature. With the shifting sands as the only obstacle to cheer their course, the waves have drawn along the beach curves such as would delight a follower of Hogarth. When they planned the outlines of the drive-way the commissioners wisely decided to follow nature. They have made no mistake. The objective point is Diversey avenue, the northern limit of the park. Here the regatta course will end, but the sea-wall and boulevard will be continued by the people of Lake View, who propose to make the Sheridan Road and the Lake Shore Drive continuous. The sea-wall will be extended to Byron avenue, opposite Graceland Cemetery. It is thought that the park commissioners will be able to complete their part of the work by the commencement of next winter. They will then have added 100 acres to the area of the park, and have given to Chicago a boulevard and regatta course unequaled in the world. Between the new boulevard and the park there will be three connecting points. There will be land connection at the north and south ends of the park and a bridge at a point opposite Webster avenue. The canal will connect with the lake at two points, one opposite Wisconsin street and the other at Fulton avenue. The boulevard will cross these connections on steel swinging bridges of a special construction. It will be several years before the dreams of the designer will be fully realized. Rows of shade trees will be planted to the east of the boulevard, and between the trees and the edge of the regatta course the sloping lawn will be beautified in the highest style of the landscape gardener's art. Between the west shore of the regatta course and the present Lake Shore Drive is a tract of land now piled high with stone and pine bark. This will be made one of the finest features of the park. Planked thus on either side by verdure-decked banks, the canal will wind its sinuous course towards what was Fisher's garden. A

ABSTRACT BUILDING,

no point will this placid stretch of water be less than 150 feet in width, while the average is nearer 200. At the ends it is widened to 350 feet, so as to permit boats to make a sweeping turn. Hardly less important is the improvement contemplated by the Lincoln Park Commissioners and the property owners who own the land fronting the lake between Elm and Oak streets. The sea-wall ends at Elm street on the south. With it the Lake Shore Drive practically comes to an end. The problem which has ever confronted the boards of park commissioners is to connect the North and South Side boulevard systems. In a recent message to the city council, Mayor Cregier suggested that Michigan boulevard be connected with a viaduct extending over the Illinois Central tracks and crossing the river at some point between Rush street and the lake. An expensive plan; there seems to be no other available. It is proposed to swing the boulevard out into the lake, starting at Elm street. It will curve out 1,000 feet from the present line and strike the existing beach at the foot of Ohio street. The Lake Shore Drive has for years been the fashionable rendezvous of the North Side. Thousands of carriages line the beautiful embankment on summer afternoons.

LINCOLN PARK.—Area, 250 acres, two and a half miles in width by one and a half miles in length; bounded by Lake Michigan on the east; Clark street on the west; North avenue on the north, and Diversey street on the south. The southern portion was formerly a cemetery tomb of the Couch family remains; all others were long since removed. First board of commissioners appointed in 1869, since which time it has been under State supervision. There is embraced within this small piece of territory perhaps more attractions than can be found in any park of the country. Where nature left off art began, and the two have contributed toward making Lincoln Park the most charming in the city. The visitor will be delighted with the undulating character of the ground, the gracefully winding and curving avenues, which stretch out in every direction; the beautiful lakes, the handsome bridges, the splendid foliage, the magnificent statuary, the gorgeous banks, beds and avenues of choicest flowers, the rare and wonderful shrubbery, the pretty little dells, knolls and nooks, that lie half concealed beneath the noble trees, and last, though not least, with the zoölogical collection, which has contributed in no small degree toward making Lincoln Park famous. Here we find the Grant monument, facing Lake Michigan on the Lake Shore drive. This magnificent work of art was presented by the citizens of Chicago, and cost $100,000. Here, also, is the Lincoln statue, by St. Gaudieur, facing the main entrance, a splendid likeness of the great president,

IN LINCOLN PARK.

and pronounced one of the finest pieces of sculpture in the world. This statue cost $50,000, and was presented, together with a drinking fountain, by the late Eli Bates. Here, also, are the "Indian Group" in bronze, presented by the late Martin Ryerson; the La Salle monument, presented by Lambert Tree, and the Schiller monument, presented by German residents of Chicago. An entire day may be spent pleasantly by the visitor in Lincoln Park. The great conservatories, flower-beds and zoölogical collection, can hardly be seen in less time. There is a comfortable refectory in the boat-house on the main lake.

LINCOLN PARK PALM-HOUSE.—The plan of the palm-house just erected at Lincoln Park, drawn by Architect Silsbee, shows a beautiful structure of steel and glass, light, airy and picturesque, sixty feet high, resting upon a bowlder foundation of split granite. The main building is 168x70 feet, with a rear extension of seventy feet, making the entire length of the structure 238 feet. In front of the main building there is to be a lobby 25x60 feet, which is approached by a vestibule twenty feet square. The interior of the main building shows an unbroken stretch, save a few light supporting iron columns for the glass roof. The conservatory is in the rear of the palm-house. It is thirty feet wide. At the extreme north end is a room 30x60 feet, which will be exclusively devoted to the culture of orchids. This room will be further beautified by a sort of observatory tower built of pressed brick and terra-cotta trimmings. The building will be erected on two terraces northeast of the present canal vista and the animal's summer quarters. The terraces occupy the space due north of the present green-houses. The latter structure will be removed as soon as the new palm-house is completed. The main approach to the palm-house will be from the floral gardens. The new house will cost $60,000.

MICHIGAN AVENUE BOULEVARD.—Michigan avenue, from Jackson street on the north to Thirty-fifth street on the south, a distance of three and a quarter miles. It is 100 feet wide from curb to curb, and skirts the Lake Front Park, the site for a portion of the Columbian Exposition. Formerly the ultra fashionable residence street of the city. Now undergoing a transformation.

OAKWOOD BOULEVARD.—Connects Drexel and Grand boulevards; 100 feet wide and half a mile long. It enters Grand boulevard at Thirty-ninth street, and touches Drexel boulevard at its intersection with Cottage Grove avenue.

WASHINGTON BOULEVARD.—The continuation of West Washington street, west from Halsted street to Garfield Park, and

AUDITORIUM BOXES.

the driveway from the center of the city to the parks and boulevards of the West Park System. Passes through Union Park, a beautiful square. This boulevard is lined for the entire distance of nearly three miles with handsome residences. Large shade trees and a continuous strip of green sward fringe either side of the avenue. On Washington boulevard are many fine churches. The Chicago Theo-

SCENE IN LINCOLN PARK.

logical Seminary is passed at Union Park and Warren avenues, the Episcopalian Seminary on the north side, west of California avenue.

WASHINGTON PARK.—Area, 371 acres; situated about one and a quarter miles west of Lake Michigan and about six and a half miles southeast of the Court-house; bounded on the east by Kankakee avenue, on the west by Cottage Grove avenue, on the North by Fifty-first street and on the south by Sixtieth street. The finest of Chicago's parks, more by reason of its magnificent entrances, Drexel and Grand boulevards, than by any great natural or artificial attraction of its own, although its flower beds are the most beautiful of any. It lacks many of the advantages which are enjoyed by Lincoln and Jackson Parks, the contiguity of the lake being of itself one of the greatest charms of the two last named. It can not boast of a zoölogical garden that will compare with Lincoln Park, nor of the magnificent monuments that are making the north shore park classical ground. But South Park has statelier trees, grander avenues, more sweeping perspectives, more charming drives than any other park in the city. It has the famous "Meadow," a stretch of velvety sward that covers 100 acres and the "Mere," with its thirteen acres of water, picturesquely sparkling behind long lines of ancient oaks and elms, and bathing the emerald banks of the mounds and knolls which almost conceal it from the view of the passing visitor. It has also its great conservatory and its splendid stables, which cover 325 x 200 feet. It has its delightful refectory, known as the "Retreat," where refreshments are served for man and beast, but its flower gardens are its greatest boast. During the months between May and November, the best exhibition of the landscape gardening art in the world are seen. Flowers and foliage are made to do, in the hands of the gardener, what the brush and palette accomplish for the artist. The designs are changed annually, and are always original, always interesting and always lovely.

THE

WORLD'S COLUMBIAN EXPOSITION.

BIRD'S EYE VIEW OF EXPOSITION GROUNDS.

PART IV.

THE WORLD'S COLUMBIAN EXPOSITION.

THE idea of holding a World's Fair at some point in the United States, in celebration of the four hundreth anniversary of the discovery of America by Columbus, was first seriously considered in the summer of 1889, and it quickly received popular approval. As soon as it seemed probable that such a Fair would be held, several cities, notably New York, Chicago, St. Louis and Washington, entered into a spirited rivalry to be designated as the place of its location, and urged their respective claims before Congress with all the force and influence they could command. It was apparent from the start, almost, that either New York or Chicago, would be selected. Chicago, with characteristic energy, formed an organization—The World's Fair Columbian Exposition, embracing the most substantial business men, raised more than $5,000,000 by subscription, and pledged itself to increase the amount to $10,000,000 to be expended in behalf of the fair. Chicago's superiority in many respects as a place for holding the Exposition was admitted, and after some discussion she was selected.

The buildings of The World's Columbian Exposition, as provided by Act of Congress, were to be dedicated on October 21st, 1892, the recognized anniversary of the discovery of America by Christopher Columbus. The Exposition, which will be the greatest universal fair the world has ever seen, will be formally opened to the public on May 1, 1893. The gates will be closed October 26, 1893. Everything will be in readiness for each of these events. The preparation for the dedicatory ceremonies have been made upon an elaborate scale, and the great buildings of the exposition will be completed and opened for the reception of the exhibits at the time named. From October 21st, 1892 to May 1st, 1893, the work of receiving and placing exhibits, and in making ready generally for the opening of the display will be carried on without intermission.

The management of the Exposition includes four organizations;
1. NATIONAL COMMISSION (authorized by Act of Congress).

2. WORLD'S COLUMBIAN EXPOSITION (organized under laws of State of Illinois).
3. BOARD OF LADY MANAGERS (authorized by Act of Congress).
4. WORLD'S CONGRESS AUXILIARY.

The National Commission, which is a supervisory body is composed of eight commissioners—at large, with alternates, appointed by the President, and two commissioners and two alternates from each State and Territory and the District of Columbia, appointed by the President on nomination of their respective Governors. This commission has held four sessions, and has now practically delegated its authority to eight of its members who constitute a Board of Reference and Control, and who act with a similar number selected from the World's Columbian Exposition.

The World's Columbian Exposition, as its corporate name reads, is composed of forty-five citizens of Chicago, elected annually by the stockholders of the organization. To this body falls the duty of raising the necessary funds and of the active management of the Exposition. Its committees supervise the various departments into which the work has been divided.

The Board of Lady Managers is composed of two members, with alternates, from each State and Territory, and nine from the city of Chicago. It has supervision of woman's participation in the Exposition and of whatever exhibits of woman's work may be made. The participation of women in the Exposition promises to be one of its most interesting as well as novel features. With a commodious and imposing building, designed by a young lady architect, and with abundance of money, and with full recognition, indorsement and aid by the United States Government, and the Exposition Directory, the women have an opportunity of showing in the most signal manner, the condition of their sex throughout the world, what are the achievements of woman in the various branches of human endeavor, and what is her adaptability to different occupations and lines of industrial and charitable work. Under the direction of the Board's President, Mrs. Potter Palmer, the work of organization, and of enlisting the interest of women throughout the United States and in foreign countries, has progressed to a most satisfactory stage.

The World's Congress Auxiliary is an authorized adjunct of the World's Fair, and aims to supplement the exposition which that will make of the material progress of the world by a portrayal of the "wonderful achievements of the new age in science, literature, education, government, jurisprudence, morals, charity, religion and other departments of human activity, as the most effective means of increasing the fraternity, progress, prosperity and peace of mankind." This constitutes the intellectual and moral branch of the Exposition. Its motto is, "Not matter, but mind," and it is organized to provide for the presentation, by papers, addresses and discussion, of the mental and moral status and achievements of the human race. Under its auspices, a series of congresses will be held in Chicago during the progress of the Exposition, in which, it is already assured, will participate a great many of the ablest living representatives in the various fields of intellectual effort and moral endeavor. The auxiliary embraces between fifteen and twenty main departments, such as literature, government, education, music, science, art, engineering, etc., in each of which are subdivisions. A program is being arranged for congress in each of these departments and divisions, in which specialists and advanced thinkers may participate in discussing the vital and important questions, and presenting the best and latest achievements of the human mind in each. During the Exposition, the auxiliary will have the use of a magnificent permanent art palace, which the Chicago Art Institute, aided by the Exposition Directory, erects on the lake front. This will have two large audience rooms, each of 3,500 capacity, and from twenty to thirty smaller rooms, of capacity ranging from 300 to 750. The great Auditorium will also be utilized for the larger congresses, and numerous other halls are available when required. Each congress will be supervised by a committee of persons actively interested in its particular field, acceptance of such responsibility having already been given. The prospects are that fully 100 congresses altogether will be held. It is the intention to publish their proceedings in enduring form.

I. The grounds of fraternal union in the language, literature, domestic life, religion, science, art, and civil institutions of different peoples.

II. The economic, industrial and financial problems of the age.

III. Educational systems, their advantages and their defects; and the means by which they may be adapted to the recent enormous increase in all departments of knowledge.

IV. The practicability of a common language, for use in the commercial relations of the civilized world.

V. International copyright and the laws of intellectual property and commerce.

VI. Immigration and naturalization laws, and the proper inter national privileges of alien governments, and their subjects, o citizens.

VII. The most efficient and advisable means of preventing o decreasing pauperism, insanity and crime; and of increasing produc tive ability, prosperity and virtue throughout the world.

VIII. International law as a bond of union and a means c mutual protection; and how it may best be enlarged, perfected an authoritatively expressed.

IX. The establishment of the principles of judicial justice, a the supreme law of international relations, and the general substitu tion of arbitration for war in the settlement of international contro versies.

The Director General is the chief executive officer of the Ex position, and the work is divided into the following great departments

A. Agriculture, Food and Food Products. Farming Machiner and Appliances.

B. Viticulture, Horticulture, and Floriculture.

C. Live-stock, Domestic and Wild Animals.

D. Fish, Fisheries, Fish Products and Apparatus of Fishing.

E. Mines, Mining and Metallurgy.

F. Machinery.

G. Transportation Exhibit: Railways, Vessels, Vehicles.

H. Manufactures.

J. Electricity and Electrical Appliances.

K. Fine Arts: Pictorial, Plastic and Decorative.

L. Liberal Arts, Education, Engineering, Public Works, Arch tecture, Music and the Drama.

M. Ethnology, Archæology, Progress of Labor and Invention and Collective Exhibits.

N. Forestry and Forest Products.

O. Publicity and Promotion.

P. Foreign Affairs.

It is hard to realize the magnitude and magnificence of this di play because there has never been anything of the kind that can l compared to it.

Looking over the list of great international fairs, we see at one

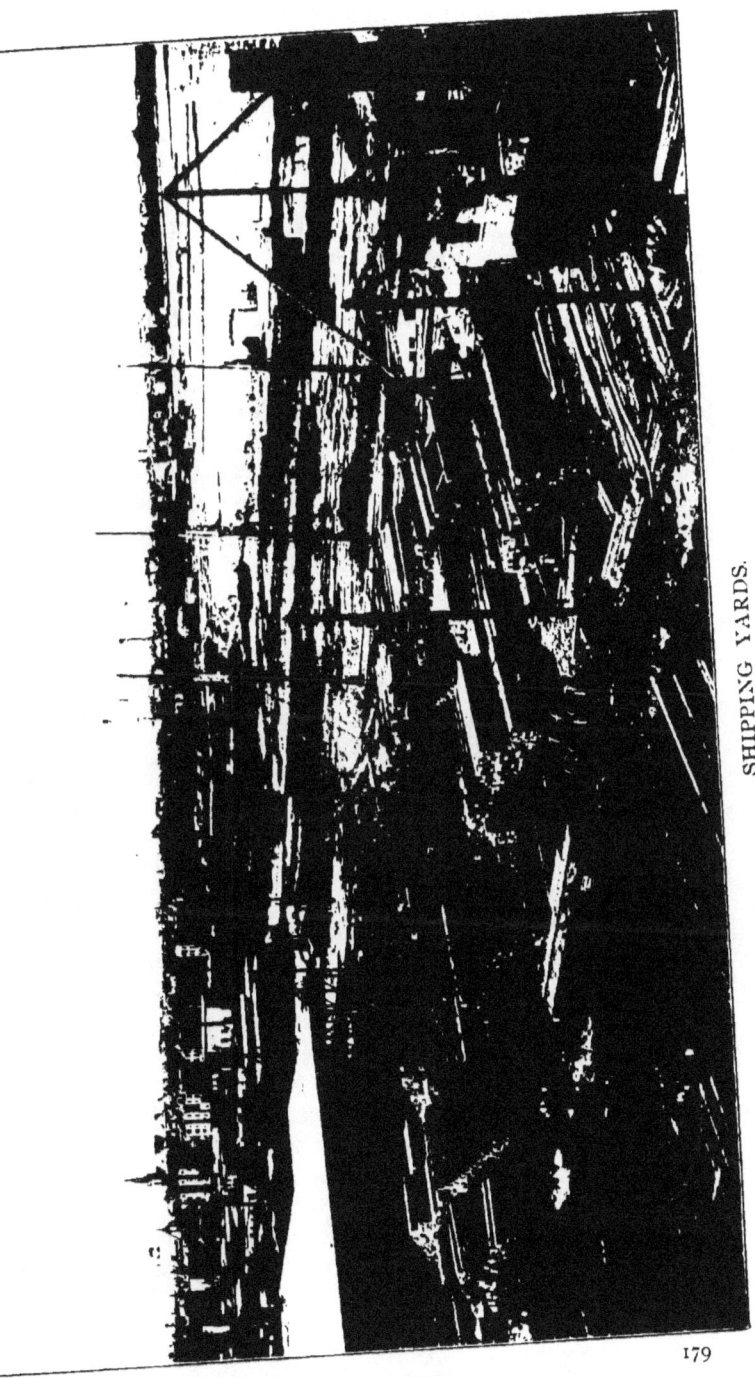

SHIPPING YARDS.

that the Paris Exposition of 1889 was the largest in every way ever held; and while (even this being the case) no comparison can be made, yet the figures of the one and the plans of the other will be of interest.

The figures showing receipts and expenditures of the Paris Exposition are briefly: Receipts, $9,900,000; expenses, $8,300,000; profit, $1,600,000.

The Champ de Mars was selected as the site of the fair. The total space occupied was 173 acres. The Machinery Palace, the largest structure on the ground, measured 1,378 feet in length, 406 feet in width and 166 feet in height. This building alone cost $1,500,000 and covered eleven acres. The Palace of Arts cost $1,350,000, the Palace of the French Section $1,150,000, and the improvements in the parks and gardens, $16,500,000. Besides the buildings and ornaments devised and provided by the Exposition management, nearly all nations contributed to the architecture. The Indian dwellings, street in Algiers, houses of New Caledonia, Tunisian Minaret, Turkish village, English dairies, Dutch bakeries, etc., which were scattered over the park were very attractive. It is hardly necessary to mention the Eiffel Tower, of which so much has been written. The structure is 984 feet high, and has occupied a more prominent place than any other attraction in Paris for the past three years. The number of exhibitors was 55,000, the largest number that has ever contributed to the success of an art and industrial exposition before. The United States was represented by no less than 1,750, and received 941 awards. It was estimated that Americans alone emptied 350,000,000 francs into the lap of Paris during the Exposition. The gold revenue in the Bank of France rose enormously. Police estimates gave the total number of strangers in Paris during the Exposition at 1,500,000.

The various railroads reported an increase over the six months of the preceding year of 1,878,747 in the number of passengers carried, and in receipts an increase of 66,000,000 francs. The City o Paris Omnibus Company reported an increase of 14,000,000 francs The Cab Company transported 29,097,111 persons from Jan. 1 to Nov. 1, 1889, the same period in the previous year only 12,000,000 with an increase in revenue of 1,558,000 francs. All other lines o business in Paris are known to have increased in revenue at a corresponding rate. Among the interesting things discovered was tha the consumption of meat increased 3,278,871 pounds and of wine 3,162,227 gallons. The total excess of the receipts of the theatres over the corresponding six months of the previous year was 10,867,-555 francs. It was estimated that the total gain to Paris must have exceeded 500,000,000 francs. The Exposition of 1889 gave very general satisfaction to visitors from all countries. Paris never looked better. The republic positively outshone the empire. There was not so much glare and brilliancy as during the Exposition of '67; there was less of tinsel and less of surface display, but the Parisians were evidently more contented, a spirit of patriotic regard for the government pervaded the masses, and strangers felt whatever appearance of prosperity they witnessed was genuine.

It was found in the spring of 1892 that the practical development of the World's Columbian Exposition had expanded away beyond the calculations of the public and the managers of the enterprise. This was the natural result of the determined effort made on all sides to eclipse everything that had been attempted before in the way of an international fair. The preparations for the greatest event of the nineteenth century were carried out upon a scale commensurate with this determination. Everything was to be better, greater and grander than the world had ever seen before, and as the grounds were laid out and the mammoth buildings began to assume form, it was seen that the management, instead of falling short in its promises and pretensions, had in every particular exceeded them. The plan and scope determined by the National Commission involved an expenditure upon the part of the local directory of about $10,000,000. It was soon evident that $20,000,000 would be nearer the amount which Chicago would be called upon to lay out on this gigantic enterprise, and that this latter sum would quite likely represent only fifty per cent. of the whole amount to be spent before the gates of the Exposition would be thrown open. The government outlay upon the federal exhibit easily exceeds $2,000,000, and additional appropriations it is thought will be necessary. The States of the Union (beginning with Illinois, which appropriated $800,000, and which was followed by Pennsylvania and New York with $300,000 each, and by a number of less wealthy commonwealths by sums ranging from $100,-000 to $150,000) have added not less than $3,000,000 to the outlay. The appropriation of foreign nations aggregates about $200,000. The international character and importance of the World's Fair will be

understood clearly when it is learned that the first sums set aside for their exhibits by such nations as Japan, Mexico and Brazil amounted to $630,000, $750,000 and $300,000 respectively. . . . The Exposition grounds cover an area of 633 acres, having a frontage of two miles on Lake Michigan. The largest building is about one mile in circumference, and its central aisle has a clean span of 368 feet and is 206 feet high. The Machinery Hall of the Paris Exposition, if placed within this aisle, would have a space 6 feet wide on each side and 11 feet on each end, with 50 feet clear for ventilation above its roof. There were used in the construction of this building 6,000 tons of iron and steel. These figures may mean much or little to the visitor, but for the purpose of comparison it may be stated that the Eiffel Tower required but 7,000 tons, and only 3,600 tons were used in the Brooklyn Bridge, and 5,600 tons in the great railroad bridge at St. Louis. The heroic dimensions of all the buildings have only lately been realized as they have appeared in their finished state and perfect outlines. The Exhibition buildings, including annexes, required a consumption of 18,000 tons of iron and steel. The buildings primarily projected, including landscape improvements, were contracted for at a saving of about $2,500,000 from the architects' estimates, but the growing necessities of the enterprise required the erection of others not at first contemplated at a cost of about $1,900,000. The total floor space of the great Exposition buildings (not including the foreign, State or special buildings) is 6,320,000 square feet or 155 acres. For the protection of these buildings and their contents, and to supply fountains and all the daily requirements within the grounds, the management provided for a possible supply of 64,000,000 gallons of water daily, which is carried through twenty miles of mains from six inches to three feet in diameter. For supplying power for machinery, etc., the management provided for boilers having a water evaporating capacity equal to 25,000 horse-power and engines for generating electricity, 18,000 horse-power; for driving line shafting and isolated exhibits, 2,000 horse-power; for compressed air, 3,000 horse-power, and for pumps 2,000 horse-power. Electrical force is supplied as power to the amount of 3,000 horse-power. The system of sewage projected is extensive and complete. The arrangements are made for the treatment of 6,000,000 gallons of sewage every twenty-four hours, the precipitated matter of which is burned and only clear water allowed to escape.

The estimated cost of the completed structures, including landscape, statuary, fountains, terminal facilities, police and fire stations, and all that may be necessary for the comfort and convenience of visitors, is $15,117,500, exclusive of the cost of administration, which is estimated at $2,770,000, up to the opening of the Exposition, May 1, 1893.

The honor of designing these great structures and of displaying to the world our progress in architecture, as well as in construction, was wisely distributed among the leading architects of the United States. Three were selected from New York City, one from Boston, one from Kansas City, and five from Chicago, making a board of ten, by whom the general arrangement and character of the grounds and buildings were determined, in conference with the distinguished landscape architects, Messrs. Olmsted & Co., of Boston, and Chief of Construction D. H. Burnham, on the Committee on Grounds and Buildings. The Paris Exposition cost about $9,500,000. The Chicago Exposition, including administration and all other expenses, will probably be from $17,000,000 to $18,000,000. In addition to this there will be perhaps from $3,000,000 to $4,000,000 expended by the General Government and by the various States. A reasonable estimate of the amount of money that will be spent for all purposes may be fairly stated to be $22,000,000 to $23,000,000. The chief buildings of the Fair are located in Jackson Park.

Many of the minor buildings, special exhibits, etc., were provided for with space in Washington Park and on Midway Plaisance. Jackson Park is beautifully situated on the lake shore seven miles southeast of the City Hall, and embraces 586 acres. Washington Park is a mile or more nearer and has 371 acres. Midway Plaisance has 80 acres. Thus a total of 1,037 acres is available for the Exposition. The spacious grounds of the Washington Driving Park Association, adjoining Washington Park on the south, may be used for certain stock exhibits.

To supply the Exposition buildings and grounds with water two plants were put in, one with capacity of 24,000,000 gallons a day, and the other of 40,000,000 gallons. Thus 64,000,000 gallons a day are available. A system for drainage, believed to be adequate and perfect, was adopted. Plans adopted for lighting the buildings and grounds provided for 138,218 electric lamps, of which 6,766 are arc lamps of 2,000 candle-power each, and 131,452 incandescent,

16 candle-power each. The electric lighting cost something like $1,500,000 and is ten times as extensive as was employed at the Paris Exposition. The light and motive plant at the Exposition require 26,000 horse-power, of which 22,000 is required for the electric plant.

Before going into a general description of the Exposition buildings and grounds it is necessary that the visitor should learn something of the details. The dimensions and cost of the magnificent structures which rear their beautiful domes on all sides of you will be interesting. The following condensed table will convey this information in a compact and intelligible form:

BUILDINGS.	DIMENSIONS IN FEET.	AREA IN ACRES.	COST.
Manufactures and Liberal Arts	787 x 1687	30.5	$1,500,000
Administration	262 x 262	1.6	435,000
Mines	350 x 700	5.6	265,000
Electricity	345 x 690	5.5	401,000
Transportation	256 x 960	5.6	370,000
" Annex	425 x 900	8.8	
Woman's	199 x 388	1.8	138,000
Art Galleries	320 x 500	3.7	670,000
" Annexes (2)	120 x 200	1.1	
Fisheries	165 x 365	1.4	224,000
" Annexes (2)	135 diam'r	.8	
Horticulture	250 x 998	5.7	300,000
" Greenhouses (8)	24 x 100	.5	25,000
Machinery	492 x 846	9.6	1,200,000
" Annex	490 x 550	6.2	
" Power House	100 x 461		
" Pumping Works	77 x 84	2.1	35,000
" Machine Shop	146 x 250		
Agriculture	500 x 800	9.2	618,000
" Annex	300 x 550	3.8	
" Assembly Hall, etc.	125 x 450	1.3	100,000
Forestry	208 x 528	2.5	100,000
Saw Mill	125 x 300	.9	35,000
Dairy	100 x 200	.5	30,000
Live Stock (3)	65 x 200	.9	335,000
" Pavilion	280 x 440	2.8	
" Sheds		40.	
Casino	120 x 250	.7	*210,000
Music Hall	120 x 250	.7	
U. S. Government	345 x 415	153.8	$7,041,000
" Imitation Battle-ship	69.25 x 348	3.3	400,000
Illinois State	160 x 450	.3	100,000
" Wings		1.7	250,000
		.2	
		159.4	$7,791,000

* Including connecting peristyle.

Two of the last named buildings were erected at the expense of the United States Government, and one at the expense of the State of Illinois, but these must be classed among the great Exposition structures. The Exposition buildings, not including those of the Government and Illinois, have also a total gallery area of 45.9 acres, thus making their total floor space 199.7 acres. The Fine Arts building has 7,885 lineal feet, or 145,852 square feet of wall space.

All of the annexes are scarcely less imposing and architecturally beautiful than the main buildings themselves. The live-stock sheds which cover an immense area as indicated, are constructed as inexpensively as possible without marring the general architectural effect. The power houses, pumping works, etc., are exhibits in themselves. There are several Exposition buildings in addition to those named, but these are mentioned in another connection. Among them are a Press building, in which every possible convenience and accommodation for the press representatives of the world is provided; and a reproduction of the Spanish convent, La Rabida, in which a wonderfully complete collection of Columbus relics and allied exhibits are gathered. The total cost of the Exposition structures alone is estimated at $8,000,000. Of course, it is understood, no reference is made here either to the numerous State or foreign buildings or to structures for the accommodation of special exhibits. These of themselves form a very important part of the Exposition.

The visitor will naturally be desirous of taking in the entire Exposition at one journey, if possible, before entering upon special views. The most delightful means by which the visitor may reach the Exposition grounds will be by steamboat on Lake Michigan. A ride of six miles from the embarking point on the Lake Front Park, with the towers and gilded domes of the Fair buildings constantly in sight, will take him there.

In the western part of the group stands the ILLINOIS BUILDING costing $350,000. Just south of the foreign and State buildings stands the FISH AND FISHERIES BUILDING, 700 feet in length, and flanked at each end by a curved arcade connecting it with two octagonal pavilions, in which is seen the aquaria and the tackle exhibit. The total length is 1,100 feet, and the width 200 feet. This building, designed by Henry Ives Cobb, of Chicago, is in the Spanish style, and conspicuous because of a liberal use of color.

A little further south across an area of the lagoon is the UNITED

INTERIOR OF AUDITORIUM.

STATES GOVERNMENT BUILDING, measuring 350 x 420 feet, and having a dome 120 feet in diameter and 150 feet high. It is constructed of stone, iron and glass, classic in style, covers four acres, and cost $400,000.

On the lake shore east of this building and in part in the intervening space, the government has a gun battery, a life-saving station complete with apparatus, a lighthouse, war balloons, and a full-size model of a $3,000,000 battle ship of the first class.

Steaming by the Government exhibits the visitor will come abreast of the largest building of the Exposition—that of MANUFACTURES AND LIBERAL ARTS. It measures 1,700 x 800 feet, with two interior courts. This building, which is of the French renaissance style, was designed by George S. Post, of New York.

Extending westward across the park, is a long avenue or court, several hundred feet wide. To the right, at the entrance of this grand avenue, is the great building of Manufactures and Liberal Arts, and farther back the other attractions already referred to. To the left is the AGRICULTURAL BUILDING, measuring 800 by 500 feet, designed by Architect McKim, of New York.

Passing the Agricultural building, the visitor will come to the great MACHINERY HALL, which lies to the westward of it, and which is connected with it by a horseshoe arcade, doubling a branch of the lagoon. It is nearly identical with it in size and cost, but differs from it considerably in appearance, being serious, impressive and rich in architectural line and detail, and the best work of its designers, Peabody & Stearns, of Boston.

Opposite Machinery Hall, and north of it in the centre of the "Long Walk," stands the EXPOSITION ADMINISTRATION BUILDING. This is one of the most imposing, and, in proportion to its size, by far the most inexpensive one of the large structures. Richard M. Hunt, of New York, President of the American Institute of Architects, is its designer. It is adorned with scores of statuary figures, and surmounted by a gilded dome rising 250 feet, or about the height of the Auditorium tower. In it are the offices of the National Commission and Local Directory, and the headquarters of all the numerous officials connected with the management and administration of the Exposition.

To the northward of the Administration building, on either side and facing the grand avenue, are two more immense buildings, one for the ELECTRICAL and the other for the MINING exhibit. These are about equal in size, covering each a little more than five acres and a half. Both are of French renaissance. The former was designed by Van Brunt & Howe, of Kansas City, the latter by S. S. Beman, of Chicago. North of these buildings in the main lagoon is an island of twenty or thirty acres in area.

To the southward of the line of buildings which are arranged along the south side of the grand avenue is a vast open expanse which is devoted to the live stock exhibit. Here immense stock buildings, a show ring and whatever else will contribute to the success of the live stock feature of the Exposition are to be found.

Jackson Park resembles a right-angled triangle in shape. The visitor has thus far, on his tour of inspection, traversed the lake shore or hypothenuse of the triangle, and across the southern end or base. It remains only to turn towards the north and note the structures ranged along the perpendicular. The first one arrived at is the TRANSPORTATION BUILDING. This is Romanesque in style and one of the largest of all, measuring 960 by 256 feet, exclusive of a great annex in the rear, which covers nine acres. North of this is the HORTICULTURAL BUILDING, another immense structure, 1,000 by 250 feet, with three domes, one at each end and a large one at the center.

Still farther north and directly opposite the park entrance of Midway Plaisance stands the WOMAN'S BUILDING, which is one of the chief objects of interest on the grounds. The exterior design was furnished by a woman architect, Miss S. G. Hayden, of Boston. Here the lady managers have their headquarters, and here is collected a wonderful exhibit illustrating the progress and attainments of women in the various branches of industry.

Passing the Woman's Building the visitor can turn toward the northeast and inspect the Foreign and State buildings in the northern portion of the park.

BIRD'S EYE VIEW.—The power of the pen is proverbial, but how inadequate and feeble an instrument it is to describe the picture presented by a bird's eye view of the Exposition Grounds and Buildings. Such beauty, such grace, such coloring! Does there exist to-day, has there ever existed, either on the canvas of the painter or in the brain of the poet, an ideal paradise that will compare with this reality? Spread out beneath him lie more than six hundred acres, upon which has been expended all the wealth of experience in art and science. The very essence of all that is elegant and unique in landscape gardening, grouped here and there are scores of graceful and imposing edifices, making a magnificent array of structures, which embody the best conceptions of America's greatest architects. Bordering this scene, and adding not a little to it, is Lake Michigan, one of the grandest of inland lakes. There is nothing to add, nothing to wipe out. Could a picture be more perfect?

To the north one sees a village of palaces; these are the buildings of Foreign Nations and some of all states of the Union. It is picturesque in the extreme because here are embodied the different tastes and characteristics of the world, national and provincial. This group is one of the most interesting parts of the exposition. These buildings are ranged on wide curving avenues, connected by numerous walks; they occupy about 100 acres of the park beautifully laid out; each building has ample grounds of its own, with lawns, flower-beds and shrubbery.

In front of the park, extending eastward into the Lake 1200 feet we see the great pier with its enclosed harbor dotted here and there by the picturesque little pleasure boats of all epochs and nations. The harbor bounded on the east, far out into the lake, by the long columned facade of the Casino, in whose free space crowds of men, women and children, in holiday attire, protected by its ceiling of gay awnings, look east to the lake and west to the long vista between the main edifices as far as the gilded dome of the Administration building. The first notable object of this vista is the colossal statue of Liberty rising out of the lagoon at the point where it enters the land, protected by moles which carry sculptured columns emblematic of the thirteen original States of our Union. Beyond this, beyond the first of many bridges, lies a broad basin, from which grassy terraces and broad walks lead on the north, to the south elevation of the enormous Main Building, and on the south to the structure dedicate1 to agriculture.

This Main Building, devoted to manufactures and liberal arts, stretches northwest one-third of a mile, The long, low lines of its sloping roof, supported by rows of arches, is relieved by the central dome over the great main entrance; and emblematic statuary and floating banners will add to its festive character.

The north elevation of the classic edifice devoted to agriculture, shows a long arcade behind Corinthian columns, supporting a series of triple arches and three low graceful domes. Liberally adorned with sculpture and enriched with color, this building, by its simplicity, refinement and grace, is ideally expressive of pastoral serenity and peace. At its noble entrance a statue of Ceres offers hospitality to the fruits of the earth.

The lofty octagonal dome of the Administration Building forms the central point of the architectural scheme. Rising from the columned stones of its square base 250 feet into the air it stands in the centre of a spacious open plaza, adorned with statuary and fountains, with flower-beds and terraces sloping at the east down to the main lagoons. North of the plaza stand the two buildings devoted to mines and electricity; the latter bristling with points and pinnacles, as if to entrap from the air the intangible element whose achievements it will display.

South of the plaza is the machinery stall with its power-house at the southeast corner. West of this and along the western limit of the park is the Transportation Building. Still further north, lying west of the north branch of the lagoon extends the long shining surfaces and the gracefully curving roof of the Crystal Palace of Horticulture. Following the lagoon northward, you see the Woman's Building, and eastward, the island devoted to the novel and interesting aquaria, in which the spectator can look upward through the clear waters and study the creatures of ocean and river.

THE ADMINISTRATION BUILDING.—The Administration Building is the finest at the Fair, it being generally conceded that this structure is the gem and crown of the Exposition Buildings. Its location is at the west end of the great court in the southern part of the site, looking eastward, across the open space and the Lagoon outwards, the Casino and the Pier. Its great gilded dome forms one of the most conspicuous objects of the Exposition. This edifice cost $450,000. The architect is Richard M. Hunt of New York, President of the American Institute of Architects, to whose established reputation it is a notable contribution. The building covers an area of 250 feet square and consists of four pavilions 84 feet square, standing at each angle of its square ground plan, and connected by a great central dome 120 feet in diameter and 260 feet high. The center of each facade has a recess 93 feet wide, within which is a grand entrance to the building. The general design is in the style of the

THE ADMINISTRATION BUILDING.

French renaissance. The lower story, comprising the pavilions, is Doric in order of architecture, 65 feet high, of heroic proportions, surrounded by a lofty balustrade, and having the great tiers of the angle of each pavilion crowned with sculpture. The second story with its lofty and spacious colonnade is of the Ionic order, 65 feet high, being a continuation of the central rotunda, which is 175 feet square. Above is the octagonal base, 40 feet high, upon which rises the great dome. This building out-tops all the others.

There are four entrances, one on each side of the edifice, which are 50 feet wide and 50 feet high, deeply recessed and covered by semi-circular arched vaults, richly coffered. In the rear of these arches are entrance doors, and above them great screens of glass, giving light to the central rotunda. Across the face of these screens, at the level of the office floor, are galleries communicating with the different pavilions.

The interior effects of this great building will be fine, and its internal features will even exceed in beauty and splendor those of the exterior. A hall or logia 30 feet square is between every two entrances, connecting the intervening pavilion with the rotunda, and giving access to offices, being provided with broad circular stairways and swift running elevators. Within the rotunda is octagonal in form, the first story being composed of eight enormous arched openings, corresponding in size to the arches of the great entrances. Above these arches is a frieze 207 feet in width, the panels of which are filled with tablets, borne by figures carved in low relief and covered with commemorative inscriptions. The second story, 50 feet in height, rises above the balcony. The interior dome rising from the top of the cornice of this story towers 200 feet from the floor below, and in the center is an opening, 50 feet in diameter, transmitting a flood of light from the exterior dome overhead. The under side of the dome is enriched with deep panelings, richly moulded, and the panels are filled with sculpture, in low relief and immense paintings, representing the arts and sciences. In size this rotunda rivals, if it does not surpass, the most celebrated domes of a similar character in the world.

The corner pavilions are four stories in height, and are each divided into large and small offices, for the various Departments of Administration, and into lobbies and toilet rooms. The ground floor contains, in one pavilion, the Fire and Police Departments, with cells for the detention of prisoners; in the second pavilion are the offices of the Ambulance Service, the Physician and Pharmacy, the Foreign Department and the Information Bureau; in the third pavilion, the Post-Office and a Bank, and in the fourth the offices of Public Comfort and a restaurant. The second, third and fourth stories contain the Board rooms, the Committee rooms, the rooms of the Director-General, the Department of Publicity and Promotion, and of the United States Columbian Commission.

THE GOVERNMENT BUILDING.—This building is erected by the United States Government at a cost of $400,000, for its own use and exhibits. One-half of the building on the south is devoted to the exhibits of the Post-office Department, War Department, Treasury Department and the Department of Agriculture, the Smithsonian Institute, the Fishery Commission and the Interior Department. The exhibit of the Department of Justice extends from the rotunda to the west end of the building, and that of the State Department, from the rotunda to the east end of the structure.

Assistant Secretary Nettleton, of the United States Treasury, has charge of the Treasury Department Exhibit, and has arranged for exhibits of the Mint, the Coast and Geodetic Survey, the Supervising Architect of the Treasury, the Bureau of Engraving and Printing, the Bureau of Statistics, the Life-saving Board, the Lighthouse Board and the Marine Hospital.

Some of the most interesting exhibits among these are by the Mint. A complete group of the coins made by the United States, and a collection of coins of foreign countries; by the Supervising Architect of the Treasury, a number of photographs all of the public buildings of the Capital, including some of the original designs of Capitol dome and extension by the distinguished architect, Thomas U. Walter, LL.D.; by the Bureau of Engraving and Printing, new bills under framing, including samples of every bill of every denomination that the United States Government now authorizes as money; a life-saving station built and equipped with every appliance and a regular crew who will go through all the life-saving manœuvers; and by the Coast Survey, of a huge map of the United States, about 400 feet square, or about the size of a square of city property,—"accurately constructed of plaster of Paris and placed horizontally on the Exposition grounds with a covering over it, with galleries and path-

THE UNITED STATES GOVERNMENT BUILDING.

ways on the inside to allow visitors to walk over the whole United States without touching it, and built on a scale showing the exact height of the mountains, the depth of the rivers and the curvature of the earth."

The War Department will exhibit lay-figures of officers and men of the United States Army, of all grades, mounted, on foot, fully equipped in the uniform of their rank and service; besides will show the uniforms worn during the Revolutionary War and the War of 1812, and thirty-one figures showing the uniform of the Mexican War. There will be also shown the use of the telephone on battlefields; the heliograph which annihilates distance; and all means of army signalling with the batteries, lines, cables, bombs, torches, and every other contrivance now in use in the army. By the arrangement of Col. Whipple, of the Ordnance Department, huge guns and explosives will be exhibited, and at special times daily there will be regular battery drills and loading and firing of pieces; many of the guns used being the finest of their kind in the world. For the use of the Medical Bureau a hospital tent will be provided, operated by a corps of hospital nurses and doctors.

THE GOVERNMENT BUILDING is classical in style, bears a strong resemblance to the National Museum and other Government buildings at Washington, was designed by Architect Windrim, is constructed of iron and glass, and covers an area of 350 by 420 feet. Its most prominent feature is a central octagonal dome, 120 feet in diameter and 150 feet high. The building fronts west and is approached on the north by a bridge over the lagoon. Its location is near the lake shore, south of the main lagoon and of the area reserved for the foreign nations and the several States, and east of the WOMAN'S BUILDING and of Midway Plaisance.

The allotment of space to the several departments' exhibits of the Government are as follows: War Department, 23,000 square feet; Treasury, 10,500 square feet; Agricultural, 23,250 square feet; Interior, 24,000 square feet; Post-office, 9,000 square feet; Fishery, 20,000 square feet, and the Smithsonian Institute, balance of space. The treasures of the latter are so numerous that it will be a task for its officers to select articles for exhibition for the world's great fair.

THE NAVAL EXHIBIT.—For the NAVAL EXHIBIT a protecting pier and breakwater have been extended into the lake, above the landing pier, behind which the United States will make a naval exhibit. A model of a coast defense battle-ship is being constructed upon a stone and concrete foundation for this part of the show, so as to observe the treaty with England which forbids a naval force or vessel of either England or the United States to be on the great lakes. This causes much comment and has given rise to the invention of the following *bon mot* about it, that, "the United States is not content with a war vessel in the abstract, but must have it in the concrete." A naval training ship is also to be brought here with a full complement of boys. It is also stated that the model of the *Victory* from the Chelsea Exhibition is to come to Chicago. A facsimile has been built in Spain of the little caravel *Santa Maria*, in which Columbus sailed on the fateful voyage that discovered America. She will first appear at the naval review in New York Harbor, in October, 1892, and be afterwards taken up the lakes to Chicago. The final resting place of this little vessel will be Washington. In coming to this country, after leaving the port of Palos from which Columbus sailed, with imposing ceremonies, the vessel will sail over the route taken by the discoverer of America upon his voyage in the original *Santa Maria* four centuries ago.

Unique among the other exhibits is that made by the United States Navy Department. It is in a structure which, to all outward appearance, is a faithful, full-sized model of one of the new coast-line battle-ships, the designs being planned by the United States Bureau of Construction and Repairs of the Navy Department, and now in course of construction at a cost of nearly $3,000,000 each by Cramp & Son, Philadelphia, and the Union Iron Works, San Francisco. This imitation battle-ship of 1893 is erected on piling on the lake front in the northeast portion of Jackson Park. It is surrounded by water and has the appearance of being moored to a wharf. The structure has all the fittings that belong to the actual ship, such as guns, turrets, torpedo tubes, torpedo nets and booms, with boats, anchors, chain cables, davits, awnings, deck fittings, etc., etc., together with all appliances for working the same. Officers, seamen, mechanics and marines are detailed by the Navy Department during the Exhibition, and the discipline and mode of life on our naval vessels are completely shown. The detail of men is not, however, as great as the complement of the actual ship. The crew give certain drills, especially boat, torpedo and gun drills, as in a vessel of war.

The dimensions of the structure are those of the actual battle-ship,

PRAIRIE AVENUE.

to wit: length, 348 feet, and width, midships, 69 feet 3 inches; from water-line to the top of the main deck, 12 feet. Centrally placed on this deck is a superstructure 8 feet high, with a hammock berthing on the same 7 feet high, and above these are the bridge, chart-house and the boats. At the forward end of the superstructure there is a cone-shaped tower, called the "military mast," near the top of which are placed two circular "tops" as receptacles for sharpshooters. Rapid-firing guns are mounted in each of these tops. The height from the water-line to the summit of this military mast is 75 feet, and above is placed a flagstaff for signaling.

The battery mounted comprises four 13-inch breech-loading rifle-cannon; eight 8-inch breech-loading rifle-cannon; four 6-inch breech-loading rifle-cannon; twenty 6-pounder rapid-firing guns; six 1-pounder rapid-firing guns; two Gatling-guns and six torpedo tubes or torpedo guns. All of these are placed and mounted respectively as in the genuine battle-ship. The superstructure contains the cabins, staterooms, lavatories, lactrines, mess-rooms, galley and fittings, mess-table for crew, lockers, berthings, and also shows the manner in which officers and enlisted men live, according to the rules of the United States Navy. On the deck and bridge of the superstructure the manner in which the rapid-firing guns, search-lights, beats, etc., are handled, is shown. The entrance to. the conning tower is from the deck of the vessel, in which are all the appliances that the captain has at his command when taking the ship into action and during the progress of a battle at sea.

An electric light plant is provided and arrangements made for heating with steam. On the berth deck are the various articles usual to the hull, machinery and ordnance; ordnance implements, including electrical machines, gun-carriage, motors and range-finders; models showing typical warships of the past and present; samples of the provisions, clothing, bunting, flags, and naval stores in general—in short, all the supplies that go to make up the outfit of a man-of-war.

The costumes of the sailors of the Navy from 1775 to 1848 are exhibited by janitors dressed in those suits of clothing. On the starboard side of the ship is shown the torpedo protection net, stretching the entire length of the vessel. Steam launches and cutters ride at the booms, and all the outward appearance of a real ship of war is imitated.

This imitation battle-ship was designed by Frank W. Grogan,

architect of the U. S. Naval Exhibit, under the direction of Capt. Meade, U. S. Navy, and Lieut. Tussing, U. S. N. The idea of having a structure to represent a man-of-war, manned with all appliances in position is new, and was conceived by Capt. R. W. Meade. Nothing of the kind has ever been attempted before, and the cost of this curious and original structure is about $100,000.

THE WOMAN'S BUILDING.—The Woman's Building is described as a new project upon an extended scale in exhibitions, and is a spacious structure designed to display woman's special achievements and work. A committee of ladies presided over most capably by Mrs. Potter Palmer, the wife of one of Chicago's most prominent citizens, has this in charge, and they propose organizing similar committees of ladies abroad and soliciting foreign exhibits. The design is to show the best things done by women. The building has a central gallery for the special display of the brilliant and artistic things done by women in art, authorship and handicraft. In other rooms there will be exemplified the charitable and industrial work carried on by women, where they labor for the benefit of humanity, in hospital service, kindergartens and schools, as housewives, and in cookery. The great achievements of famous women will have full representation, and as exhibition within this building will be upon special invitation based upon merit, this is expected to be a most attractive part of the Fair. At any rate, the ladies are enthusiastic about its prospective success, and they only fear that their building, which covers nearly two acres, may be found far too small for what they will have to put into it.

"Encompassed by luxuriant shrubs and beds of fragrant flowers, like a white silhouette against a background of old stately oaks, is seen the Woman's Building, situated in the northwestern part of the Park, separated by a generous distance from the HORTICULTURAL BUILDING on the one side, and the Illinois State Building on the other, and facing the great lagoon with Wooded Island as a vista. A more beautiful site could not have been selected for this daintily designed building."

There was a large number of designs for the building prepared by women architects from all parts of the land. The President of the Board of Lady Managers selected from them all the sketch by Miss Sophia G. Hayden, whose sketch showed harmony of grouping and gracefulness of details, which indicated the architectural scholar.

THE WOMAN'S BUILDING.

and to whom was awarded the first prize of one thousand dollars and also the execution of the design. The second prize was given to Miss Lois L. Howe, of Boston, and the third to Miss Laura Hayes, of Chicago. Miss Hayden, who is a graduate, with high honors, of the School of Technology, in Boston, went from there to Chicago, and personally made the plans and elevations for the building.

The lagoon, directly in front of the structure, takes the form of a bay about 400 feet in width, from the centre of which a grand landing and staircase leads to a terrace six feet above the water. Crossing this terrace other staircases give access to the ground, four feet above, on which, about 100 feet back, the building is situated. Flower beds, in artistic designs and low shrubs, cover the first terrace, forming, together with the creamy white balustrades rising from the water's edge, and also in front of the second terrace, a charming foreground for the fine edifice. Four hundred feet is the extreme length of the principal facade, the depth of the building being two hundred feet. Italian renaissance is the style selected.

This large edifice consist of a center pavilion flanked at either end with corner pavilions connected in the first story by open arcades, forming a shady promenade the whole length of the building. The first story is raised about ten feet from the ground line, and a wide staircase leads to the center pavilion. This pavilion, forming the main triple arched entrance with open colonnade in the second story, is finished with low and beautiful proportioned pediment enriched with a highly elaborate bas-relief. The corner pavilions being like the rest of the building, two stories high, with a total elevation of 60 feet, have each an open colonnade added above the main cornice. Here are located the Hanging Gardens, and also the Committee rooms for the use of the Board of Lady Managers.

The structure is adorned with an open rotunda 70 by 65 feet reaching to the full height of the building and covered by a richly ornamented skylight. A lobby 40 feet wide leads into this rotunda, which is surrounded by a two-story open arcade, as delicate and chaste in design as the exterior, the whole having a thoroughly Italian court-yard effect, admitting abundance of light to all rooms facing this interior space. On each side of the main entrance and occupying the entire space of the curtains and on the first floor, are located on the left hand a model hospital, on the right a model kindergarten, each occupying 80 by 60 feet. On the floor of the south pavilion is the retrospective exhibit, the one on the north, to refor: works and charity organization, and each of these floors is 80 by 20 feet. The curtain opposite the main front contains the librar; bureau of information, records, etc. Ladies' parlors, committ(rooms and dressing rooms are located on the second story above tl main entrance and curtains, and all leading to the open balcony : front, and commanding a splendid panorama of almost the enti ground. The great Assembly-room and Club-room is on the secor floor of the north pavilion. The Assembly-room is provided with ɛ elevated stage. A model kitchen, refreshment rooms, receptic rooms, etc., are in the south pavilion. The building is encased wit "staff," the same material used on the rest of the buildings, and as stands with its mellow decorated walls bathed in the bright sunshii the women of the country are justly proud of the result.

The Board of Lady Managers was not created without some mi givings, nor encouraged without some fears. Established prejudic had to be overcome, numerous barriers removed and countless o˙ structions swept away before the necessary recognition was secure⋅ The election of Mrs. Potter Palmer, of Chicago, a beautiful, an i: tellectual, and above all, an energetic woman, has contributed fro the outset to establish the character of the undertaking and to insu its success. Mrs. Palmer infused life into the movement, inspir(the women of the world with her own enthusiasm, planned a sy tematic campaign, and conducted the executive department of tl board with a degree of judgment that marked her as a person of wo: derful administrative ability. The woman of fashion, the leader society, the devoted wife of one of the most prominent and wealthie citizens of Chicago, her conduct of the great responsibility which w. placed upon her shoulders not only surprised but amazed those wl were actively employed in other departments of the Exposition, ai who for that reason could understand and appreciate the magnitu(of the task which she was called upon to perform.

The women of every country on earth were invited to take pa in this exhibit; Mrs. Palmer communicated with the female sove eigns and with the consorts of sovereigns in foreign countries, askir for their assistance; the women of every State and territory in tl North American republic were organized into Boards; the women ⋅ Canada, of Mexico, and of the South American Republics we⋅ brought into correspondence; not a moment nor an opportunity w;

CHICAGO UNIVERSITY, WHEN COMPLETED.

lost in creating an interest in the Women's department everywhere, and the result is before us now.

Regarding application for space in the Woman's building, exhibits could only be entered there by invitation from the Board of Lady Managers. The space at its disposal was comparatively small and the Board wished to reserve it for the most select and distinguished things. The general design of the Women's exhibit, as outlined by Mrs. Palmer, was as follows: The Board wished to mark the first participation of women in an important national enterprise by preparing an object lesson to show their progress made in every country of the world during the century in which educational and other privileges have been granted them and to show the increased usefulness that has resulted from the enlargement of their opportunities.

The Board decided that in the general Exposition buildings, where the competitive exhibits were placed, it would not separate the exhibit of women's work from that of men, for the reason that as women are working side by side with men in all the factories of the world it would be practically impossible, in most cases, to divide the finished result of their combined work; nor would women be satisfied with prizes unless they were awarded without distinction as to sex and as the result of fair competition with the best work shown. They are striving for excellence, and desire recognition only for demonstrated merit. In order, however, that the enormous amount of work being done by women might be appreciated, a tabulated statement was procured and shown with every exhibit, stating the proportion of woman's work that enters into it. The application blanks sent out to manufacturers contained this inquiry.

Besides the foregoing extensive exhibit women had another opportunity of displaying work of superior excellence in an advantageous way in the Woman's building, over which the Board of Lady Managers exercised complete control. In its central gallery is grouped the most brilliant achievements of women from every country and in every line of work. Exhibits here were admitted only by invitation, which was considered the equivalent of a prize. No sentimental sympathy for women caused the admission of second-rate objects, for the highest standard of excellence was here strictly maintained. Commissions of women organized in all countries as auxiliaries to the Board of Lady Managers were asked to recommend object of special excellence produced by women, and producers of such suc cessful work were invited to place specimens in the gallery of the Woman's Building. The platform for the guidance of commissions and organizations throughout the world who desired to coöperate with the Board of Lady Managers was laid down as follows:

1. To procure, for competition in the main buildings, a representative exhibit showing the work of women in all the varied occupations in which they engage.

2. To procure as far as possible statistics as to the amount of woman's work that enters into every exhibit, and interesting data connected with the same.

3. To recommend to the Board work of such supreme excellence as to be worthy of admission to the gallery of the Woman's Building.

4. To recommend to the Board such women as have the requisite expert knowledge to serve on various juries of award.

5. To see that the educational work being carried on by women, from the primary to the highest branches of education, is exhibited when possible, and when not possible that it be illustrated by means of maps, charts, photographs, monographs, relief models, etc.

6. To see that the charitable and philanthropic work, as well as that to promote recreation, healthfnlness, reform, etc., inaugurated by women, is either exhibited or made matter of record as above.

7. To aid in giving suitable publicity to the plans of the Board of Lady Managers in all the leading papers, through the agency of press women when possible.

8. To aid in the collection of a loan exhibit of old lace, embroideries, fans, etc.

9. To secure books written by women for the woman's library, especially such as relate to the exact sciences, philosophy, art, etc.

10. To secure from every country a chronological exhibit, showing the evolution and progress of woman's industries from the earliest time to the present.

THE MACHINERY HALL.—Machinery Hall is second only to the ADMINISTRATION BUILDING in the magnificence of its appearance. It is 850 by 500 feet. It presents the appearance of a grand church and palace of the old world combined and on the largest scale, and was designed, with the other buildings on the great plaza where it stands, with a view to making a grand background for display, and in order to conform to the general richness of the court and add to the striking appearance, the two facades of the Machinery Hall in the court are rich with colonnades and other features. The design follows classical models throughout, the detail being followed from the renaissance of Seville and other Spanish towns, as being appropriate to a Columbian celebration. An arcade in the first story admits passage around

MACHINERY HALL.

the buildings under cover, and as in all other buildings, the front is formed of "staff" colored to an attractive tone ; the ceilings are enriched with strong color. A colonnade with a cafe at either end forms the length between MACHINERY and AGRICULTURAL HALLS, and in the center of this colonnade is an archway leading to the Cattle Exhibit. From this portico there extends a view nearly a mile in length down the lagoon, and an obelisk and fountain in the lagoon for the southern point of view.

Machinery Hall with the Machinery Annex, somewhat smaller but of similar construction, and the Power House cost nearly one million and a quarter dollars. Machinery Annex is on the west of Machinery Hall, and is an annex in fact and not a detached edifice. The Annex covers between four and five acres and increases the length of the machinery building to nearly 1,400 feet, making it the second largest of all the EXPOSITION BUILDINGS, the great manufactures structure alone exceeding it in size.

It is spanned by three arched trusses and the interior presents the appearance of three railroad train houses side by side, surrounded on all sides by a gallery fifty feet wide. An elevated traveling train runs the entire length of the long naves for moving machinery.

The location of the Hall is at the extreme south end of the Park, midway between Lake Michigan and the west line of the Park. It is west across the lagoon from the AGRICULTURAL BUILDING, and just south of the ADMINISTRATION BUILDING. Peabody & Stearns, of Boston, are the architects.

All the power for running the machinery is supplied from the separate Power House, adjoining Machinery Hall, which will contain the steam-boilers, the engines and the dynamos, provision being made to supply the largest amount of electrical power ever made. A number of steam-engines of various types will furnish 16,000 horsepower, operating the dynamos for light and power, and driving the shafting. It is only in Machinery Hall and Annex that steam-power will be used. All the power elsewhere will be required here contrasts with the 6,000 at the Paris Exposition, and the 1,456 horsepower Corliss engine driving the machinery at the Philadelphia Centennial Exposition.

The display of machinery is large and more interesting than any ever made before in an International Exposition. The electrical machines are confined, of course, to the electrical department, and some of the mining machinery to the mines and mining department, but nevertheless every inch of space is taken up in the machinery building and the scene is one of the greatest animation from one end of the great hall to the other. Everything from the smallest to the most ponderous machines of the age is to be seen in the building and its annexes, and everything is in motion. The visitor is struck at once with the great diversity shown in the construction of engines, some of which exhibit movements that he little dreamed of. The nations of the earth are in competition here. England, Germany, France, Holland, Belgium and other European countries have sent the best examples of their machinery, and the United States makes an exhibit which alongside of the best any of the other nations has to offer is creditable. This is the land of invention, and the application of steam to all sorts of purposes was never before so fully illustrated. Machinery is doing everything, and more than the hands of man were employed in doing a century ago. Some of the ingenious contrivances one would imagine almost think, so thoroughly do they perform the task assigned them. Here the machinery used in every branch of manufacture is in operation. The arrangement is perfect, and from the trains which move around the building above, the visitor can take a splendid observation of the entire exhibit. The enormous extent of space under roof in the buildings devoted to machinery, in round numbers nearly eighteen acres, is proof of the appreciation of the importance of this branch of the Exposition by the management.

THE MANUFACTURES AND LIBERAL ARTS BUILDING.— The mammoth structure of the Great Columbian Exposition is the MANUFACTURES AND LIBERAL ARTS BUILDING. It is symmetrical throughout in its proportions. It is the largest exposition building ever constructed, being 1,688 feet long by 788 feet wide, and covering nearly thirty-one acres. A gallery fifty feet wide extends around the entire building inside, on all four sides, by which is added more than eight acres to the floor space available for exhibits, and making the total floor area of the building forty acres in all. In addition to this there are eighty-six smaller galleries, twelve feet wide, projecting from the great gallery, from which can be seen the vast array of exhibits and the throng of people on the floor below. An avenue fifty feet wide extends throughout the length of the building, on the main floor, called "Columbia Avenue;" and this is crossed at right

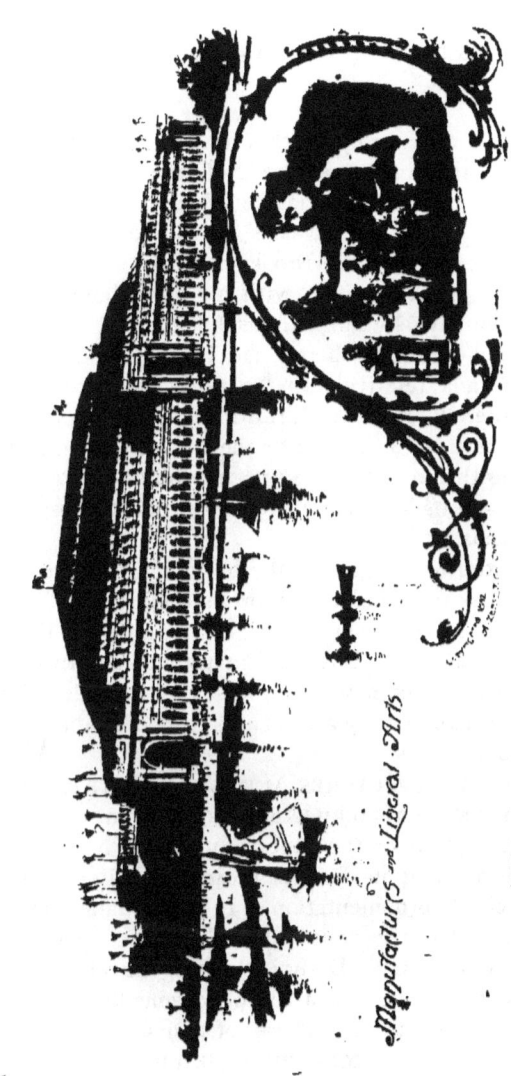

THE MANUFACTURES AND LIBERAL ARTS BUILDING.

angles at the center by another avenue of the same width. The roof covering this immense edifice is of iron and glass, and arches an area of 385 by 1400 feet, and has its ridge one hundred and fifty feet from the ground. The steel trusses for the roof will contain more metal by 50 per cent. than the Brooklyn bridge.

This gigantic edifice, with all its elaborate ornamentation, cost one million five hundred thousand dollars. It occupies a most advantageous position, facing the lake, with lawns and promenades between; and relatively to the other exposition buildings,—on the west is the ELECTRICAL BUILDING and the lagoon separating it from Wooded Island; on the south the harbor and in-jutting lagoon; and on the north the UNITED STATES GOVERNMENT BUILDING. Its own vastness and its location make it the most conspicuous building on the grounds.

In exterior appearance the building is covered with "staff," and so treated as to be made to represent marble. The great fluted columns and immense arches are apparently of this substantial and beautiful material. There are many fine entrances to the building but those at the corners and midway at the sides of the structure are grand, with their lofty arches and piers of elaborate design and ornamentation.

THE MANUFACTURES AND LIBERAL ARTS BUILDING is in the Corinthian style of architecture, and in point of being severely classi excels nearly all of the other edifices. The long array of column and arches which its facades present is relieved from monotony b very elaborate ornamentation. In this ornamentation female figures symbolical of the various arts and sciences, play a conspicuous an very attractive part. Designs showing in relief the seals of the di ferent States of the Union and of various foreign nations also appea in the ornamentation. These, of course, are gigantic in their pr portions. THE AGRICULTURAL BUILDING perhaps is the only on which has a more elaborately ornamental exterior than has this c lossal structure.

This building is regarded as one of the marvels of the Expos tion, for its architectural success. George B. Post, of New York, the architect.

It is no exaggeration to say that one might spend an entire mont in the Manufactures and Liberal Arts building, giving ten hours day to the inspection of exhibits without seeing all that is displaye here. The term "World's Fair" may be appropriately applied to this department alone, for here are the evidences of the progress of mankind in every section of the habitable globe. Whatever machinery or inventions may have accomplished; whatever the soil may have produced or the produce of the soil nourished, the results are here. Science, art and industry have their special departments; steam and electricity are represented fully; but these may be denominated causes; the effects of all our knowledge in science, art and industry, of the inventions in electrical and steam force, in navigation, in transportation, in culture, are made manifest in the Manufactures and Liberal Arts building. Here are the higher products of the age, the necessaries and luxuries of the civilized world. If the visitor, after passing through the Art, Agricultural, Machinery, Forestry, Horticultural and all the other departments and sections, is desirous of obtaining an insight into the results of man's achievements in all these branches of intellectual development and refinement, he will find it in the Manufactures and Liberal Arts building. The Liberal Arts department alone covers an immense space, and here the educational institutes and all that enters into educational systems of the various countries are fully represented.

THE ELECTRICAL BUILDING.—The Electrical Building has all the imposing appearance to qualify it to stand among the noble structures about it devoted to older arts and sciences. There will be represented in it a wonderful growth in a very short period of time.

This structure has an open portico running along the whole of the south facade, the lower or Ionic order of architecture forming an open screen in front of it. Its various pavilions are furnished with windows and balconies. The exterior orders are richly decorated in details, and friezes, pediments, panels and spandrils have received a decoration of figures in relief with architectural *motifs;* the general tendency of which is to illustrate the purposes of the building.

The architects have designed the building in its details and general outlines so that they might be capable of producing an illumination by night on a scale hitherto unknown, the flag-staffs, the open porticos, all being arranged with this in view. By day a fine effect is produced by the color of the exterior which is like marble, but the walls of the hemicycle and of the various porticoes and loggia are highly enriched with color, the pilasters in these places being decorated with scagliola and the capitals with metallic effects in bronze.

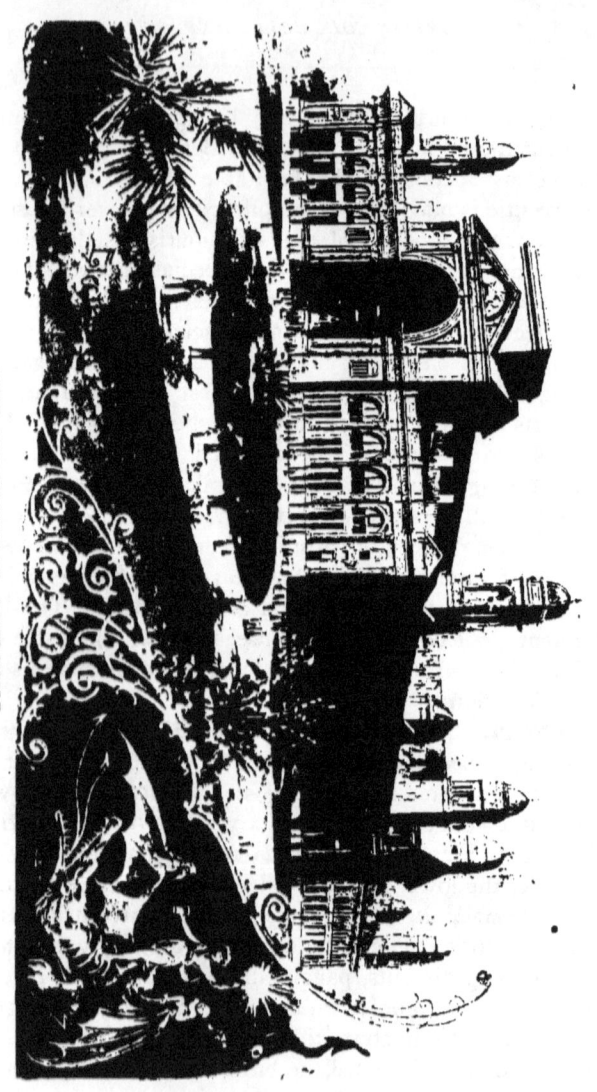

THE ELECTRICAL BUILDING.

This building is 351 feet wide and 769 feet long, the major axis running north and south. It fronts south on the great quadrangle or court, north on the lagoon, east opposite the MANUFACTURES BUILDING, and west the MINES BUILDING.

The general plan is as follows: A longitudinal nave 115 feet wide and 114 feet high, crossed in the middle by a transept of the same width and height. The nave and the transept have a pitched roof with a range of skylights at the bottom of the pitch and clerestory windows. A flat roof covers the rest of the building, averaging 62 feet in height and provided with skylights. The second story is composed of a series of galleries connected across the nave by two bridges, with access by four grand staircases. The area of the galleries in the second story is 118,546 square feet, or 2.7 acres.

The exterior walls of this building are composed of a continuous Corinthian order of pilasters 3 feet 6 inches wide and 42 feet high, supporting a full entablature, and resting upon a sylobale 3 feet 6 inches. Thus it is seen that these columns extend throughout the first and second stories. The total height of the walls from the grade outside is 68 feet 6 inches.

There are two great semi-circular projections to the structure, flanked by two towers 195 feet high, and the north pavilion is placed between these two projecting portions of the building. The great semi-circular window is the central feature of the edifice, and above it 102 feet from the ground, is a colonnade forming an open loggia or gallery, commanding a view over the lagoon and all the north portion of the grounds.

There are central pavilions on the east and west which are composed of towers 168 feet high. In front of these two pavilions is a great portico composed of the Corinthian order with full columns.

On the south there is a a pavilion semi-circular in form, 78 feet in diameter and 103 feet high. The opening of this niche is framed by a semi-circular arch, which is crowned by a gable or pediment with smaller gables on the returns and surmounted by an attic, the whole reaching the height of 142 feet. In the center of this niche, upon a lofty pedestal, is very appropriately placed, a colossal statue of FRANKLIN, "whose illustrious name intimately connects the early history of the Republic with one of the most important discoveries in the phenomena of electricity." Van Brunt & Howe, of Kansas City, are the architects. The cost of this structure is $375,000.

The Electrical Department of the Columbian Exposition wil be a revelation to even those who attribute almost miraculous powers to the great force. A hundred thousand incandescent lamps placed harmoniously about the grounds and buildings, and 10,000 arc lamps distributed advantageously to light up the beautiful architecture and pleasing landscape, would alone furnish almost a fairy spectacle; but combine with these, electric fountains, pointing rainbow sprays toward the sky, glittering lamps of many colors sparkling under the clear waters of the lagoons and at night setting out in all their dainty colorings the floral beauties and the most brilliant kaleidoscope will fade in an every-day dull contrast.

The Electrical Building itself is beautiful beyond description. Beside general ornamentation made under the direction of the chief of that department each exhibitor has been on his mettle to outdo his neighbor in uniqueness of design and grandeur in result. The laying out of arbitrary aisles in the building resulted in leaving a circular space thirty feet in diameter in precisely the center of the building. This space was the most desirable of course, and upon designs for it nearly twenty firms set at work. One firm, engaged in the business of artistic lighting, undertook to construct a great tower reaching to the dome of the building, 160 feet in height, the whole to be made of Bohemian crystal, vari-colored and in hundreds of dainty designs, all lighted from within by opalescent and tinted incandescent globes wrought into figures, designed to contrast pleasingly with the shimmering exterior.

Other exhibitors designed evanescent arches of incandescent lamps to span the main aisles of the building, the designs being so constructed that the figures could be changed instantaneously from a switch board hidden from view at the exhibitor's space. The best talent was secured by the larger electrical companies for the work of preparation of the department exhibit, and $2,000,000 were appropriated for the purpose.

A model house has been built to demonstrate in actual operation every economic application of electricity for use in the home.

Thomas A. Edison, the greatest of living electrical inventors, has been deeply interested in this department. His company it is believed has invested half a million dollars in its display.

All of the great electrical companies, telegraph and telephone companies, street railway and lighting and machinery companies of

CENTRAL MUSIC HALL.

the United States and the world at large are represented in the Elec trical Building. An especially good display of engines and dynamo comes from England, and in fact the leading features of the electrica exhibition held in London in 1892 are all here. Eugene and Pau Champion, of Neuilly-sur-Seine, France, have a series of electrica fireworks for the Exposition. Neither gunpowder, dynamite, no other explosive material is used in producing the dazzling effects Among the novelties is a model light house prepared for the World' Fair by Sauter, Harle & Co., of Paris.

The German electrical firm of Shuckertt & Co., of Nuremberg makes a general exhibit in the electrical department, and, at the sam time, gave one of the Shuckertt ground glass reflectors for the ser vices of the Exposition, and asked that it be given a prominent loca tion in a convenient point to light the lake shore and the harbor o the Exposition. A complete system, demonstrating the Europea: idea of long-distance transmission, is exhibited. A large multiphas dynamo of the five-wire system is also among the European exhibits A 1,500 horse-power direct current dynamo, a 500 horse-power alter nating current dynamo, and a 1,000 horse-power motor are feature of the exhibition of the Siemens & Halske Company. A new street car motor for conduit operation, developed by Herr Hasselwander, o Germany, the Buda-Pesth conduit railway of Siemens & Halske, an a number of storage battery systems of different European firms ar likewise exhibited. The electrical display made by Siemens & Halske, of Germany, is probably the most extensive and costly eve witnessed.

In this connection it might be well to say that the following i the arrangement of electric lights: Arc lights—Machinery Hall, 600 Agricultural, 600; Electricity Building, 400; Mines and Minin; Building, 400; Transportation Building, 450; Horticultural Hall 400; Forestry Building, 150; Manufactures Building, 2,000. Th Fine Arts Building is completely lined with incandescent lamps, an one mile of wall space, on which pictures are hung, is lighted. Th number of lamps is 12,000. There are no arc lights in this building The Woman's Building is lighted by both systems. It was decidec to place in it 180 arc lights and 2,700 incandescent lamps. The re ception and dressing rooms are furnished with the incandescent lamps The Administration Building is supplied with 1,000 incandescen lamps. The Machinery and Agricultural Annexes are supplied witl arc lights. Each building is furnished with wires for incandescent lighting in order to accommodate the exhibitors.

The saw mills are run by electricity. The Manufactures Building is supplied with electric power, and the saw mill employed there is worked by that force. At the Paris Exposition but three buildings were furnished with electric light. Each structure at the World's Columbian Exposition has a plant which may be used night and day.

In all there are used, approximately, 127,000 electric lamps, of which 7,000 are arc, of 2,000 candle power each, and 120,000 incandescent sixteen candle power lamps. To run the plant 22,000 horse-power is required. The World's Fair directors spent $1,-000,000 for these electric plants. Exhibitors are not required to pay anything for light, except in cases where they call for more lamps than are furnished by the construction department.

It was the aim of the management to make the World's Fair site and the buildings one grand exemplification of the progress that has been made in electricity. The electrical exhibits are confined to a few of the buildings, but on every hand there is a display of electricity. The grounds, including the water-ways, the wooded island, the streets and avenues, and boulevards approaching the World's Fair site, are all lighted by electricity, and in harmony with the general effect which it is desired to produce. The great structures of the Exposition are turned into a panoramic view at night by the aid of powerful electric search lights. On the gilded dome of the Administration building, on the centre pavilion of the Casino, and at other suitable points these search lights are placed. During the evenings on which the Exposition is open, the lights are turned on the several main buildings and water-ways so as to flood them with a sudden burst of electric splendor. Glimpses of the outlines of woods, water and buildings suddenly flash before the eye. And this panoramic view may be had from different points of observation.

THE TRANSPORTATION BUILDING.—The Transportation Building is a long structure and is much of the Romanesque in its style of architecture. It is exquisitely refined and simple in architectural treatment, although it is very rich and elaborate in detail. Its interior is treated much after the manner of a Roman Basilica, with broad nave and side aisles. The roof is in three divisions, the

THE TRANSPORTATION BUILDING.

middle one rising much higher than the sides, with a beautiful arcaded clerestory. The cupola, exactly in the centre of the building, rises 165 feet from the ground. The main entrance is an immense single arch, enriched to an extraordinary degree with carvings, bas-reliefs and mural paintings, the entire feature forming a rich and beautiful, yet quiet color climax, treated entirely in leaf, and called the "Golden Door." There are numerous other entrances and with them are grouped terraces, seats, drinking fountains and statues. This leads to the central open space, surmounted by a cupola rising 165 feet, and reached by eight "lifts" which will be themselves exhibits. These carry visitors to the galleries running along the sides of the building. The remainder of the architectural composition falls into harmony with the highly-wrought entrance, and is duly quiet and modest in treatment. The main building of the Transportation Exhibits is 960 feet front by 256 feet deep, and will extend westward to Stony Island avenue. Adjoining on the west is the Transportation Annex, a triangle of nine acres, consisting of one-story buildings, each 64 feet wide, set side by side. These will contain in spaces 16 feet wide, long railway lines, to exhibit trains of both freight and passenger cars and engines. This display is expected to be stupendous, and hence the large space devoted to it. There will be at least 100 locomotives arranged so that each will face a central avenue, making a fine perspective effect. Everything in the way of transportation is expected to be exhibited, ranging from a baby carriage to a huge "Mogul" engine. Technically this exhibit will include everything comprised in class G of the official classification. It forms, with other buildings, the northern or picturesque quadrangle. It is situated between the HORTICULTURAL HALL and the MINES BUILDING. Its arcial relation is with the MANUFACTURERS' BUILDING on the east side of the quadrangle; the central feature of each of the two buildings being on the same east and west line.

The cupola of the TRANSPORTATION BUILDING, viewed from the lagoon, will form the effective southwest accent of the quadrangle, while from the cupola itself, reached by eight elevators, the Northern Court, the most beautiful effect on the entire Exposition, may be seen in all its glory. These elevators of themselves will naturally form a part of the TRANSPORTATION EXHIBIT, and as they will also carry passengers to galleries at various stages of height, a fine view of the interior of the building may be easily obtained. The main galleries of this building will prove quite accessible to visitors because of the abundant placing of passenger elevators.

If we add to the effect of the exhibits the architectural impression given by the long vista of richly ornamental colonnades, it may be easily imagined that the interior of the Transportation Building will be one of the most impressive of the Exposition. A transfer railway with 75 foot tables will run the entire length of the structure and immediately west of the main building, to assist in the placing of exhibits. Adler & Sullivan, of Chicago, are the architects. The Transportation Building cost about $300,000.

For the first time in the history of world's fairs it was decided to give the science of transportation in its broadest meaning that attention to which its importance entitles it. Every method of transportation, except the back of the mule and the foot of man, is shown. The development of modern transportation has been so recent and rapid that its significance has hardly been understood. Already its early history is in many instances fading away or utterly lost. Judged by their relations to the every day life of the world, no other industry surpasses it in utility or equals it as a power in the progress of civilization. Considered from the stand-point of the amount of capital invested, it overshadows every other industry. Prof. Arthur T. Hadley of Yale College says:

"The railroads of to-day are worth from $25,000,000,000 to $30,-000,000,000. This probably represents one-tenth of the total wealth of civilized nations, and one-quarter, if not one-third, of their invested capital. It is doubtful whether the aggregate plant in all manufacturing industries can equal it in value. The capital engaged in banking is a trifle beside it. The world's whole stock in money of every kind—gold, silver and paper—would purchase only a third of its railroads."

If to the railroads be added the shipping of the world and all means of conveyance on common roads, the magnitude of the interests represented in this department of the World's Columbian Exposition may be fairly estimated.

It was the intent of this department that it should fully and fairly present the origin, growth and development of the various methods of transportation used in all ages and in all parts of the world. As far as possible the means and appliances of the barbarous and semi-civilized tribes are shown by specimen vehicles, trappings and craft. Past history is illustrated by relics of the earlier days. The development of water craft, from the crudest forms to the modern ocean steamship; of the wheeled vehicles from the first inception of the idea of the wheel to their present seeming perfection; and of that greatest of all means of transportation—the railway—is also further illustrated by accurate models, drawings, plans, and designs, in cases where the actual apparatus, appliance or machine itself could not be exhibited. It was the aim of this department to keep the historical feature clearly in view, and even to magnify it. By so doing the greatest exhibition of the actual means of transportation employed throughout the world to-day stands out in high relief by contrast, and the wonderful achievements of recent years bear more weighty testimony to the genius of the age in which we live.

Exhibits in this department are divided into six general classes —railways, intramural transit, carriages and other vehicles for common roads, bicycles, aerial and pneumatic machines, and marine transportation. Of these the railways, as most important, demand most space. A space of over eight acres is devoted to this interest. The plan adopted provides for the best possible utilization of space. Exhibitors have every opportunity for showing their appliances and devices to the best advantage. As far as possible, arrangements were made by joint agreement for showing everything in its proper place and relations. Locomotive appliances are best shown on locomotives and the appurtenances and furnishings of cars on cars.

It is believed that nearly all of the establishments engaged in locomotive, car and bridge building are represented. A large number of the leading railways of the world also make exhibits of their standard roadbed, track, and equipment. Street railways—surface, underground, and elevated—are shown very completely in this department.

A large portion of the floor space of the Transportation building proper is devoted to the display of carriages and vehicles for common roads.

Bicycles, the most recent of all road vehicles, receive the attention to which their popularity and rapidly increasing use entitle them.

Transportation through the air and by means of air is yet in a comparatively undeveloped condition. Whatever is worthy in past achievements is sent here, and whatever there is of present success or future promise. Whether or not this realm is ever conquered by

THE MINES AND MINING BUILDING.

human ingenuity, the subject will ever be a fascinating one. Montgolfier's early attempts in this field are exemplified, and the modern schools for the training of aeronauts have space allotted to them.

Every known method of transportation on water is shown in this division. Small craft of all kinds are exhibited in full size; vessels, from the nature of the case, must be shown by models. For fuller illustration, drawings, plans and paintings are shown. Much attention is given to the merchant marine. The navigation of the inland waters of the world, especially the great lakes and rivers, is illustrated more fully than in any previous exposition.

THE HALL OF MINES AND MINING.—THE MINES AND MINING BUILDING is of classic architecture. The architect, S. S. Beman, of Chicago, has followed mainly the early Italian renaissance, with which he has taken sufficient liberty to adapt it to its place in a great general Exposition. A decided French spirit pervades the exterior design; but it is kept subordinate. Its plan is simple and straightforward, embracing on the ground floor spacious vestibules, restaurants, toilet rooms, etc. This building is 700 feet long by 350 feet wide, and its location is at the southern extremity of the Western Lagoon or lake, and between the ELECTRICITY and TRANSPORTATION BUILDINGS.

There are entrances at the sides; but two grand entrances are placed at the ends, north and south, each 110 feet high, their enormous arched ways richly embellished with sculptural decorations, emblematic of mining and its allied industries, and opening into a vestibule 88 feet high. To the right and left of each entrance inside start spacious flights of stairs leading to the galleries, which are 60 feet wide, 25 feet from the ground floor, and lighted on all sides by large windows, and from above by a high clerestory extending around the structure.

The main front south looks out on the great Central Court, and the north front on the western and middle lakes and a beautiful thickly wooded island. Each corner of the building is a spacious square pavilion, each being surmounted by a dome, and the entire roof is of glass, elevated 100 feet above the floor, and all lighted by arched windows extending through the galleries. The cantilever system applied to the roof is the only one used in the Exposition buildings excepting the laxedomes, and not been used before for the support of roofs as in the Mines Building.

Between the main entrance and the pavilions are richly decorated arcades forming an open loggia on the ground floor and deeply recessed promenade on the gallery floor level, which commands a fine view of the lakes and islands to the northward and th great Central Court on the south. These covered promenades ar each 25 feet wide and 230 feet long, and from them is had access t the building at numerous points. The loggias on the first floor ar faced with marbles of different kinds and hues, which will be cor sidered part of the Mining Exhibit, and so utilized as to have ma ketable value at the close of the Exposition. The loggia ceiling will be heavily coffered and richly decorated in plaster and colo The ornamentation is massed at the prominent points of the facade The exterior presents a massive, though graceful appearance.

The great space of the interior is one story high and 630 fee long by 230 feet wide, with an extreme height of 100 feet at the cer ter and 47 at the sides. This is spanned by steel cantilever ro trusses supported on steel columns placed 65 feet apart longitudinall and 115 feet and 57 feet 6 inches transversely, thus leaving clear spa encumbered with only 16 supporting steel posts. The canti-leve are of pin connection to facilitate erection. The inner and high ends of the cantilevers are 46 feet apart, and the space between the is spanned by riveted steel trusses with an elliptical chord.

The exterior of this structure, like that of all the others, will l made of "staff," similar to that used in facing the recent Paris E position buildings. The cost of the MINES BUILDING is $250,00 This large building is to contain a most interesting exhibition of tl minerals and metals of this country, with the methods and applianc for mining and working them.

In no other department of the World's Columbian Expositio perhaps, is seen a greater diversity of exhibits than that of Mines ar Mining. Not only is there a dazzling array of diamonds, opals, eme alds and other gems, and of the precious metals, but a most exte sive collection of iron, copper, lead, and other ores, and of the product; of coal, granite, marble, sandstone and other building ston of soils, salt, petroleum, and, indeed, of almost everything useful beautiful belonging to the mineral kingdom. The mineral resourc and products, not only of this country as a whole, but of each Sta and section as well as of foreign countries is of the most complete ar representative description.

THE ART INSTITUTE.

The exhibit of coal at the Exposition, of course, is qualitative rather than quantitative. Not only are the different varieties of coal which the different localities produce, shown, but chemical analyse of each and the results of tests determining economic value and adap tability to various uses. The coal resources of the different State and sections are shown by geological maps and drawings giving con figuration, stratification, etc., which render apparent the extent an accessibility of the coal beds and veins.

So, too, as regards iron. The most strenuous efforts were mad to have an exibit worthy of that great branch of industry. Thi country is now the first nation in the world in iron production, hav ing recently forged ahead of Great Britain, its only real competitor Our production of pig iron now exceeds 10,000,000 tons annually, c nearly four times what it was ten years ago, and the production c steel now aggregates about 5,000,000 tons a year, a growth of nearl 300 per cent. in the decade. The development of the iron resource of the Southern States has been especially great and rapid.

Another exhibit which is very extensive and varied is that building stone. Granite, limestone, marble, sandstone and bluestor in scores of colors, are shown by the finest specimens procurable Nearly every State has quarries of native material of excellent qua ity. From one to half a dozen of twenty or more recognized varietie of granite, for example, are quarried in twenty-eight states, Mass chusetts, Maine, California and Connecticut being the largest pr ducers. The value of the granite output in 1889 was $14,464,095, a increase of more than $9,000,000 over that of 1880. Limestone quarried in almost every State, Pennsylvania and Illinois taking th lead. The value of the output in 1889 was $19,095,179. This is e: clusive of the output of marble, which, as is well known, is a speci of limestone, the quarrying of which in a number of the States is a important and extensive industry. Sandstone, including bluestone was quarried in 1889. to the value of $11,758,081.

One of the greatest attractions of the mines department of th Exposition is the remarkable collection of minerals owned by Profe sor A. E. Foote, of Philadelphia. It is the finest private collectic in the world, a complete history of mineralogy, and is so arrange that the mineralogy of the States is shown. This collection w shown at the Centennial, at London, and at Paris, and in each i stance received the highest award.

The Canadian Copper Company, of Sudbury, Canada, makes a mineral exhibit which includes the Canadian Company's exhibit.

In its exhibit the government geological survey places on view a sort of synoptic picture of the mineral resources of this country. Big chunks of native gold and silver are shown just as they were dug out of the earth, together with remarkable ores of all sorts, particularly those of what are called "economic minerals," such as iron, copper and tin. Accompanying these are maps drawn for the purpose of assisting the illustration. Professor Clarke, the distinguished chemist and mineralogist, was given charge of the whole matter, and he collected a wonderfully fine assemblage of precious and semi-precious stones also, which form part of the display. This collection, although it is largely composed of gems found in the United States, is not limited to those. Dozens of big boxes and trays full of such jewels of all sorts were sent from the National Museum.

Henry A. Ward, of Rochester, N. Y., whose display of minerals was one of the features of the Louisville Exposition, consumes 5,000 square feet of space for his mineral cases, and sends enough to fill 10,000 feet in a geological display. The exhibit of coal, iron ore, building stone and clays from Indiana is very extensive. There is also a special cabinet exhibit of what may be called commercial minerals. Gov. J. V. Aycardi, of Panama, tendered for exhibition at the World's Fair a beautiful piece of carved marble, a bas relief representing the landing of Columbus, which was presented to the State of Panama, nearly ninety years ago, by the Empress Josephine, who, at the same time, gave the colossal bronze statue of Columbus which now stands in Aspinwall. Pueblo, Col., makes a special exhibit. The celebrated Westerman and Briggle collection of gold specimens is seen, among other things.

The Columbian Exposition appropriately and properly yields a conspicuous place to the mining display. Interest centers in the Mining building as a museum of those metals and minerals that were such an incentive to the enterprise of the great Spanish voyager. More especially because here is placed an historical exhibit, illustrating by means of models, drawings, or original tools and appliances themselves, the successive advances made in the metallurgical art from the primitive methods in vogue among the natives of the new world at the time Columbus landed.

The evolution of the metallurgical industry is illustrated by

relics of early days. Mexico furnishes some of the old-fashioned Catalan forges for ironmaking with their crude hammers and water blasts. Catalonia was a province in Spain where this antique implement was first employed and from which skilled ironmongers were exported to the new world. This primitive affair will make a strong contrast with the modern improved forging press of 4,000 tons worked by 2,000 horse-power engines and commanded by traveling cranes capable of lifting 150 tons.

The iron industry of the United States has much to show for its development since the days of Columbus. It was as early as 1619 that a London Company sent over to Virginia 100 persons skilled in the manufacture of iron. On the banks of the James River they established the first works for the smelting of ores in America, and erected one of the Catalan forges. Unfortunately the colony was, within a few years, annihilated by Indians and the works demolished. The first blast furnace in Maryland dates back to 1724, and was christened the "Principio." Some years ago two pigs of iron bearing the lettering "Principio, 1751," were raised by fishermen from the Patapsco river. One of the pigs is exhibited at the fair.

The growth of Bessemer steel operations is the most stupendous fact in the development of the metallurgical industries. In 1865 two Bessemer converters combined gave a total annual product of 500 pounds. In 1890 there were eighty-two and the product over 4,000,000 tons. This great expansion is to be accounted for largely through the perfection of the machinery used in these processes. The most striking illustration of this is seen in the iron and steel section of the Mining building. In a conspicuous place is exhibited the original steel converter, upon which, in 1857, Mr. Kelly, of Kentucky, obtained his patent. In comparison with this relic is placed the ponderous equipment of a steel plant, presented either by a model or by a working apparatus. There are blast and puddling furnaces, open-hearth furnaces, rolls, steel trains, and every conceivable process of manufacture together, flanked by artistically arranged stacks of the product in its various forms of bars, rods, sheets, wire, etc.

The mineral exhibit from Michigan is sure to attract much attention. This includes, besides extensive collections from museums, etc., granites, marble, and other building material of rare and beautiful qualities, but which have not yet been marketed to any great extent; raw material from the iron mines, in plates 69 to 70

per cent. pure, as taken from the mines; and especially, specimens o
copper, which, in its pure state, is found only in the Michigan mines.
A copper exhibit, the "largest and most extensive ever attempted,'
is made by the Calumet and Hecla mines. It includes "obelisks o
pure copper ranging in weight from fifty to five hundred pounds, also
quantities of wire and sheet copper that has been drawn and rolled
from the native metal just as it was taken from the mines; rods o
copper bent into different shapes, and even tied into knots, as one
would tie a cravat, without breaking or splintering, as would be the
result of such an operation on the copper produced by other mine
and containing an alloy which renders it less ductile. A curious fac
concerning the silver deposits sometimes found in the copper, is, tha
nature has welded the silver and copper together without mixing
them, whereas no process has ever been discovered by mineralogist
by which the same thing can be done artificially. Examples of this
phenomena are included in the exhibit."

Nearly all the mineral-producing states of the Union make large
exhibits. Geological societies at home and abroad are well repre
sented.

THE AGRICULTURAL BUILDING.—Standing very near the
shore of Lake Michigan and almost surrounded by the lagoons tha
lead from the lake into the Park is the magnificent structure known
as THE AGRICULTURAL BUILDING. It is classic renaissance in its
style of architecture, and is 600 feet wide, and 800 feet long, its
longest dimensions being east and west. The north side of the
structure is almost on a line south of the Pier extending into the lake,
on which stand the heroic columns emblematic of the Thirteen Ori
ginal States. The front of the building runs for its entire length
along the lagoon. On the east the building faces a harbor for plea
sure boats. On the west is a continuation of the lagoons, for the
whole length of the front. For a single story building the design is
bold and heroic. The general cornice line is 65 feet above grade,
while on both sides of the main entrance are mammoth Corinthian
pillars 50 feet high and 5 feet in diameter. There is a pavilion or
each corner and in the center of the building, the center one being
144 feet square. The corner pavilions are connected by curtains,
forming a continuous arcade around the top of the building. The
main entrance is 64 feet wide, and its vestibule leads to the rotunda
100 feet in diameter. The dome is mammoth in its proportions,

THE AGRICULTURAL BUILDING.

being 130 feet high and 100 feet in diameter, and made of glass. I[n] the main vestibule statuary is placed, having for design the illustra[tion] of the Agricultural industry. And about all the entrances simila[r] designs are grouped in the most elaborate manner. The corne[r] pavilions are surmounted by domes 96 feet high and above thes[e] tower groups of statuary. The design for these domes is that of thre[e] women, of herculean proportions, supporting a mammoth globe.

This immense structure covers more than nine acres of groun[d] and together with the DAIRY and FORESTRY BUILDINGS, which cove[r] 7 and 4.5 acres respectively, costs about $1,000,000. The idea [is] new as agricultural interests are promoted by this Exposition. [A] large building stands on the south of the Agricultural Building, de[-] voted to a Live Stock and Agricultural Assembly Hall. It is nea[r] the Elevated Railroad. Like the other important buildings of th[is] great Exposition it is a very handsome structure. On the first floo[r] are located—A Bureau of Information; suitable Committee and othe[r] rooms for different live stock associations of every character; tw[o] large and handsomely equipped waiting-rooms for ladies, loungin[g] rooms for gentlemen, and ample toilet facilities. From this floo[r] broad stairways lead to the Assembly room in the second story, whic[h] has a seating capacity of 1,500. Lectures will be provided by qual[i-] fied persons upon Agricultural subjects. Here will be set forth t[he] theories to be illustrated in the other buildings.

The building and annexes devoted to the Agricultural exhibi[t] which include the products of the soil, agricultural implement[s,] machinery, etc., will attract great attention from those visitors wh[o] are interested in this branch of industry. The history of no previo[us] Exposition attested such general interest among all classes of peop[le] as to the general character, extent, the benefit it is believed wi[ll] follow, and the possibilities for good awaiting agriculturists from t[he] exhibit in the Agricultural Department of the Exposition. A grea[t] advancement has been made since the Philadelphia Centennial Expo[-] sition in all branches of farm work. Since that time the Depar[t-] ment of Agriculture has been given a position in the Cabinet; ha[s] attained a firm foothold in the estimation of the people, and has n[ot] only become one of the most prominent of the government depar[t-] ments, but has been productive of most beneficial results to t[he] commerce of our country, and every one engaged in farm worl[d.] Another advance in agricultural work is the Experiment Statio[n] that are now connected with the Agricultural Colleges of the country, supported by the Government, with trained scientists and educators at their head, their work reaching out into all the fields of scientific research, seeking to assist in a practical way those engaged in farm-work and to advance the standard of excellence in this great industry to a foremost place in the estimation of mankind. The subject of irrigation and its possibilities has, within a few years, become one of intense interest, and this Exposition presents the subject in such a way that it will attract very great attention. The great advance made in the study of dairying and the successful breeding of live stock has been one of the marvels of the past decade, and with the impetus that will be given these industries by the Dairy School and the immense Live Stock exhibit at the Exposition, the good result likely to follow cannot be estimated.

The interest throughout the country in beautifying road-ways by tree planting, the setting aside by several of the State legislatures of one day in the year to be devoted to this purpose, known as Arbor Day, and the encouragement given this excellent practice in the common schools; the popularity of and interest taken in Farmers' Institutes throughout the country by the farming community, are all indicative of the rapid advancement that has been made in agricultural pursuits since the Philadelphia Centennial Exposition. The present Exposition is the focusing point at which all the best results, the thought, intelligence, and energy of those interested in the great problems connected with the agricultural life is centered. As an instance: the question of the production of sugar from sorghum and the sugar beet is one that is attracting great interest in many sections of the country, notably in the west. The Experiment Stations in connection with the Agricultural Department at Washington are devoting time and attention to this work and the results that are shown in the Exposition, as to what can be done with an acre of ground devoted to producing sugar from these products is a source of wonder and amazement to the visitor. It attracts attention to the localities adapted to this industry, and is the means of building factories and their industries connected with the production of sugar in this manner.

The South is represented at the Exposition by so great a variety of products that one ceases to wonder at the great material advancement made by that part of the agricultural area of the country. One

THE POST OFFICE.

purpose of the Exposition of 1893 was to show to the assembled world such a magnificent result of the energy, advancement and culture of our agricultural population.

For the first time in the history of Expositions, a magnificent building is devoted entirely to the use of agricultural organizations, with a splendid auditorium or lecture-room in which to meet and deliberate.

The products of every State in the American Union and of nearly every colony and country on earth are collected here. The arrangement of the exhibits will excite the wonder and compel the admiration of the visitor. Taste of the highest order has been displayed in every section, and the interior of the great agricultural building is a scene of enchanting beauty. Illinois makes a magnificent display in this department. In the Agricultural implement and machinery section Chicago takes first place. Here are produced the greatest harvesters known. The McCormick Harvester Company has made the leading exhibit at many international expositions, and has eclipsed itself at this one. The State Board of Agriculture of Illinois has offered the prizes to exhibitors in this form :

> All samples shown in this class are to become the property of the Board of Agriculture, from which selections will be made for the purpose of exhibition at the World's Fair.
>
> For the best and largest display from any county in each of the grand divisions of the State of Illinois, $200 ; second prize, $150 ; third prize, $100.
>
> All counties competing, but failing to receive one of the foregoing prizes, will each be paid $50 by an award of that amount to the best and largest display sent from them respectively.

There were expended on the display of farm products of the State of Illinois the sum of $20,000.

The exhibit of the agricultural experiment stations of the United States is not one of the least interesting features of the Chicago Exposition. One portion of the proposed exhibit, which is to attract general attention, is *an experiment station in operation*, with its office, laboratories, etc., illustrating how the indoor work of a station is actually carried on. In another portion of the exhibit each station presents, by means of maps, diagrams, pictures, sets of publications, etc., a full statement of its location, equipment, lines of work, etc., so that the visitor can, if he desires, follow out in detail the history and the work of any particular station. The main feature, however, is a topical exhibit of the work of the stations as a whole. In this is made not the full showing of the work of any single station, but a unified exhibit showing the kind of work done by the stations, the way in which they do it, and some of the more important results which they have reached. The preparation of the exhibit was in the hands of the Committee of the Association of American Agricultural Colleges and Experiment Stations co-operating with the United States Department of Agriculture.

LIVE STOCK.—The Live Stock Exhibit will open upon June 2, 1893, with the kennel show, which will undoubtedly comprise the largest and finest collections of dogs ever seen. The rules adopted by the Live Stock Department provide only for dogs of unquestioned pedigree, and even in such cases applications will be considered strictly upon their own merits, by a committee of three experts. The kennel clubs and dog fanciers of both Europe and America are deeply interested in the exhibition, and those best informed say not less than 3,000 dogs will be exhibited. The various kennel clubs propose to supplement the already handsome premium list by a number of very handsome medals. Lord Bute, reputed to be the biggest dog in the world, and the winner of twenty-six first prizes in cups at various bench shows, will be placed on exhibition. Lord Bute is a pure-blooded St. Bernard and is owned by Knowles Croskey, proprietor of the Menthon Kennels, Phœnixville, Pa. He is a noble dog, bred in England, and cost the present owner $3,750. He is thirty-six inches high and weighs 247 pounds.

Members of the Mascoutah Kennel Club, of Chicago, expect to play the part of host to the various kennel clubs of the country which may visit the Exposition. The club passed resolutions calling upon similar clubs in all parts of the world to make a special effort to create an interest in the World's Fair.

The period devoted to the exhibition of animals for awards is as follows: Cattle, Sept. 11 to 27; horses, jacks and jennets, Aug. 24 to Sept. 27; sheep and swine, Oct. 2 to Oct. 14; kennel show of dogs June 12 to 17; poultry, pigeons, pet stock, etc., Oct. 18 to 30. Exhibitors of horses and cattle must accompany their application with pedigree of animals offered for entry. This written evidence implies a description or pedigree in the standard live stock records. Animals unregistered, but which have some peculiar value, historical or otherwise, may be exhibited, but may not compete for prizes.

The exhibit of blooded and fat cattle, sheep, swine, horses, etc.,

it is expected, will be the greatest ever held in this country. Cattl and horses will be here from England, France and Germany, at leas Some magnificent Normans are expected. Every State in the Unio will send contributions. Prizes will be given, sometimes by the Stat boards and sometimes by private people for the best exhibits. Th great stables of trotting horses in France and many famous Englis racers will be here. England, Ireland and Scotland will send ove larger exhibits than they have ever made at a foreign expositio before.

FORESTRY.—The Forestry Building is in appearance the mos unique of all the Exposition structures. Its dimensions are 200 b 500 feet. To a remarkable degree its architecture is of the rusti order. On all four sides of the building is a veranda, supporting th roof of which is a colonnade consisting of a series of columns com posed of three tree-trunks each 25 feet in length, one of them from 1 to 20 inches in diameter and others smaller. All of these trunks ar left in their natural state, with bark undisturbed. They are contr buted by the different States and by foreign countries, each furnish ing specimens of its most characteristic trees. The sides of th building are constructed of slabs with the bark removed. The win dow frames are treated in the same rustic manner as is the rest of th building. The main entrances are elaborately finished in differer kinds of wood, the material and workmanship being contributed b several prominent lumber associations. The roof is thatched wit tan and other barks. The visitor can make no mistake as to th kind of tree-trunks which form the colonnade, for he will see upo each a tablet upon which is inscribed the common and scientifi name, the State or country from which the trunk was contributed and other pertinent information, such as the approximate quantity of such timber in the region whence it came. Surmounting the cornic of the veranda and extending all around the building are numerou flagstaffs bearing the colors, coat of arms, etc., of the nations an States represented in the exhibits inside.

The forestry display, like the Forestry Building, is one of th most unique of the Exposition. It is likewise comprehensive an instructive. Forestry is rapidly becoming a vital subject of study both for the States of the Union and the nation at large. As science it is perhaps more feebly developed in the United States tha in any other civilized nation. The depletion of our natural forests alarming to those who have made this subject a study, and a rational forest management is becoming a necessity in our civil governments. The forestry exhibit at the Fair will probably give more instruction and arouse more interest in this vital question than anything else possibly could. The plan followed out in this department is simple. The government makes the exhibit which treats of forestry as a science, while the States make exhibits which have for their object the illustration of existing forestry conditions. The plan of the exhibit is the work of Dr. B. E. Fernon, Chief of the Forestry Division of the Government Department of Agriculture, and one of the highest authorities on the question. By his plan the States make an exhibit showing the forestry resources of the country, and methods of forestry development, wood-working and all industries relying on forest products and the work necessary to forest management. The government exhibit is calculated to give the student of forestry a comprehensive view of the subject. The government shows all the trees native to the United States—about four hundred and twenty-five species—and the most important of these trees—about one hundred species—are elaborately exhibited. This exhibit also shows the nature of raw wood materials, the difference of structure and quality of woods grown in different sections. There is shown a collection of fruits and seeds, planting tools, illustrations of planting methods and statistics of forest management.

In the construction of the Forestry Building, the idea of exhibiting the woods of the different States was beautifully carried out.

Many foreign nations have contributed to this picturesque exhibit. There are trees from Asia, Australia and all parts of South America among these specimens of growth of which people read but never see. The orange, lemon, banana, fig, rubber, palm, cork, date, calisaya, tar, and every species known is represented here. As in the Agricultural and Horticultural departments, the exhibits of the different States and countries are grouped.

THE DAIRY.—The Dairy Building, by reason of the exceptionally novel and interesting exhibits it will contain, is quite sure to be regarded with great favor by World's Fair visitors in general, while by agriculturists it will be considered one of the most useful and attractive features of the whole Exposition. It was designed to contain not only a complete exhibit of dairy products but also a Dairy School, in connection with which will be conducted a series of tests for

WASHINGTON PARK RACE TRACK—GRAND STAND.

determining the relative merits of different breeds of dairy cattle as milk and butter producers.

The building stands near the lake shore in the southeastern part of the park, and close by the general live stock exhibit. It covers approximately half an acre, measuring 95x200 feet, is two stories high and cost $30,000. In design it is of quiet exterior. On the first floor, beside office headquarters, there is in front a large open space devoted to exhibits of butter, and farther back an operating room 25x100 feet, in which the Model Dairy will be conducted. On two sides of this room are amphitheatre seats capable of accommodating 400 spectators. Under these seats are refrigerators and cold storage rooms for the care of the dairy products. The operating-room, which extends to the roof, has on three sides a gallery where the cheese exhibits will be placed. The rest of the second story is devoted to a cafe, which opens on a balcony overlooking the lake.

The Dairy School, it is believed, will be most instructive and valuable to agriculturists.

This department belongs properly to the agricultural exhibit, but it has been deemed advisable to separate them. No feature of the Exposition, probably, possesses greater interest or value to the agriculturist than the Dairy School. The school includes a contest between both herds and individuals of the chief breeds of dairy cattle with a view of ascertaining the respective merits of each in milk giving and butter and cheese producing. Each herd is charged each day with food consumed accurately weighed, and is credited with the milk, butter and cheese produced. Manufacturers of dairy utensils and appliances gladly furnish all that is required in their line. Accommodations are provided so that spectators may view the processes of butter and cheese-making.

The tests and all details of management are under rules prepared by a committee composed of one member from each of the dairy cattle associations in the United States, three from the Columbian Dairy Association, three from the Agricultural Colleges and U. S. Experimental Stations, and one from the manufacturers of dairy utensils.

The manufacture of the product takes place in the Dairy building, in an operating space 25x100 feet, above which on either side is a gallery which accommodates fully 500 spectators. The school in all probability will continue through four months, and each participating herd is represented by a given number of cows. The results of this test and of the exhibition which will be made of the latest and mos advanced scientific methods known in connection with the feedin; and care of cattle, the treatment of milk and the production of butte and cheese, cannot fail to be of very great value to the dairy interest of this country. These interests, it is scarcely necessary to state, ar of enormous importance and extent and, indeed are scarcely surpasse by any other branch of industry in respect of the amount of mone invested. It cannot be doubted that the Exposition Dairy Schoc will cause a more economic and scientific management of the dair interests of the entire country and consequently a greater return fron the capital and labor invested.

Representatives of seven breeds of dairy cattle have furnishe herds for the test which will be the longest in duration, and the mos thorough and exhaustive so far as cows are concerned that has eve been held. From twenty-five to fifty gilt-edge cows of each of th dairy breeds of Devons, Brown-swiss, Short-horn, Guernseys, Rec polled and Jerseys will contest with each other for the prizes whic will be awarded both to herds and individual cows.

THE HORTICULTURAL BUILDING.—The HORTICULTURA HALL faces east upon the largest lagoon, immediately south of tl entrance to Jackson Park from the Midway Plaisance, and has i front a flower terrace for an outside display, including tanks for nyn pheas and the Victoria Regia. The structure is 1,000 feet long wit a width of 286 feet, and cost $400,000. The front of this terrac having a low parapet between large vases, borders the water, and h: a boat landing at the center. The plan of this fine hall included central pavilion, with two end pavilions, each connected to the ce: ter by front and rear curtains, thus forming two interior court These courts, each a parallelogram of a half-acre, will be decorate in colors and planted with ornamental shrubs and flowers. A cryst dome surmounts the central pavilion 187 feet in diameter and 1 feet high, and under this will be the palm house. The curtains w contain the hot-houses and the plants under glass. There are gɛ leries in the end pavilions, designed for cafés, being surrounded l arcades giving charming views over the grounds and the interic which will present an attractive floral and horticultural display.

The exhibits in this building consist of all the varieties of plant vines, seeds, horticultural implements, etc. The roof will be of glɛ not far removed from the plants, so that those plants requiring su

THE HORTICULTURAL BUILDING.

shine light will be provided for, while provision is made to heat such parts as need it. The front curtains and space under the galleries are designed for exhibits that require only the ordinary amount of light. The exterior of the building is in "staff," tinted in a soft warm buff, color being reserved for the interior of the courts.

The cost of this building was about $300,000, and W. L. B. Jenny, of Chicago, is the architect.

The horticultural display is greater and grander than anything ever attempted before. The description already given of the magnificent HORTICULTURAL BUILDING indicates in itself the great attention which the management has given to this branch of the Fair. While only portions of buildings or small structures have been devoted to horticultural displays heretofore, the World's Columbian Exposition has created an immense, beautiful and cosy structure, and dedicated it to this purpose.

To the Horticultural Department belongs the distinction o the first installed exhibit of the Exposition. This consists of three great trees, an elm, an ash, and a sugar maple, which were planted near the HORTICULTURAL HALL. The elm is seventy-five feet high, two feet in diameter and weighs ten tons. Mr. Peterson, the Rose Hill nurseryman, planted these trees as a permanent exhibit the planting and transferring requiring 22 men, 12 horses and the expenditure of $600, all of which was at Mr. Peterson's individua expense.

The States of the Union have contributed some wondrous ex hibits to the Horticultural display, such a collection of fruit as perhap has never been seen before. The great fruit-bearing states from Nev York to California and from Michigan to Louisiana have rivaled eac other in the extent and costliness of their exhibits. California a was to be expected takes the lead. Missouri, New York, Delaware Indiana, Iowa, Nebraska, Virginia, Florida, in fact, every state in th Union, has exhibited its specialties in fruit growing magnificently The immense oranges of Louisiana, Florida and southern Californi are brought into contrast with the beautiful grapes of Missouri, th big red apples of Michigan, the mammoth watermelons of Mississipj and Georgia, and the luscious strawberries of southern Illinois. Th Citizens' Association of California alone occupies two and a ha acres and makes a wonderful exhibit. The Southern Californi World's Fair Association has a space 88 by 270 feet in which an e) hibition of oranges trees in full bloom is to be seen. Five acres out doors for oranges, lemons, limes, etc., and 3,000 square feet of table space for an exhibition of fruits were also granted this association. England, France, Germany, Switzerland, Austra, Russia, Turkey, Italy, Spain, Portugal, and in fact every country in Europe, as well as portions of Asia, Africa, Australia and all the Latin-American Republics and the numerous colonies are represented here. The Michigan peach orchard in full bearing is not the least attractive feature. The exhibits are changed frequently, and the odor of the tropics mingles with that of the temperate zones.

FLORICULTURE.—The floral exhibit is to be found in the HORTICULTURAL BUILDING also and it passes description. Not only the republics and colonies of the American continents, but the nations and colonies of the earth, have contributed toward making this the most gorgeous display ever beheld by man. All of the State horticultural societies, the royal and imperial horticultural societies of European nations, the associations of nurserymen everywhere, and the owners of private conservatories and hot-houses in every part of the world, have taken an active interest in this beautiful display. It required five acres in addition to the original allotment of space to accommodate the floral exhibits. The space at first intended for the Indian exhibit on the Wooded Island was given over to a rose garden; 20,000 feet of space are given to an exhibit of flower seeds alone; five acres are given over to a nursery exhibit; two beautiful greenhouses, one of them 1,000 feet long and 24 wide and the other 500 by 600 were added to the space in the summer of 1892. Half a million pansies, one hundred thousand roses, and millions of other flowers, including every known variety and species, are seen at the Exposition. The horticultural exhibit is on a scale never before attempted in the history of the world. Mr. Thorp, of the floricultural division, estimated that the equipment of the Horticultural Building, including the purchase price of plants, would be $350,000, and the total expense of the display $750,000. The floriculturists of the country donated a large share of the plants. Ten of the sixteen acres of ground on the wooded island are planted in flowers. The shores are left wild for scenic effect, and the waters around the margin are bright with water lilies and other aquatic vegetation, while the interior is planted with roses, rhododendrons, and lilies, besides a variety of wild flowers, preserved in a nursery.

THE FISH AND FISHERIES BUILDING

In addition to all this the roof of the WOMAN'S BUILDING, the interior of nearly all the department, State and foreign buildings, the grounds surrounding them, the beautiful terraces along the lagoon, etc., are all decorated with flowers.

THE FISHERIES BUILDING.—The Fisheries Building is, as far as the exterior of the structure is concerned, in the Spanish Romanesque style of architecture contrasting agreeably with the classic architecture of the neighboring buildings. The length of the building is 1,100 feet and the width 200 and cost about $200,000. There are two smaller polygonal buildings or wings connected with the main or middle structure and curving outward at either end. This gives a concave curve to the group which has a most pleasing effect. It is built on a banana-shaped island, and subdivided into three parts to conform to the curved shape of the island on which it stands. The general Fisheries Exhibit is in the central part of the building. In one of the polygonal buildings is the exhibit of the angling paraphernalia, and in the other is the water pool and aquaria, in which live fish are displayed and which constitute a wonderful exhibit. Marine fishes are transported to Chicago from the coast in sea water. An addition of 3,000 gallons of pure sea water was required for the supply on each trip.

The building for the display of live fish is circular, 134 feet in diameter, standing near one extremity of the Marine Fisheries Building and in a great curved corridor connecting the two. A rotunda 60 feet in diameter is in the center of this building, and under this rotunda, and in the middle of it, is a basin or pool 20 feet wide, from which rises a towering mass of rocks covered with moss, lichens and other aquatic plants. Crystal streams of water gush from the clefts and crevices in the rocks and fall upon the reeds, rushes, and ornamental semi-aquatic plants in the basin below.

Gorgeous gold fishes, golden ides, golden tench and others swim in this pool. Here also are ten large aquaria and a number of smaller ones. From the rotunda one side of the large series of aquaria may be viewed, which are ten in number and have a capacity of 7,000 to 27,000 gallons of water each.

Passing out of the rotunda and into a great corridor or arcade, the opposite sides of this series of great tanks, another line of tanks somewhat smaller, ranging from 700 to 1,000 gallons each in capacity, can be viewed by passing through a great corridor about 15 feet in width and reached from the rotunda through the entrance. The glass fronts of the aquaria are in length about 575 feet, through which the fish may be seen swimming in their native element, and have 3,000 square feet of surface. They make a panorama never before seen in any exhibition, being the finest exhibition of the kind ever seen in the United States, and rival the great permanent aquariums of the world not only in size but in all other respects. The United States Government Fish Commission will provide much of this display. These aquaria have a capacity of 18,725 cubic feet of water, or 140,000 gallons, which weighs 1,192,425 pounds or about 600 tons. Of this large quantity 40,000 gallons is, including reservoirs, used for the Marine Exhibit. In the entire salt water circulation, including reservoirs, there are 80,000 gallons. The pumping and distributing plan for the marine aquaria is constructed of vulcanite. The pumps are in duplicate and each has a capacity of 3,000 gallons per hour. The sea water is supplied by the United States Fish Commission from Wood's Hall Station, and the fresh water supply is secured from Lake Michigan. The sea-water supply is obtained by evaporating the necessary quantity to about one-fifth its bulk, thus reducing both quantity and weight for transportation about 80 per cent. The fresh water to restore it to its proper density is supplied from Lake Michigan.

To the close observer the exterior of the building cannot fail to be exceedingly interesting, for the architect, Henry Ives Cobb, exerted all his ingenuity in arranging innumerable forms of capitals, modillions, brackets, cornices and other ornamental details, using only fish and other sea forms for his *motif* of design. The roof of the building is of old Spanish tile, and the side walls of pleasing color.

One of the most interesting exhibits at the World's Columbian Exposition is that of FISH and FISHERIES. Therein not only will visitors of piscatorial inclinations find much to engage their attention, but others who have been wont to regard "fishy" and "incredible" as synonymous and equally inconsequential terms will undoubtedly have reason to change their minds as to the interesting features of a fish display after visiting this department of the Exposition. The Fisheries Building is a corner where the public will wish to linger, a spot where it will be possible to realize the words of John Bunyan when he wrote:

> You see the way the fisherman doth take
> To catch the fish, what engines doth he make!

A STREET SCENE.

> Behold how he engageth all his wits,
> Also his snares, lines, angles, hooks and nets.

Much has been said and written of the magnificence of the World's Columbian Exposition, by way of comparison with previous expositions, which it is proposed to eclipse. The immense strides made in every department of art, science and industry during the second half of the present century have been fittingly illustrated at the various international expositions held since the late Prince Consort of England inaugurated the great London Exposition of 1851.

Everything that science has rescued from the depths of ocean, sea, lake or river, is displayed at the fisheries exhibit. Inhabitants of deep-sea grottoes; the coral animal—builder of islands and continents; sea anemones, that blossom miles below the surface of the ocean; monstrous devil-fish, sharks and other terrors of the deep are seen, beside the speckled beauties of stream or lake, the plebeian catfish, perch and sucker, suggestive of the boyish angler and the shallow stream. From ocean depths are brought specimens of subaqueous life so marvellously delicate and so richly beautiful that the microscope will only reveal in part their wondrous beauty and film-like tracery. The methods, too, by which the mysteries of the deep are penetrated, the paraphernalia of the United States Fish Commission, the inventions by which the finny tribe is cultured, the wonderful progress made in the art of fish farming, in addition to the implements of commercial fishing and the latest tackle for angling—all these are displayed to their fullest extent.

Not the least interesting portion of the exhibit is the Aquarial or Live Fish Display. This is contained in a circular building, 135 feet in diameter, standing near one extremity of the main Fisheries building, and in a great curved corridor connecting the two in the center of the circular building is a rotunda sixty feet in diameter, in the middle of which is a basin or pool about twenty-six feet wide, from which arises a towering mass of rocks covered with moss and lichens. From clefts and crevices in the rocks crystal streams of water gush and drop to the masses of reeds, rushes and ornamental semi-aquatic plants in the basin below. In this pool gorgeous gold fishes, golden ides, golden tench and other fishes disport. From the rotunda one side of the larger series of aquaria may be viewed. These are ten in number, and have a capacity of seven thousand to twenty-seven thousand gallons of water. Passing out of the rotunda by the entrances, a great corridor or gallery is reached, where on one hand may be viewed the opposite side of the series of great tanks, and on the other a line of tanks somewhat smaller, ranging from 750 to 1500 gallons each in capacity. The corridor or gallery is about fifteen feet wide. The entire length of the glass fronts of the aquaria is about 575 feet or over 3,000 square feet of surface. They make a panorama never before seen in any exhibition, and rival the great permanent aquariums of the world not only in size, but in all other respects.

The total water capacity of the aquaria, exclusive of reservoirs, is 18,725 cubic feet, or 140,000 gallons. This weighs 1,192,425 pounds, or almost 600 tons. Of this amount about 40,000 gallons are devoted to the marine exhibit. In the entire salt water circulation, including reservoirs, there are about 80,000 gallons. The pumping and distributing plant for the marine aquaria is constructed of vulcanite. The pumps are in duplicate, and each have a capacity of 3,000 gallons per hour. The supply of sea water is secured by evaporating the necessary quantity at the Woods Hall station of the United States Fish Commission to about one-fifth its bulk, thus reducing both quantity and weight for transportation about 80 per cent. The fresh water required to restore it to its proper density is supplied from Lake Michigan. In transporting the marine fishes to Chicago from the coast there was an addition of probably 3,000 gallons of pure sea water to the supply on each trip.

It is a matter of importance that provision was made in the upper part of the building for an eating saloon in which a specialty is made of supplying food composed of fish and other animals taken from the water. This is a practicable and most excellent illustration of our fisheries, and this special work is so conducted as to give those who patronize fish dinners at the Exposition a better conception than the majority of them now have of the value of fish as food.

Under the direction of Henry Elliott, the only artist who has ever drawn and painted the seal and walrus in their native haunts, an interesting exhibit for the World's Fair was prepared by the Smithsonian Institution. This exhibit consists of models in papier mache representing the fur seal and walrus fisheries on the Alaskan coast. The animals represented, as well as the men who catch them, are modeled in clay. One of the models shows a seal "drive." This model includes hundreds of mimic seals which Aleuts are driving along to the killing grounds by waving cloths and shouting. Another illustrates a "rookery" on which the full grown seals, bellowing and pugnacious, have hauled up out of the surf upon the islands to breed. Another model shows a hauling ground of bachelor seals. The killing of seals is also shown, a group of Aleuts being represented in the act of smashing their heads with clubs. There is also represented a number of hair seals, which are not useful for their fur, but merely for food supply to the natives of that region. The walruses, now rapidly becoming extinct, are also reproduced in material that gives them a remarkably life-like appearance. Hundreds of models in clay are made of these animals, in order to represent the different species and sizes of each. They are cast in papier mache and painted.

THE ART PALACE.—The FINE ART GALLERY is intended to be a perfectly safe depository for the art collection, and it and the UNITED STATES BUILDING will be, considering size, the costliest structures of the Fair. Many of the art exhibits herein contained will probably be bought for the permanent gallery Chicago intends establishing after the Fair is over, as its memento. Among the paintings already here is Moro's picture of Columbus, executed in 1540, and bought in London to exhibit at the Fair. The ART BUILDING is in reality a group of galleries. The chief structure is cruciform with a nave 320 feet long by 96 feet wide, and transepts stretching 500 feet. The four exterior angles are filled in with lower constructions, thus making it a parallelogram or oblong, 500 feet by 320 feet, with a wide projecting portico in the middle of each side, the roof extending from all the cornices back to a central dome, and intersected north, east, south and west by a great nave and transept 100 feet wide and 70 feet high, and at the intersection of which is the great dome 69 feet in diameter. This magnificent structure is in the Grecian-Ionic style of architecture and is a pure type of the most refined classic architecture. It is 125 feet to the top of the dome, which is surmounted by a colossal statue of the type of famous figures of winged Victory. The transept has a clear space through the center of 60 feet being lighted entirely from above. On either side are art galleries 20 feet wide and 24 feet above the floor. The cost of this ART PALACE is between $500,000 and $600,000 and was planned in the World's Fair Construction Department, under the eyes of Supervising Architect D. H. Burnham and Chief Designer P. B. Atwood.

THE ART PALACE.

On the main floor of the nave and transept the collections of sculptures are displayed, and on the walls of both the ground floors of the galleries are ample areas for displaying the paintings and sculptured panels in relief. The corners made by the crossing of the nave and transept are filled up with small picture galleries. And around the entire building are galleries 40 feet wide forming a continuous promenade around the classic structure.

Separated from the main gallery, and 100 feet distant on the east and west sides, are two annexes, each 320 feet by 120 feet. These annexes are one-storied and divided into large and small galleries. The annexes are brought forward so that the whole group surrounds three sides of a court 300 feet by 700 feet, which will be made an attractive feature. The architect of the annexes in its facade at least, is George W. Root.

The entrance to the main building is by four great portals, richly ornamented with architectural sculpture, and approached by broad flights of steps. The walls of the loggia of the colonnades are highly decorated with mural paintings, illustrating the history and progress of the arts. The frieze of the eastern walls and the pediments of the principal entrances are ornamented with the sculptures and portraits in bas-relief of the masters of ancient art The general tone or color is light gray stone. The building, though of a temporary character, is necessarily fire-proof. The main walls are of solid brick covered with "staff," architecturally ornamented, while the roof, floors and galleries are of iron.

This palatial structure is beautifully located in the northern portion of the Park, with the south front facing the lagoon. Beautiful terraces separated the structure from the lagoon. They are ornamented with balustrades, with an immense fight of steps leading down from the main portal to the lagoon, where there is a landing for boats. The north front faces the wide lawn and the group of State buildings. Groups of statues, replica ornaments of classic art, such as the Choriagic monument, the "Cave of the Winds," and other beautiful examples of Grecian art, ornament the immediate neighborhood of the building. The ornamentation also includes statues of heroic and life-size proportions.

It was the general impression for some time after the holding of the Columbian Exposition at Chicago had been decided upon that the department of Fine Arts would be the weakest. The point was raised that Europe would not contribute its art collections or any considerable portion of them for the reason that Chicago was generally believed abroad to be a city far removed from the centre of education and culture in the United States. This point was raised, however, by persons who under-rated European knowledge with regard to Chicago. It very soon became evident that the choice of Chicago as the location of the World's Fair was not only received favorably abroad, but with more satisfaction than if New York had been selected, and by no class was the selection of Chicago received with more satisfaction than by that interested in the development of art. Scarcely had the invitations to foreign governments been sent out by the State department before applications for space began to pour in. The amount of wall space asked by England, France, Germany, Austria, Italy, Belgium, Switzerland, Russia and other European States was greater than they had consumed at the last Paris Exposition, and was a pleasant surprise to the Exposition management. In 1892 Halsey C. Ives, chief of department, made a six months' tour through Europe. He visited every important art center on the Continent, and returned convinced that England, France, Germany, Belgium, Holland and Italy would make magnificent displays.

The Art Building, as planned, had approximately 125,000 square feet of space for pictures. This was exclusive of the space allotted to Sculpture and Statuary. Mr. Ives found that 200,000 square feet would be necessary for pictures. He based his opinion upon the fact that early in 1892 all the available space had been practically consigned, while a dozen foreign countries at least were still to be heard from. France alone had asked for 82,000 square feet. Eighty-two thousand square feet for an art exhibit was more than twice the combined amount asked for by England and Germany. The former secured 20,000 square feet and the latter a like amount. Belgium asked for 8,000 square feet; Holland, 3,000; Denmark, 3,000; and Japan 2,000, making a total of 56,000 square feet. It became necessary, therefore, that the two annexes to the building should be considerably enlarged. Even with the additional space the visitor will find that the walls and floors of the magnificent building are crowded.

No one thing exhibited at the Centennial attracted more general attention, or was more distinctly remembered than the "Sleeping Iolanthe," in butter, by Mrs. Caroline S. Brooks. Since that won-

AUDITORIUM CURTAIN.

derful success, the artist has done several notable bits in a characteristic vein, the best known being "Lady Godiva," a bas-relief which was also in butter. The World's Columbian Exposition, however, has another, and a full length "Sleeping Iolanthe" in marble. Mrs. Brooks worked upon the exquisite creation for several years, and found difficulty in securing a block of marble, flawless in quality, which should also be large enough.

The statue of Shakespeare, by William Ordway Partridge, intended for Lincoln Park, and the statue of Alexander Hamilton, intended for Boston, by the same sculptor; a life-size portrait of Columbus, by Sallus, the celebrated painter of Ecuador; two ancient Greek vases made of baked clay and which are twenty-two centuries old; a marble tablet representing the landing of Columbus, from Colon, United States of Colombia; the Spitzar art collection, the most comprehensive collection of European art in the world, and valued above $4,000,000; an immense display of ceramics from many nations; the $10,000 portrait of Columbus, executed by the famous Moro in 1540; the display of the American Society of Wood Engravers which attracted so much attention at the last Paris Exposition; displays by the etchers of the United States and foreign countries; the display of the National Lithographers' Association; an immense exhibit by the photographers of this and other countries; the paintings of G. A. P. Healy, the famous American artist; the large and valuable collection of Rudolph Crenan, of Leipsic, representing scenes and incidents in the life of Columbus; the greatest paintings of France, Germany, England, Belgium, Holland, Italy, Spain, Switzerland and other European nations; the choicest specimens of art from Asiatic, Australian, African and South American centers; the rarest and most costly sculptures, statues, arts, etc., from the greatest galleries in the world, and the most impressive collection of the works of American artists, will be among the attractions of the Art Building.

Architecture is represented strongly in the Art Building. The American Institute of Architects took a decided stand in favor of making the exhibit a prominent and a worthy one. This Institute includes in its membership all the well-known names, in different parts of the country, of men to whom the growth of American architecture, as distinguished from mere building and construction, is due, and of which they are to-day the honored representatives.

THE PALMER HOUSE.

The rules governing the Art exhibit may be briefly stated as follows: "All work to be admitted must be originals, with the exception that casts from original works by modern artists are placed in the same class with original figures and groups in marble. There will be three sections in the department—an American section, a section for foreign countries that are represented by a commission, a section comprising private collections and the works of artists from countries not represented by a commission. All works must be examined by the official jury before they can be admitted. Progress in American art and architecture is to be a special feature of the exhibit."

THE CASINO AND PIER.—The Pier, extending out into Lake Michigan from the eastern extremity of the Grand Court or avenue running from the ADMINISTRATION BUILDING to the lake, is one thousand feet long and eighty feet wide. At the extremity of the Pier is the beautiful Casino. Along the shore from which the Pier projects runs a beautiful promenade large enough to hold the thousands of visitors that will throng it during the fair.

From the Pier will be in full view the entire line of Exhibition Buildings. Passenger steamers will ply to and fro from the Pier and the City.

The architecture of the Casino is of the Venetian order, and was planned by Architects Burling and Whitehouse, of Chicago. It is a composite structure embracing nine pavilions, and is meant to be a representation, on a small scale, of Venice in the waters of Lake Michigan. It is built on piles, and is 180 by 400 feet. It has nine pavilions two stories high, except in the middle, where the central pavilion rises to the height of 180 feet. The communication between the nine pavilions, separated as they are by water, is by means of gondolas and bridges, in imitation, as far as possible of the way of getting about in Venice. The aspect is truly Venetian,—with its gondolas, bridges and water.

In front of the Casino is the harbor for small pleasure boats. At night this harbor is lighted by incandescent lamps sunk beneath the surface of the water. A gallery fifty-six feet wide surrounds the central pavilion, while at the west end of the Pier stands thirteen columns designed by sculptor St. Gaudens to represent the THIRTEEN Original States of the UNION.

The material of the Casino is of wood, and the walls are covered with "Staff," in resemblance of marble, highly and variously colored,

At the Casino the visitor will be furnished with excellent music and light refreshments, as well as permitted a view of water, city and exposition palaces while enjoying the cool breezes.

THE STATE BUILDINGS AND EXHIBITS.—Sites for buildings or space for special exhibits were allotted by the Exposition management to every State and Territory of the American Union. Every one of them is represented in some manner on the Exposition grounds ; most of them creditably, some of them magnificently. The foreign visitor must understand that each of the States and Territories is perfectly independent in all such matters, and that it is only by a vote of the respective State or Territorial Legislatures, involving the appropriation of funds to meet the expenses of the exhibit, that action could be taken. It is a matter in which neither the Federal government nor a neighboring state or territory can interfere. Some of the State legislatures were generous in their appropriations ; some delayed action until the last moment. As a rule, when the legislatures failed to act, or when their action was considered inadequate to the importance of the event, private citizens contributed, in order that their States should not be left out in the cold or misrepresented by a poor display. Chicago being the chief city of the State of Illinois' the latter commonwealth very naturally takes the lead among her sisters.

The Illinois building is one of the grandest on the grounds, and the Illinois exhibit ranks among the first. For convenience sake the State buildings and State exhibits are arranged alphabetically rather than with regard to their prominence, politically or otherwise. The following is a description of some of the State buildings.

ALABAMA.—Provision was made for a state building for Alabama. The state is represented in miniature at the Exposition by a series of comprehensive relief maps. It is proposed to show the mineral deposits, cotton belt, vegetable farms and everything else of interest in the state on a series of maps covering 20,000 square feet. Besides this an exhibit of the state's industries and products will be found grouped in the Department buildings. Alabama likewise contributed to the general display.

ARKANSAS.—Arkansas has no special state building, but she makes an exhibit of her industries and products that will be representative and worthy. While the legislature did nothing toward furthering the exhibit of the state, the citizens organized and the result is apparent to the visitor. Arkansas also contributed to the general Exposition. In the forestry display there are some noted specimens of her pine trees. In the agricultural building also she has made a creditable showing.

CALIFORNIA.—The California building is characteristic of the great Pacific Coast State, picturing in its exterior the California of the Padres, and in its interior the California of to-day. While the architect has closely followed the old mission style, he has interjected enough of the more ornate Moorish to relieve the somewhat somber effect of the old churches, and he gives the required light and roominess. Therefore there is a charming simplicity of detail. Outside there is a clear story with a great, flat central dome as the crowning feature and a roof-garden to heighten the semi-tropical appearance. From the ground to

the eaves is fifty feet and to the highest point of the roof proper sixty-five fee
while the elevation of the dome is eighty feet. Those portions of the roof n(
devoted to the garden are closely copied after the quaint adobe buildings of th
early Spanish settlements, with genuine earthen-ware tiles, deep red in colo
semi-cylindrical and overlapping. The dome and middle portions are tiled wit
iron plates curled and shaped like the original roofing. The material of th
walls is wood, treated with some sort of cement and worked into a close imit;
tion of the yellowish-gray adobe of the old days. On the four corners and flan]
ing the dome are towers designed after the mission belfries, and in them a1
swung some of the old Spanish bells which have outlived the Padres and the
crumbling churches. The interior carries a gallery giving an area equal to tw(
thirds of the ground floor. This is set apart for offices, which are grouped so a
to command a clear view of the main floor. The ground-plan is one vast exh
bition hall, the arrangement of compartments conforming to the extent of th
displays as decided upon by the Commissioners. The total floor space is 100,00
square feet, of which the gallery affords 40,000, the extreme measurements (
the building being 500 feet by 110 feet main width. The cost of the building i
$75,000.

A wonderful exhibit is presented by California. The state has long bee
famous for the size of its trees, some of which are the largest in the world. Thi
exhibit is nothing more nor less than a complete railway car, excepting only th
trucks, fashioned and carved from the trunk of a "Sequoia Giganta," or bi
tree of Tulare county. The originators of the idea are Messrs. Doyle, Meyei
and Bachman, of the county named. The tree used is about twenty-eight fee
in diameter and something more than four hundred feet long. The immense lo
was cut down to the size of a car, or about eleven feet square and fifty-five fee
in length. All this had to be done by hand with long saws made expressly fc
this purpose. It was then hollowed out inside by first cutting doors at each enc
working out the insides and polishing the inside surface; the roof is the natur;
bark of the tree. The material taken from the inside and cut off in squarin
the log was manufactured into useful little souvenirs of this wonderful produc
tion. A full-sized railway car made of but a single piece of wood will surely b
a feature of great interest. California will show as a part of its exhibit th
finest collection of minerals in the United States. Instead of making a specie
collection, as was done for the New Orleans, Philadelphia and Paris exposition
the state sends the magnificent collections belonging to the State Mining Burea
Museum. The State University had the collection of the State Geological Sui
vey, the Voy collection, Hanks collection, Keene collection, and several others
These are all classified, arranged, identified and labeled. Each county and dis
trict in the state is properly represented. Every department of the mining in
dustry has its separate place with locality indicated. No other state or territor,
of the Union has any such collection as belongs to California now. Among th
exhibits from Southern California is a model constructed to illustrate irrigation
Of course the California exhibit is one of the greatest and grandest on th
grounds. The state appropriated $300,000, and every cent of this, and a grea
deal more, has been spent in securing an exhibit worthy of the golden state
The wine and fruit exhibits alone are superb. Besides California's special dis

MARYLAND.

PENNSYLVANIA.

ILLINOIS.

NEW JERSEY.

WEST VIRGINIA.

CALIFORNIA.

play she has contributed largely to every other department of the Exposition, and the visitor will be amazed at the extent of her resources. The state's various exhibits are mentioned in connection with the different departments.

COLORADO.—This young state has a granite and marble palace. The Colorado Marble and Mining Company contributed the material for the building. Besides the mineral, agricultural and educational exhibits, the flora and fauna of the state are shown in great completeness. More than 1,000 specimen plants were pressed ; nearly 200 varieties of fruit were duplicated perfectly in wax and more than 2,000 species of insects were mounted long before the Exposition was opened. Colorado contributed largely to every department of the Exposition· The women of Colorado subscribed $10,000 for the purchase of Powers' famous statue " The last of his race," which appears in connection with the Colorado exhibit. The statue represents a dying buffalo with an Indian standing by its side with uplifted spear. This state makes a specially fine mineral exhibit. The exhibit of Colorado is both technical and economic in its character, and forms a popular and massive display of the state's resources in ores, building stone, coal, iron, commercial clays, gold and silver.

CONNECTICUT.—The state of Connecticut made no appropriation for the World's Fair, but $50,000 was raised by general subscriptions, the city of Hartford contributing alone $10,000. This money has been spent in a manner that insures Connecticut a favorable representation in the several departments, and also a special exhibit.

DELAWARE.—The little state of Delaware lost no time in subscribing its loyal adherence to the World's Columbian Exposition, and considering the extent of its area opened its coffers with a liberality which is highly complimentary to its citizens. The first donation was $10,000, which was to be followed by a further sum of $15,000. It occupies a position in the Exhibition buildings, but its headquarters will be in the space allotted in Jackson Park to the different states. The building which is constructed wholly of native woods and materials of the state of Delaware, is very picturesque and elaborately finished, measuring 58 feet by 60 feet. The cost was $7,500. A room in the building is fitted up in Colonial style, with hangings, pictures, and furniture all in representation of Colonial days. There are figures in clay of the old Swedes' Church in Wilmington, Barratt's Chapel, near Frederica, the home of Methodism, and Christ Church, near Laurel. Old Swedes' Church was founded in 1699 at a cost of £800. Barratt's Chapel, located in Kent county, near Frederica, and eleven miles south of Dover, was founded in 1780. Christ Church, Broad Creek, about two miles east of Laurel, Sussex county, was built more than a hundred years ago of heart pine. It is without a particle of paint. It has the high-backed pews, the chancel at one end, the servants' gallery at the opposite end, while midway on the east side is the lofty pulpit, and immediately below are the reading-desk and the clerk's desk. The first consignment of Delaware's exhibit comprised six cars loaded with native woods, three cars from Sussex, two from Kent, and one from New Castle counties. The consignment was placarded " From the World's Fair Commissioners of ़Delaware to the Columbian Exposition, Chicago." This was one of the earliest consignments received.

FLORIDA.—The design of the Florida state building is modeled after old

Fort Marion, which is one of the most picturesque as we'l as the oldest structure in North America, and an interesting relic of Spanish conquest in the new world. Begun in 1620, when the Pilgrim Fathers were landing at Plymouth Rock, this curious four-bastioned fortress was ancient long before the white man reared his cabin on the spot on the shores of Lake Michigan which is now a center of interest throughout the civilized world. The form of the building renders it peculiarly well adapted for the display of Florida's varied resources, the mast and ramparts affording opportunity for a series of sunken and hanging gardens of remarkable interest. The cost of building and exhibit was $100,000. In addition to her special exhibit, Florida occupies three acres of space in the exhibition of flowers.

GEORGIA.—Georgia has a handsome building and a creditable display, the cost of which was provided by private subscription. The sum of $100,000 was raised by the citizens of the state. The state is represented in nearly every department of the Exposition.

IDAHO.—Idaho has a state building peculiar to herself. Recognizing the folly of attempting to compete with the older states in the erection of an elaborate building, she constructed one somewhat rustic in appearance and costing $15,000. In its exhibit Idaho pays special attention to the mining industry. It may not be generally understood, but the fact remains that the state has contributed $175,000,000 of money in gold and silver to increase the wealth and enrich the commerce of the land. It produces one-half the lead product of the United States. In consideration of these facts a special effort was made to have a mining exhibit commensurate with the importance of the state as a valuable mineral producer. The state legislature appropriated $20,000. Private citizens contributed $100,000 additional.

ILLINOIS.—The state of which Chicago is the chief city very naturally takes the lead among her sisters, both as regards her special building and her special exhibit. Aside from private contributions, which were numerous, the state legislature appropriated $800,000 to defray the expenses, to begin with. The Illinois building has come to be looked upon as one of the main structures of the Exposition. It occupies one of the most favored spots on the grounds, in the northern or "improved" portion of Jackson Park, where on the south for nearly one mile there is a view of a beautiful water-way, and on the north and east are the unique buildings of other states and foreign nations. Illinois was the first state to be ready with its building, and in its construction there was expended $250,000. The building, with its dome 200 feet high, is located near where the boat-house formerly stood on the artificial lake. A broad channel about sixty feet wide was extended from the southeast portion of the park up to this lake. The grand entrance to the building faces this water-way, and passengers up this channel discover the Illinois state building looming up at the end of the route. The structure is placed on a terrace four feet high, and in front of the entrances there are stone terraces with railings, statues, and stone steps leading down to the roadway. The main features are the terraces north and south, the south the more important of the two, as from this point may be viewed the panorama of all the magnificent Fair buildings, as well as the water-way. The building is embellished with fine carving and statuary, the material being cast blocks of approved composition. It is thoroughly lighted, first from the side windows, which are placed about fourteen feet above the floor to permit cases to be placed against the walls; second, with skylights placed in the flat roof of the side aisles; and third with continuous skylights on the ridge of pitched roof or nave. Ventilation is provided for through windows placed a story above the flat aisle roof and the foot of the sloping roof over the nave. The building is constructed of Illinois stone, brick and steel. The Memorial hall and school were formerly designed to be separate buildings, but it was decided to incorporate them in the main structure. Fountains and flowers decorate the adjacent grounds, and allegorical statuary finds a place in the decorative features of the building. The interior of the structure is appropriately ornamented. There are no competitive exhibits in the Illinois state building. It is "a collective, departmental exhibit for the state, which shall illustrate its natural resources, together with the methods employed and results accomplished by the state in its municipal capacity through its several departments, boards, commissions, bureaus and other agencies in the work of promoting the moral, educational and material welfare of its inhabitants, so far as such methods and results are susceptible of exhibition." A feature is a model common school-room of high grade, fully equipped and furnished, under the direction of the state superintendent of public instruction. This includes the following: An illustration of the methods and results of educational work as pursued in the normal universities, the public, technical and art schools and the high schools of the state; an exhibit by the University of Illinois of the equipment, methods of instruction and achievements of that institution in its several departments; an exhibit of the educational and industrial work as conducted in the state charitable institutions. There are also collections, correctly classified and labeled, illustrating the natural history and archæology of the state; an exhibit by the state fish commission of native and cultivated live fish, with hatchery and appliances and equipments for transportation, models of fishways in use; also a special collection of the cultivated products in the several branches of agriculture; architectural drawings (with elevations) of every public building erected and now used or maintained in whole or in part by the state; also maps, charts, diagrams and tables for the state, and, so far as practicable, for each county. In the memorial hall, which is fire-proof, there are placed such relics and trophies belonging to the state as the governor has designated. The control and general management of the exhibit devolves upon the state board of agriculture. The board in turn invited the co-operation of Illinois members of the national commission and of the board of lady managers.

There are three entrances—the prominent one to the south, one to the west facing the Midway Plaisance, and the other on the north end of Memorial hall from the boat landing or the edge of the lagoon. The building in the main is 160 feet wide by 450 feet long, with the school-house, about 75x60 feet, taken out of the east end and within the building. The dome is 72 feet in diameter and about 200 feet high, with a lookout about 80 feet high and another in the lantern about 175 feet high. The side walls are 47 feet high, while the center wing on the south is 72 feet high, and both ends 54 feet, with a still higher projection in the center. On the north the Memorial hall forms a wing 50x75 feet,

while on the south is placed the executive offices in a wing 75x123 feet, carrie up three stories, with a public hall in the third story. In addition to thes offices, there are others in each of the four corners for the departmental officer: The Memorial hall has a gallery. There is a gallery around, inside and outsid of dome piers for viewing the exhibit hall.

The figure which crowns the main entrance of the Illinois building is fro1 the hands of the sculptor Taft. It is a draped figure with arms outstretchec and is called "Illinois Welcoming the Nations." Another allegorical group t be seen on this building is "The Birth of Chicago." Chicago, a rare an radiant maid of grace divine, garbed in trailing robes, is pictured coming fro1 earth like a new Pallas Athene springing full-armed from the forehead of Zeu: Nymphs of the lake, the forest and the stream attend the nativity of fa Chicago, and all their unstinted offerings are poured out in glad profusion ; the feet of the new queen and goddess. "La Salle and his Companions" an "Education" are other groups that will command attention and admiratio1 All are by Taft. There are twelve groups in all, and the cost was $12,500.

One of the most interesting features of the Illinois exhibit is the Worthe collection of fossils and library. There is a splendid coal exhibit here showin the product of the Illinois mines. The state fish commission is well repr(sented among the exhibits ; there are exhibits of the state charitable and crim nal institutes ; of the various products, and mineral and industries ; a geologic: exhibit, an emergency hospital exhibit, a kindergarten exhibit, an education: exhibit, besides great displays of fruit and flowers. Illinois does not confir her exhibits to this building, however. Her competitive exhibits will be foun in every department of the Exposition. The following was the apportionme1 of the funds at the disposal of the state commission : woman's exhibit, $40,00(construction, $195,800 ; statuary, $17,700 ; architect's fees, $11,500 ; grounds an exterior ornamentation, $10,000 ; interior furnishing, $60,500 ; normal and con mon schools, and university, $30,000 ; board of charities, $20,000 ; natural hi: tory, geology, archæology, $40,000 ; fish commission, $5,000 ; agriculture, etc $25,000 ; live stock, $40,000 ; horticulture, $20,000 ; agricultural drawings, map: etc., $27,000 ; state and county statistics, $8,000 ; printing and stationer: $30,000 ; administration, including cost of ceremonies, receptions, expenses (board, salaries, freight transportation, rents, care of buildings, contingencie etc., $175,000.

INDIANA.—The World's Fair commissioners of Indiana offered prizes ($300, $200 and $100 respectively for the first, second and third best plans for tł Indiana building. The building cost about $25,000, and it contains about 6,0(square feet of floor space. Instead of costing $25,000 the building whe completed is said to have cost double this sum. Indiana is represented i every department of the Exposition, and everywhere creditably.

IOWA.—"The Blue Grass Palace" of Iowa is one of the attractive noveltic of the Exposition. The state appropriated a preliminary sum of $50,000, whic was greatly increased to meet the expenses of the Iowa building and exhibi The Iowa building, a handsome structure, cost alone $25,000. The corn, educ tional, horticultural, mechanical and industrial exhibits generally of the sta· are among the attractions of the Exposition.

KANSAS.—The Kansas state building is cruciform in design, two stories high, and cost $20,000. It is constructed entirely of Kansas material. The building consists of 13,934 square feet. There are 4,058 square feet in the rear for the natural history exhibit of the state university; 3,340 square feet in the front of the building for headquarters accommodations, leaving a balance of 6,336 square feet for odd bits in the center of the building. The second floor contains 3,840 square feet for exhibits and 3,340 square feet in the front of the building for further consideration. The building combines the idea of a clubhouse and a building for the state exhibit. Kansas contributes largely to the attractions of nearly every department of the Exposition. Aside from the state appropriation, her citizens raised by private subscription $150,000 to defray the expenses of a creditable exhibit.

KENTUCKY.—Kentucky is represented by a handsome building and a worthy exhibit. She contributes to every department of the Exposition. The legislature appropriated $100,000, and private citizens contributed generously.

LOUISIANA.—Louisiana is represented in many of the departments of the Exposition. Her exhibits are not as complete as they should be, but they are not unworthy of the great gulf state.

MAINE.—The Maine building is constructed entirely of native granite, and cost $10,000. The building is used principally as a club or reception house. Maine contributes exhibits to every department of the Exposition.

MASSACHUSETTS.—The designers took for their model the old Hancock house that stood for so long a time the most familiar structure on Beacon street, Boston, and which is an admirable representative of the old colonial residence, with such modifications only as the purposes of the structure demand. The reproduction of this type of our architecture is a happy idea, and will undoubtedly meet with general appreciation. The cost of reproduction was about $40,000. The building is used exclusively as a state headquarters and club house. Massachusetts contributes very largely to every department of the Exposition, particularly to the art, educational, horticultural and mechanical displays. The exhibit of the state cost $75,000.

MARYLAND.—The Maryland building, a reproduction of the state house, is constructed of granite, and cost $35,000. Maryland's canning and oyster interests are represented on a large scale. The canned goods exchange of Baltimore has a canning house in which a practical illustration of the work done is given. The exhibit of the state, aside from the building, cost $30,000.

MICHIGAN.—The legislature of Michigan appropriated $20,000 for the State Exposition building, but most of the material was contributed, so that the structure, as it stands, represents an outlay of about $50,000. Its dimensions are 100x140 feet. The building is constructed wholly of Michigan materials.

MINNESOTA.—The Minnesota building is one of the handsomest on the grounds, a prize of $500 having been awarded the successful architect. The legislatnre subscribed only $50,000, but this sum was increased to $150,000 by private subscription. Every county in the state contributed generously, and the result is a creditable building and a creditable exhibit in nearly every department of the Exposition.

MISSISSIPPI.—Mississippi makes a very creditable showing, particularly in

18

ILLINOIS CENTRAL RAILROAD TRACKS.

the agricultural and horticultural departments. The state and citizens subscribed generously toward the exhibit.

MISSOURI.—The exhibit of the state of Missouri is one of the most extensive at the Exposition. The state is rich in agricultural and mineral land, and besides, is one of the foremost of the manufacturing states of the Union. The state very early applied for 20,000 square feet of space in the horticultural department alone. The Missouri building cost $50,000, and is one of the handsomest structures of the state group. The state originally appropriated $250,000, but this was increased to $500,000, an appropriation equal to New York's.

MONTANA.—The legislature of this young but wealthy state appropriated originally $50,000 for the state's exhibits. Later on this amount was doubled. Montana's exhibits will be found principally in the department of mines and mining. One of the interesting exhibits from the state is a relief map of Butte, the greatest mining camp in the world. The state board set aside $5,000 for the woman's exhibit.

NEBRASKA.—The style of Nebraska building is Romanesque, and its arrangement combines to a remarkable degree the qualities of utility, beauty and small cost for construction. The building covers 9,652 square feet, not including a large veranda on the side adjoining the little lake. The agricultural and general exhibit is arranged in a hall 100x60 feet. Facing the exhibit hall on the first floor are offices, balconies and a lobby. The exhibit from this state is one of the grandest to be seen. Nebraska is represented particularly in the agricultural, horticultural and forestry departments.

NEVADA.—Nevada is represented almost wholly in the mines and mining department.

NEW HAMPSHIRE.—This state is represented in every department of the Exposition, notably in the geological and mining displays. New Hampshire also contributes valuable works of art and exhibits for the educational display.

NEW JERSEY.—The appropriation of this state was $70,000, a portion of which was set aside for the building of a state headquarters. The state has contributed exhibits to every department of the Exposition.

NEW YORK.—New York appropriated $300,000 to defray the cost of its building and exhibit at the World's Fair. This amount was increased later on, and greatly added to by private subscriptions. There was considerable delay on the part of New York, and active work did not begin until the spring of 1892. From that time on, however, New York's interest in the Exposition lacked nothing in enthusiasm. The building of the state of New York represents, with very slight modifications, the historical old Van Rensselaer residence, which was for so long a time one of the most familiar landmarks in Gotham. New York contributes, of course, to every department of the Fair, and more largely than any other American state excepting, perhaps, Illinois. Her exhibits are prominent in the art, agricultural, horticultural, musical, electricity, mechanical and manufactures departments.

NORTH CAROLINA.—North Carolina has reproduced for its building what is known as the "Tyron Palace." This structure, constructed of material brought from England the middle of the eighteenth century, is a fine type of colonial architecture. A circular colonnade connects upon the right and left of the main building two similar structures; and to reproduce it entire in full si: occupies the entire space allotted to North Carolina. This state is represent in every department of the Exposition. One of the oldest states of the Unic its contribution of art treasures and curios is very interesting.

NORTH DAKOTA.—The North Dakota building is 70x50 feet. A space 46x feet in front of the main assembly hall, between two committee-rooms, is us as a court-yard. From this court-yard the main assembly-room is entei through a large stone arch, above which on the exterior is an elaborately carv panel containing the coat of arms of North Dakota. The main feature of t interior is the assembly hall, which includes a space 24x56 feet. North Dakc of course pays great attention to the exhibit of her principal product, whe but, also, makes a good showing in several other departments. The educatioi advantages of the young state are fully presented, and her school exhibit among the best. She makes contributions to the department of forestry.

OHIO.—The style of architecture of the Ohio building is distinctive a much unlike that of any of the other state buildings. The original idea was have the building constructed of material furnished gratis by contractors, a thus make it in itself an exhibit of the building materials of the state. Ho ever, the contractors were slow in taking the matter up, and so many obstac stood in the way that it was determined to build it of wood. The estimated c was about $35,000. The building is two stories, the lower one being of nu than the ordinary height. The state of Ohio sends exhibits to the Fair valu at between $5,000,000 and $6,000,000. The appropriation of the state w $100,000.

OREGON.—The state of Oregon is represented very fully in the agricultur mining and other departments. It has also contributed to the forestry depa ment. The real work of the state did not commence until late in 1892, but 1 exhibit is nevertheless creditable.

PENNSYLVANIA.—The Pennsylvania building, as is quite appropriate, is c of the costliest and handsomest of the group. One of the main attractions the old "liberty bell" from Independence Hall, which hangs in the tower rotunda directly opposite the gallery on the second floor. The entire height the building is 165 feet. Over 800 electric lights are used to light it. Porcl 20 feet wide surround the building. The whole structure is practically a rep duction of Independence Hall, Philadelphia. Pennsylvania appropriated $3c 000 to defray the cost of its building and exhibits, but this represented onl: small portion of the state's contributions.

RHODE ISLAND.—The building of the little state of Rhode Island is a tv story structure, modeled after the Doric style of architecture, with toweri pillars resting on porches at either end. The entrance at the front is throu three circular arches into a circular porch twenty feet in diameter, which op< into a main hall 20 x 42 feet. The first cost was estimated to be $8,000. Rhc Island contributes largely to the manufactures and liberal arts department, well as to every one of the great sections of the Exposition.

SOUTH CAROLINA.—South Carolina, owing to the defeat of an appropriat bill in the legislature, was late in securing a place among her sister states ;] the exhibit made, though small, comparatively, is creditable.

MARSHALL FIELDS—WHOLESALE.

SOUTH DAKOTA.—The state building of South Dakota is in the style of old French farm-house. The walls are of bricks. Its dimensions are 60 x 72 f(On the first floor is an assembly hall with towering mantels and house f places at each end. The state raised between $80,000 and $100,000. The leg lature was late in acting, but the energetic and enterprising people of the you state made full amends for its neglect. South Dakota is well represented in agricultural, horticultural, mineral and forestry departments.

TENNESSEE.—The private citizens and counties of the state of Tennes subscribed liberally toward securing an adequate exhibit at the World's F the legislature having failed to pass an appropriation bill. The funds rai were ample to provide for a very creditable display, and the state is represen in nearly every department.

TEXAS.—This great state has one of the most notable buildings of the gro The structure is 85 x 250 feet. The main height is 70 feet. Constructed entir after the style of the old Spanish missions, it is a good example of Span renaissance architecture. The structure is built of Texas materials. Te took unbounded interest in the Exposition from the very first. The city Galveston alone raised over $150,000. There were over $300,000 raised by c tributions throughout the state. Texas is represented, and represented well every department.

VERMONT.—One hundred of the substantial citizens of Vermont subscri $100 each, and the building, costing $10,000, was erected without drawing uj the state treasury. Vermont is represented in the geological, agricultural, ho cultural, mechanical and art departments, and quite fully in the mineral ; forestry departments. A $6,000 monument of Barre granite is one of the hibits from Vermont.

VIRGINIA.—The best exhibits of the Virginia State Fair of 1892 are offe the visitor at the Exposition of 1893. The state appropriated about $80,(which was increased by private subscriptions. Virginia makes a good sh ing, but one hardly commensurate with her age or high position among states of the Union.

WASHINGTON.—Washington's is a unique state building. It is construc almost entirely of material brought from the state, and forms an illustration the building materials and industries peculiar to that young but vigorous co monwealth. The building is 220 x 140 feet. The exterior is of timber fr Puget Sound region and all the lumber entering into it was donated by the st lumbermen's association. The main entrance is made one of the features of building, and is of granite, marble and ore quarried in the state. In addit to what was contributed, the state expended $50,000 in constructing and ela rating the details of the building. It is surmounted by a flagstaff 175 feet hi and there are four towers of unique design. A peculiar incident in connect with the acceptance of the design for this building was that the one which first was considered third in merit was adopted, and the architect who recei the first prize in the competition was relegated to the rear. The state sp $100,000 on the collection of an exhibit, and contributes largely to the departme of agriculture, forestry, mines, fisheries, education, electricity, live stock, : arts, woman's work and transportation. Her displays are very creditable.

NEBRASKA.

KANSAS.

VIRGINIA.

KENTUCKY.

WASHINGTON.

SOUTH DAKOTA.

WEST VIRGINIA.—West Virginia has a beautiful little building which cost about $20,000. The state contributes very extensively to the departments of mines and mining, forestry, agriculture, floriculture, horticulture, manufactures and liberal arts, and machinery.

WISCONSIN.—The Wisconsin state building is a handsome structure. It is commodious, and the interior is arranged with special reference to the products of this wealthy state, which in variety and character make the exhibit one of the most attractive and interesting to be seen at the Fair. It is two stories high, with not less than 10,000 feet of floor space exclusive of porches. The whole structure is built of Wisconsin material. The exterior walls are of stone, brick and terra cotta, and the roof of slate, tile or iron made in Wisconsin. The interior is ornamented and furnished with plate, beveled and mirror glass, Wisconsin pine and hardwood, and encaustic tile. The cost of the building was $30,000. Douglas county appropriated $2,000 to pay for a stained-glass window at the head of the main staircase. Wisconsin is represented in every department of the Exposition.

WYOMING.—The Wyoming building is in style a model club house. The dimensions are 70 feet in length by 50 feet in width. The cost of the building was $20,000. Wyoming contributes to the agricultural, mines and mining and other departments of the Exposition displays, which show her to have made wonderful advancement.

THE TERRITORIES.—The territories of the Union are well represented. Beginning with far-away *Alaska*, each and every one of them makes a creditable exhibit. The government takes care of the Alaskan display, which is a novel and interesting one in many particulars. The seal industry is represented among others. *Arizona* contributes largely to the mines and mining departments and to the Indian exhibit. *New Mexico* raised over $75,000 and in consequence the visitor sees a great many attractions from this wealthy territory, notably in the mines and mining department and Indian exhibit. *Oklahoma*, youngest of the territories, has made a splendid effort to bring herself properly before the world, and her efforts have been crowned with success. *Utah* ought not properly to be classed among the other territories, so much is she in advance of them. Her building is a "Salt Palace," and her exhibits are really deserving of a first place among those of the great agricultural and mining states. *District of Columbia.*—The display made by the district in which is located the seat of government includes pictures of the school buildings, views of the streets and avenues, and probably a fac-simile in miniature of the city and its public buildings. There is to be also a collection of historical relics.

A GROUP OF STATE BUILDINGS.—The four states of Wisconsin, Indiana, Michigan and Ohio, are grouped together on a triangular plat of ground near the western limit of Jackson Park, just north of Fifty-ninth street. How to arrange these four state buildings so that each would have a commanding view of the fine art galleries and the pretty little lake near by has been one of the problems for the construction department. The buildings are so placed that each commands a fine view of the art galleries, the picturesque lake and the buildings of a number of foreign nations. The Indiana building cost about $100,000, of which amount $70,000 was to be donated by lumber associations.

The Michigan building represents an outlay of $40,000, most of which was donated from private sources. The Wisconsin and Ohio buildings cost about $50,000 each, and as in the case of Michigan and Indiana, most of the building material was donated.

OTHER BUILDINGS.—Notwithstanding the generous provision made for space by the management, the great size of the buildings as originally planned, and the number of them, exceeding that of any previous exposition, it was found in the spring of 1892 that others must be erected to meet the demands of exhibitors and the public. Some changes were also made in the original designs, more especially with relation to *The Casino*. No casino is to be seen as originally designed, at the end of the pier 1,000 feet from shore, and there is no curved mole bearing columns emblematical of the thirteen states. In place of the latter there is a peristyle, 60 feet wide and 500 feet long, extending north and south and spanning the lagoon entrance by a grand arch. Ranged along this peristyle are emblematic columns representing all of the states and territories. At the north end of the peristyle is *The Music Hall*, which for a time it was thought would have to be put on the wooded island. It measures 140 by 200 feet, and has an auditorium large enough to seat 2,000 people, with an orchestra of 75 pieces and a chorus of 300 persons. It also has a rehearsal hall 50 by 80 feet, capable of seating 600 people. This music hall is designed to be used by musical talent and connoisseurs of the art rather than by the mass of the people who will visit Jackson Park. It is intended that here shall gather the fine singers and instrumentalists who may wish to be heard and criticized by the best representatives of their art or profession. The grand choruses and band concerts—the proper musical entertainments—will be held in an amphitheatre accommodating 15,000 people or more. This is located in the extreme Southern part of the park, and after the close of the projected musical programme will be transformed into a live-stock show ring. At the south end of the peristyle there is a restaurant and cafe, of the same size and style as Music Hall. This is constructed to supply the main features of the abandoned Casino. The cost was $206,000. The pier, extending 1,000 feet into the lake, is one of the greatest features. At its extremity, in place of the Casino, is erected a *Tower* 250 feet high. This is of iron, covered with staff, and resembles a lighthouse in appearance. From its summit electrical displays of exceeding brilliancy are made, and by means of electric "search-lights," the grounds, or any particular portion of them, can be flooded with light on fete nights. *Department Building.*— The building, which is two stories high, cost $58,000. Its dimensions in feet are 165 by 310. In the center is an open court, and about this court are located four important departments of the Exposition management. The northeast section is devoted to general offices for the Chief of Construction and his assistants. The southeast quarter furnishes room for a hospital. In this hospital are three wards, 39x19 feet each. Two wards are for male patients and one for female patients. The hospital is complete in all appointments. The south end of the building, running west from the hospital, is devoted to the fire department. Here are located steam and chemical engines, police patrol-wagons, ambulances, fire and police alarm offices, stalls for horses, etc. Running east and west through the center of the building is a driveway eighteen feet wide.

On the west side of the structure, between the driveway and the fire department, is stable room for twenty horses and a number of carriages and other vehicles. Across the driveway, just north, are police headquarters. Here Col. Wright will assemble his Columbian Guards. Cells for lawbreakers are also provided. The northwest section of the building is devoted to a large restaurant. The upper story is largely used for dormitories. *Convent of La Rabida.*—It may be remembered that early in 1492 Columbus, while traveling on foot and in a destitute condition, applied for food at the Franciscan convent of La Rabida in Spain, and was kindly and hospitably received. The prior of the institution, Father De Marchena, was a man not only of education and culture, but of large influence with Queen Isabella. Columbus explained his plans for the discovery of the new continent to the prior, who became interested, and secured for him a reception at the court of Ferdinand and Isabella, who were then in camp with the besieging army in front of Grenada. There is little doubt but that for the timely assistance of the good abbot Columbus would have completely failed in his endeavors to secure assistance to discover the new world, as he had previously failed in his endeavors to obtain aid from the governments of Spain and Portugal. A fac-simile of the convent, costing $50,000, is among the structures on the grounds. It is alluded to elsewhere. *Shoe and Leather Building and Mineral Display Building.*—These are located in the grand central court of the Manufactures and Liberal Arts building. Their dimensions in feet are 325x425 each, and their cost $100,000. It was the original intention to leave two great open courts in the center of the Manufactures building, each about 400 by 500 feet. After the shoe and leather industries of the country made such a determined fight for the building, and agreed to raise all the money necessary to put it up, it was decided that the two buildings named could be erected in the court which it was originally intended to decorate with flowers and fountains. The buildings are one story high, and are separated from the walls of the main building by streets about fifty feet wide. *Bridges.*—The bridges over the lagoon and canals are all worthy of attention, and have been constructed at a great expenditure of time, labor and money. The cost of the viaducts and bridges was $125,000. *Lavatories, Closets, Etc.*—The lavatories, closets, etc., at the World's Fair required the expenditure of between $450,000 and $500,000. There are 3,000 closets, 2,000 urinals and 1,500 lavatories. The contract for the construction and care of all these was said to be the largest contract of the plumbing description ever let. At the Centennial and the Paris Expositions the plumbing and sanitary precautions were very unsatisfactory. It was the determination that they should be as perfect as possible at the Chicago Exposition. *Streets in Reproduction, etc.*—Many streets, villages, etc., in imitation of streets and villages in foreign towns and countries, are reproduced. These will represent portions of North, South, and Central America, streets in Cairo, Egypt, etc., all of which are referred to elsewhere. *Towers.*—The decorations of the towers involves a great deal of attention and a great outlay. The towers, it is seen, are not bare shafts of iron, but their exterior framework is surrounded with an additional structure which makes them appear like columns of masonry. At the first landing of the tower on the pier, 200 feet high, will be a big clock with bells and chimes. At the second landing, 250 feet high, is an electric plant and an

GUNTHER'S CONFECTIONERY.

immense searchlight for giving panoramic views of the Exposition grounds and buildings. *Religious Exhibits Building.*—The Evangelical Alliance (at this writing) proposes the erection of a great building for religious exhibits. *Band Stands.*—Visitors to the World's Fair will find on every hand bands of music for their entertainment. Fifteen music-stands are provided for the accommodation of the different bands anxious to visit the Exposition and make music for the visitors. *Natatorium.*—A natatorium, or swimming school, will be found directly west of the location assigned to the Dutch Settlement on Midway Plaisance Its dimensions are 200 by 250, and cost $60,000. *Bank.*—The Chemical National Bank has established a branch in the Administration building for the accommodation of visitors. *Additional Buildings.*—As up to the very last moment changes were made in the general arrangements for special buildings, it is impossible to enumerate them all in this connection. Two handsome structures, however, in addition to those already named, will be found by the visitor in all probability—one for the accommodation of the brick tile and terra cotta manufacturers, the other for exhibits of heavy machinery, such as drop hammers, forges, etc.

SPECIAL ATTRACTIONS.—In addition to the many other useful and attractive features of the exhibition, the following will be found of special interest to the visitor :

ARCHÆOLOGY AND ETHNOLOGY.—All possible phases of pre-historic man in America and the life of the aborigines at the time of the landing of Columbus are illustrated at the World's Columbian Exposition by the department of Archæology and Ethnology. Prof. F. W. Putnam, of Harvard University, is the chief of this department and is pronounced the most competent man in America for the position.

GOVERNMENT EXHIBIT.—The Government Exhibit has been treated in this volume in connection with the several departments, under the head of "Fish and Fisheries," "Battle Ship," "Naval Exhibit," "Post Office," "Indian Exhibit," etc.

INDIAN EXHIBIT.—This exhibit is partly under the direction of the United States' Government, and partly under the direction of Prof. Putnam, chief of the Archæological and Ethnological department.

NOVEL, QUAINT AND CURIOUS THINGS.—There are many novel, quaint and curious things exhibited. These include exhibits—sometimes in the department buildings, sometimes in the state and foreign buildings, and sometimes in the special exhibits made by private individuals, firms and corporations. The following comprise the most conspicuous of these exhibits, and include such features as "A Street in Cairo," "Bazaar of All Nations," "Esquimaux Village," strange things from foreign lards, antiquities, etc. Two anchors that Columbus carried in his ships are exhibited. A bell 790 years old, from Carthagena, Columbia, South America, is on exhibition. Capt. William A. Andrews, known as "the Lone Voyager," from his trips in his wonderful little boats, Nautilus, keel fifteen feet, and Dark Secret, keel twelve feet, makes an exhibit in the Marine department of the World's Fair. The Very Rev. Doctor Peralta, Bishop of Panama, tendered for exhibition at the World's

MASSACHUSETTS.

MAINE.

FLORIDA.

IDAHO.

RHODE ISLAND.

IOWA.

Fair his very remarkable historical and ethnological collection, which has been for some years in a museum connected with the bishop's palace.

Australia contributes the most wonderful astronomical clock that has ever been exhibited. It was constructed in New South Wales. This clock is in many respects similar to the celebrated time piece at Strassburg, showing numerous figures during the hour and performing many marvellous mechanical feats. The case is forty feet high, by twenty-five feet square and is made of colonial cedar. Captive Balloon Ascensions may be made from the grounds or from grounds in the vicinity daily. The "Bazaar of all Nations" is established near Midway Plaisance. Persons having a concession to sell goods in the bazaar were allotted space in which to erect buildings suitable for the purpose. These buildings were expected to be erected in the style of architecture that prevails in the country in which the articles are produced.

H. W. Young, of Augusta, Ill., sends a Bible printed in 1615, the ownership of which in this country he has traced back to 1660. Some novelties may be seen around the California and other buildings. The Monterey Cypress, a yellow fir tree 111 feet high, a California "Big Tree," and others, are visible outside the forestry exhibit. A continuous clam-bake is one of the attractions which epicurean visitors will find at the Exposition. One of the two old sunken vessels in Lake George is on exhibition as a relic. Van Houten & Zoon, the manufacturers of cocoa at Weesp, Holland, set apart $100,000 with which to make an exhibit. The Hercules Iron Company was granted the privilege of constructing and operating a cold storage warehouse on the Exposition grounds. It has a capacity of 600,000 cubic feet, and cost $150,000.

The congregation of the little colored church at Haleyville, in Cumberland County, N. J., contributes an interesting historical relic. It is the bell that has for years called them to church. In the year 1445 the bell, it is said, hung in one of the towers of the famous mosque at the Alhambra. After the siege of Granada the bell was taken away by the Spanish soldiers and presented to Queen Isabella, who in turn presented it to Columbus, who brought it to America on his fourth voyage and presented it to a community of Spanish monks who placed it in the Cathedral of Carthagena, on the island of New Granada. In 1697 buccaneers looted Carthagena and carried the bell on board the French pirate ship, La Rochelle, but the ship was wrecked on the island of St. Andreas shortly afterward and the wreckers secured the bell as part of their salvage. Captain Newell, of Bridgeton, purchased it, brought it to this country, and presented it to the colored congregation of the Haleyville church. The bell weighs sixty-four pounds and is of fine metal.

Rudolph Cronau, the eminent author and scientist of Leipsic, Germany, has contributed his extensive collection of paintings, sketches and photographs, representing scenes in the life of Columbus, and places visited by Columbus during his voyages to the new world.

W. L. Libby & Son Company, of Toledo, Ohio, were granted a concession for the operation of a big cut-glass factory. The Company invested between $50,000 and $75,000 on its plant, which is located at 59th street, in the Midway Plaisance, on a plat of land 150 by 250 feet. One of the events of the Exposition will be a Cyclist's parade, in which many of the 24,000 members of the League

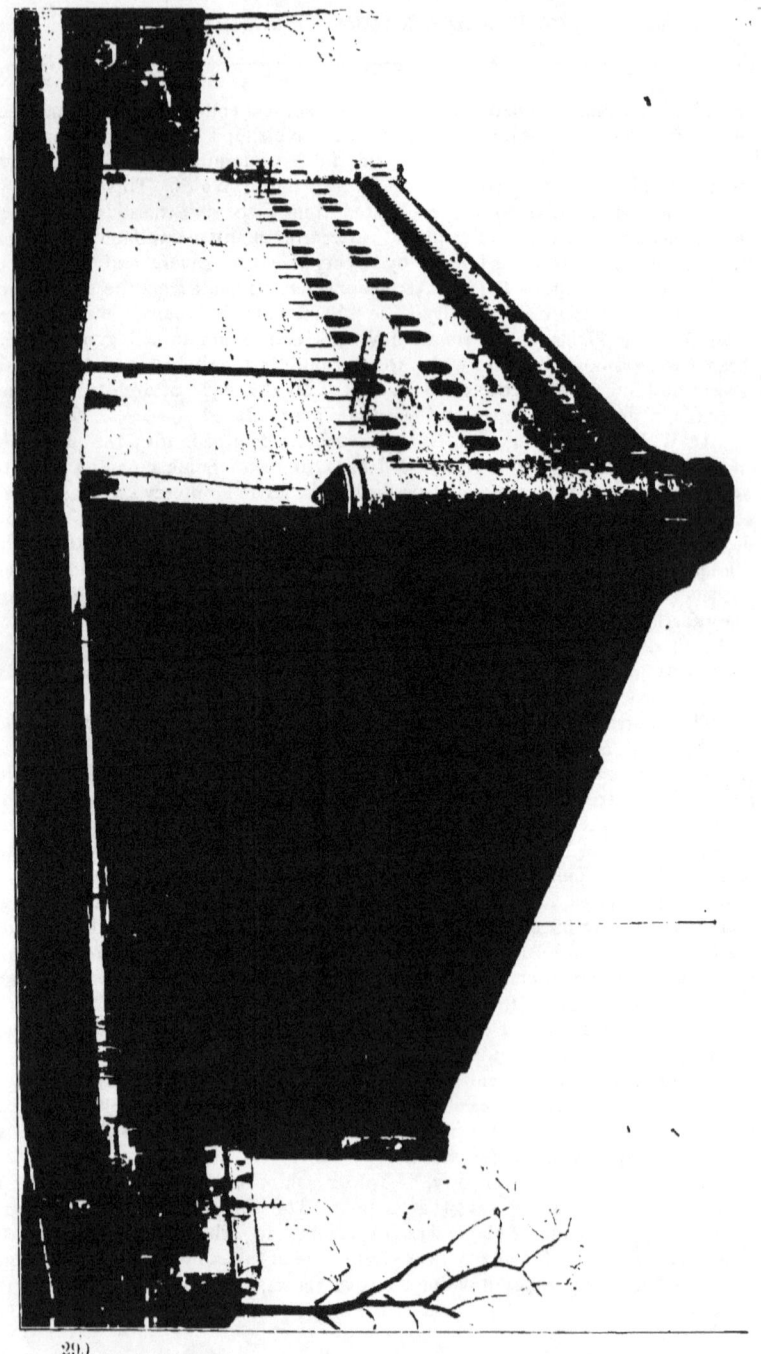

ARMORY.

of American Wheelmen will take part. The date will be announced in due season. Among the transportation exhibits are coaches used in the early days of railroading, formed after the style of stage coaches, and many other curiosities, sent by the Old Colony railroad company. An East Indian village and exhibit occupies 200,000 square feet of space on Midway Plaisance. It is conducted by the East Indian Exhibit Co. A reproduction of the famous Eddystone Lighthouse may be found by the visitor on the lake shore, used as an exhibit and a beacon light. John W. Stiles & Co., of Spokane, Wash., was granted a concession for the reproduction of an Esquimaux village on the Exposition grounds. M. O. Jaensch, of Wahoo, Neb., sends a valuable collection of arms. The collection includes 100 pieces, including swords, pistols, guns, etc.

Not the least interesting feature of the government exhibit at the Fair is the fast flight of carrier pigeons. Captain R. E. Thompson, of the signal service, has this feature of the display in charge, and at frequent intervals he will liberate birds for flights to within 200 miles of Chicago. George W. Childs, the Philadelphia philanthropist, has taken a great interest in this feature of the government display, and offers a prize valued at $100, which will be on exhibition at the Fair, to the owner of the bird making the greatest distance in one day. The first cotton gin made by Eli Whitney is exhibited by the New Orleans Machinery Company, which also makes an extensive exhibit of cotton gins, sugar mills and other machinery. Dr. West, a collector of curios at Antigonish, Nova Scotia, is entitled to the credit of having shipped to the Columbian Exposition the first exhibit from a foreign country. It consists of useful and ornamental articles purchased from the Antigonish Mountain Indians. The first locomotive ever used is exhibited in the Transportation Department. Other curiosities connected with the early days of steam transportation are also to be found there. The first map of the world ever made is exhibited. Pope Leo consented to its loan from the Vatican library. It is known as the Diege Ribere map, and was begun in 1494 and finished in 1529.

W. A. Alexander and Louis Gelder, representing the insurance associations of Chicago, were granted space, 50 by 100 feet, to construct a building to constitute an exhibit of the most improved methods of fireproof construction and the appliances used in saving goods from burning buildings. The building may be occupied by a salvage corps during the Fair. The Western Union Telegraph Company exhibit, handsomely framed, the first telegraph message ever sent, which was in May, 1844. The message was received by Prof. Morse at the Capitol in Washington, from an assistant in Annapolis. It is seen in the Electricity Department. One of the exhibits that the Baltimore & Ohio road makes in the Electricity Building is a model of the first telegraph wire strung along that line by Morse. The line was nine miles long, and extended from Baltimore to Relay Station. The line was laid in a lead pipe.

An eagle measuring almost 20 feet between wing tips perches above the main entrance of the Manufacturers' Building. The old gunboat "Niagara," which was sunk in Massasauga Bay, Erie Harbor, in 1812, is exhibited. The Manufacturers' Club, of Philadelphia, has a building constructed entirely of material made by members of the club, as headquarters for manufacturers. A building in the form of an iceberg in which to make a polar exhibit is projected.

One of the novelties of the Fair is a building 200 feet square used as a skatin
rink. This rink is to be supplied with a 16-inch layer of ice summer and winte
by artificial means. A Government Life Saving Station is on exhibition.
magnificent microscope was made by the Munich Poeller Physical and Optica
Institute for the Chicago Exposition, at a cost of $8,750. It possesses a magn
fying power of 11,000 diameters. John McAdams & Co., of Brooklyn, exhib
on Lake Michigan a device to prevent boats from coming in collision. It is
marine brake, powerful enough to stop boats running at a high rate of speec
A genius at Muhlenberg, Pa., completed a marvellous clock for exhibition at th
Fair. Around the dial is a railway track, on which a miniature locomotiv
makes the round every five minutes. It requires a magnifying glass to see th
delicate machinery.

Sir Walker Bullard contributes the finest collection of native Maori curios
ties and paintings in the world. Maj. John Wilson, of Auckland, has brougt
a colony of Maoris to the Exposition. The United States Consul to Merida
Yucatan, sent to the Exposition a Maya house, with its native inmates and the
belongings, and a Maya potter who makes native vessels in public. Meteori
stones of various sizes are exhibited. One of the finest specimens was ser
from Marengo, Ill. Charles P. Southard, of New Jersey, has erected a mode
home, valued at $2,000, built through the medium of a co-operative building loa
association. Models of all the warships of the United States Navy are show
in the battle-ship Illinois, in which is made the naval exhibit of the governmer
at the World's Fair. A concession was granted to M. Stepanni to erect th
Moorish Palace. One of the many attractions which are exhibited in this pala
is $1,000,000 in gold coin in one pile. A space 200 by 250 is used for the palac
which cost $400,000. There is a $60,000 natatorium in operation on the Exp
sition grounds. It includes bath-rooms, a swimming pool, a cafe, and a stan
for the sale of cigars and flowers. This concession was granted to L. J. Kadis
of Chicago.

The most gruesome exhibit at the Exposition is that made by the Nation
Prison Association. The exhibit is a comprehensive expose of the devices ar
methods employed for inflicting punishment from the beginning of history
the present time, and shows the progress which humanity has made in th
quality of mercy. A special building is used for the exhibit, and in it
arranged cells of every description, many of them reproductions of places whic
have detained persons famous in history. Mr. Sell, the London advertisir
agent, exhibits specimens of all the leading newspapers of the world whic
have been printed during the last two centuries. The Clayden model of th
ocean currents is exhibited by the Navy department. This is a kind of hu;
scientific tank show. Mrs. Lou Barnes, of Vicksburg, granddaughter of th
late Col. J. W. Nailor, sends the samples of cotton which her grandfather e
hibited at the World's Fair in London in 1851, and at the New York Cryst
Palace in 1853, with the medals awarded him at each. The cotton is still we
preserved. A panorama of the Volcano Killean, of Hawaii, is exhibited on tl
ground. The original volcano has a crater one-half mile in diameter, in whic
there is constant volcanic action. The exhibit is under the auspices of tl
Hawaiian Government.

LAKE FRONT, MICHIGAN AVENUE.

A full-sized model of the Parthenon of Athens is one of the most interesting of the Exposition buildings. It contains the World's Fair in miniature. A company embracing several very wealthy men will operate a permanent circus after the style of the Hippodrome in Paris. A building, with seating capacity of 5,000, and having a garden on the roof, has been erected, and the attraction will be in operation to entertain World's Fair crowds. Among the wonderful things to be seen is a petrified log from Oregon. This is probably the largest petrifaction ever exhibited.

A business house in Chicago has established a physicians' bureau of service and information, which it proposes to make of great value to the medical profession who may visit the Exposition. A tribe of African Pigmies may be seen by the visitor at the midway plaisance. A chronometer, supposed to have been the property of one of Pizarro's men, recently found in Ecuador, is exhibited. A perfect reproduction of a street in Pompeii, the pavement of which is made of lava from Vesuvius, showing several houses as they appeared before the eruption which destroyed the place, together with relics, etc., is among the attractions. The visitor to the Exposition will have an opportunity of learning among other things, just how a first-rate post-office is managed. A working model of such an office is a part of the U. S. Government exhibit. It is a branch of the central Chicago Post-office so far as mails are concerned, but entirely independent in its exhibition features. It handles all mails of officials, exhibitors, and others to and from the Exposition grounds, and has a special delivery service of its own.

In the model post-office building heretofore referred to is located the Government postal museum. Among this collection are the most interesting foreign exhibits. The building erected on the grounds by the publishers of Puck is one of the most interesting attractions of the Fair. It shows fully every detail of the process of editing and publishing a humorous paper. A miniature model of the town of Pullman, 30x80 feet, is a part of the exhibit made by the Pullman Palace Car Company. The State of Ohio sends a number of valuable and interesting relics of the Mound Builders. These are from 100 mounds in Ohio and are 20,000 in number. Saginaw, Mich., has a miniature reproduction of a Salt plant.

The cottage in which George Fox, the founder of the Society of Friends or Quakers, was born, in Leicestershire, England, was brought over and appears on the Fair Grounds. A cast-iron slack trough which was captured by General Sam Houston from Santa Anna, at the battle of San Jacinto, has been sent from Texas. The old locomotive "Sansom," built in England in "the thirties" by the celebrated Timothy Hackworth and brought to this country in 1838, is shown in the Transportation Building.

When Columbus was made a prisoner in San Domingo, the governor who arrested him feared there might be an attempt at rescue. So he trained a big gun on the entrance of the citadel, or castle, in which Columbus was confined. That cannon laid in the same place until Mr. Ober, a World's Fair representative, recovered it, and with the permission of the Governor of San Domingo, brought it to the United States. It is on exhibition.

A very novel feature of the Historical Exhibit at the Exposition is a fac-

TERRITORIAL.

MINNESOTA.

DELAWARE.

NEW YORK

NORTH DAKOTA.

simile reproduction of the little ship "Santa Maria," in which Columbus sailed. It is proposed that the vessel will be taken to Washington after the Exposition and there anchored in the park south of the White House. Shakspeare's historic home at Stratford-on-Avon is also reproduced here and is located on the space set apart for the British Government exhibit.

No side shows are permitted within the Exposition grounds. The Directory decided that the entrance fee shall entitle the visitor to see everything within the inclosure. There are, however, several theatres built and kept running, at which the finest talent in the world appears, and visitors who choose to attend the performances have to pay an admission fee. Such sights as "A Street in Cairo" is free, but natives of oriental countries in a few cases are allowed to charge a small fee to special performances of a theatrical nature.

A silversmith of Monterey, Mexico, sends a piece of silver which is an exact reproduction of the Agricultural building. It is eight feet wide, contains a quantity of silver valued as bullion at $10,000, and is valued at $20,000. A $10,000 model of a stamp mill for reducing copper, the property of the State Museum of Michigan, is shown at the Fair. This model was made and presented by the Calumet and Hecla Copper Company.

Some magnificent statues adorn the grounds. Notable among these is the statue of Franklin, at the main entrance to the Electricity building ; the statue of Columbus, belonging to the city of Baltimore ; and the statue of Columbus, by St. Gaudens, at the entrance to the Administration building. A colossal statue of the Republic rises from the basin in front of the Administration building. This is by Daniel C. French, of New York.

An immense wooden box, bound in iron, was recently found at Helsinfors, in Finland, by workmen engaged in excavating in the cellar of an old house. Upon opening the box the men found that it contained a large parchment and a quantity of pieces of iron of odd shapes. Being unable to make out the contents of the parchment, they carried it to Mr. Rizeff, the nearest magistrate, who found that it was written by Father Suger, one time minister to Louis VII., of France. It was an elaborately written treatise upon the use of steam as a motive power, and further examination revealed that the bits of iron were numbered parts of a rudimental but complete steam engine. The pioneer steam engine has been put together, and is exhibited.

The concession for the reproduction of "A Street in Cairo," was granted to George Panyolo, of Egypt. The space occupied is 600 by 300 feet. The location is the Midway Plaisance. The exhibition is open to visitors, free of cost, except upon occasions of a special street spectacle, as, for example, during the passing of the wedding procession, which will form one of the features of the display.

One of the most novel buildings at the Paris Exposition was the tea house erected by the Palais Indian Tea House Company, of London. This same concern has constructed on the Exposition grounds a series of tea houses which are finer than anything seen at Paris.

The leading theatrical managers of the country will probably erect a building in which theatrical and musical entertainments may be given during the progress of the Fair. An exact reproduction of the Tower of London, costing $250,000, will probably be one of the attractions of the Fair. The North Ameri-

can Turner Bund displays gymnastic apparatus, literature on the subject of physical exercises and development, and representations of gymnastic organizations. Eight days during each month of the Exposition the Turners give gymnastic exhibitions. The Washington Park Club perfected arrangements for a most notable race meeting during the Fair. The stakes in the American Derby are $50,000; in the "Queen Isabella" one mile for three-year-old fillies, $25,000; in the "Columbus Handicap" for three-year-olds upwards, $25,000; in a race for two-year-olds, $25,000; and large stakes are provided for a number of other races. The racing track is close by the World's Fair grounds.

Waukesha mineral water is furnished to consumers on the Exposition grounds at one cent per glass. Space of 8,000 square feet was granted the White Star Steamship Co., for an exhibition of models of the "Greyhounds" of its line. Similar exhibits are made by other ocean steamship lines. A Wild West Show will be given near the Exposition grounds daily, but it will have no connection with the Exposition. The location of the show is south of the Exposition grounds. One million signatures of people directly or indirectly connected with the Exposition are being collected by the World's Fair Mammoth Autograph Album Co. Copies of these collections of autographs will be bound in three volumes of 2,500 pages each, to be presented, respectively, to the President of the United States for the Smithsonian Institution, to the Governor of Illinois for the State Library, and to the Mayor of Chicago for the City Public Library. The names will be collected from all parts of the world.

FOREIGN EXHIBITS.—The civilized world, sections of the semi-civilized and many portions of the uncivilized, are represented at the World's Columbian Exposition. The Chicago World's Fair of 1893 has a stronger claim upon the term Universal than any of its predecessors. For the first time in history the great nations of Europe are able to exhibit their progress in science, art, and industry, on what may be justly termed neutral ground. The political and social rivalry which has ever been a menace to different nations in international expositions heretofore, finds no place here. While the United States comes into competition with all nations, in every department of human activity, the narrow environments and prejudices which exist abroad are unknown here, and every nation is certain to be treated fairly, impartially and justly, not only in the allotment of position and space, but in the distribution of honors. The foreign department of the Exposition, from the beginning, has been intelligently and wisely managed. The sending of a commission into the countries of Europe in 1891 was the most politic and judicious step that could have been taken. The effect of their mission was felt almost immediately. Europe was awakened to a sense of the importance and magnitude of the World's Fair, and upon the return of the commission two of the greatest empires on earth—England and Germany—sent representatives to inquire further into the status of the enterprise and to report to their respective governments the result. The reports of Sir Henry Wood and James

Dredge, on the part of England, and of Herr Wermuth, on the part of Germany, as well as the active interest these envoys have since taken in the success of the Exposition, are fresh in the minds of the public. Not only has their friendship and enthusiasm interested the exhibitors of the two empires named, but they have stimulated every European nation, many of which, for a time, at least, were inclined to be apathetic. The visit of the ambassadors of foreign nations accredited to Washington in 1891 also served to enlighten the Old World as to the magnitude of the preparations being made here. Later on, the sending of additional commissioners—notably the departure of Mr. H. N. Higginbotham and T. B. Bryan for southern Europe—served to renew the interest of foreign nations in the World's Fair.

The organization of a Latin-American Commission likewise resulted in bringing the Spanish-American republics into line, and the exhibit made by our neighbors on this continent demonstrate how well the bureau having this department in charge has been conducted by Mr. W. B. Curtis Finally the appointment of Walker Fearn as chief of the foreign exhibit department gave an impulse to this branch of the executive service of the Exposition, the favorable effects of which have continued to be felt up to the present time. The passage of the McKinley bill by Congress for a time had a depressing effect upon the prospects of the Exposition Foreign manufacturers were inclined to hold aloof, in the hope, perhaps that by so doing the government might be influenced in the direction of more liberal customs laws; but as our system of government can not be thus influenced, and as foreign governments and foreign manufacturers began to realize that outside pressure of this kind would probably have an effect quite contrary to that which was desired, they gradually accepted the situation and set about making the best of it.

It has been decided that agents in this country of articles manufactured in foreign countries cannot have the same entered for exhibition as American products. Although the capital of residents of the United States may be employed in the manufacture of such goods, the exhibits will have to be entered as foreign ones and space be assigned for them by the World's Fair Commission of the country in which the articles are produced.

The following are the nations and colonies represented at the World's Columbian Exposition, with all information concerning their respective exhibits in possession of the Exposition management:

ALGIERS.—The Governor of Algiers has taken a deep interest in the Exposition. It was the wish of exhibitors in that colony to have a distinct sub-section of the French exhibit. The Algiers display is novel and brilliant. It may be seen in the French section.

ARGENTINE REPUBLIC.—The President of the Argentine Republic appointed a World s Fair Commission early in 1891, and no time was lost in collecting and forwarding exhibits. The sum of $100,000 was placed at the disposal of the commission and visitors can readily see how judiciously this sum was expended. The Argentine display is a handsome one.

AUSTRALIA.—Australia is one of the most important exhibitors at the World's Fair. Not less than 1,000,000 feet of space were demanded by her exhibitors, and this was placed at their disposal. New South Wales took a lively interest in the Exposition from the first, as did New Zealand and Queenland. The merchants and manufacturers of Sydney and Melbourne were enthusiastic, and the public of Australia in general determined upon making a display which should attract the attention of the world to the progress the great island is making.

AUSTRIA.—The Austro-Hungarian Empire was a little late in responding to the President's invitation, but finally decided to participate, although not officially. The premier notified the U. S. minister that the Empire would give its utmost support to anything that private parties might do toward making an exhibit. Private interests at once took up the matter, and the exhibits from Austria and Hungary in the several departments of the Exposition are fully up to the standard established by the great powers of Europe. As a strong evidence of her friendship, Austria postponed the International Art Jubilee, which was to occur in 1893, until 1894, so that it should not interfere with the World's Fair.

BELGIUM.—Belgium from the first displayed the greatest interest in the World's Fair, and determined upon taking an active and conspicuous part in the Exposition. She made a grant of 600,000 francs, and has sent an art exhibit much more extensive than that displayed at the last Paris Exposition. Belgium is represented in all the leading departments. A supplementary grant of 300,000 francs was made to aid the private exhibitors.

BOLIVIA.—Bolivia has an excellent exhibit. It is among the best from the Latin-American Republics. Bolivia's appropriation for the Fair was $150,000.

BRAZIL.—The government of Brazil makes a magnificent display. The cost of the exhibit was over half a million dollars. The Brazil building is in itself a leading attraction. In addition to the $550,000 appropriated by the Federal government of Brazil, $250,000 were appropriated by the different states of the Republic. Brazil's exhibits will be found in the art, agricultural, forestry, horticultural, floricultural and other departments, and always occupying a conspicuous and creditable position.

BRITISH COLUMBIA.—British Columbia is represented by a building which is a novelty in architecture, composed of every variety of wood known to the British Columbia forests. British Columbia is represented in nearly all of the principal departments.

BRITISH GUIANA.—British Guiana appropriated $20,000 for an exhibit and appointed a commission to collect and display the same. A space of 60x30 feet is allotted to the exhibit from this colony, close to the exhibit and building of the Dominion of Canada. The location was chosen by British Guiana so as to afford an opportunity for contrasting its exhibits with those of other British

WYOMING

COLORADO.

LOUISIANA.

INDIANA.

OHIO.

TEXAS.

American colonies. A local exhibition of the resources of British Guiana was held previous to the shipment of the exhibits to this country, so that the choicest might be selected.

BRITISH HONDURAS.—This colony makes an excellent exhibit, consisting principally of woods, plants, fruits, tropical flowers, native minerals, etc.

BRITISH WEST INDIA.—The display made by British India in various departments and sections is an interesting one. Exhibits from Burmah are particularly attractive. The commissioner for British West Indies was granted 25,000 square feet of space. Much of the exhibit from these colonies consist of tropical plants, etc., which are to be seen in the horticultural department.

BULGARIA.—Bulgaria has a surprisingly fine art and industrial display. The kingdom is represented worthily for the first time at an International Exposition.

CANADA.—Canada early in 1892 asked for 96,000 square feet of space, but this did not represent the total space desired. In the fine arts and fisheries annexes additional room was necessary. Canada was granted in all about 100,000 square feet.

CEYLON.—Ceylon has a special building on the grounds. Among the attractions of its display is a large tea house.

CHILE.—The position of Chile as to its participation in the World's Columbian Exposition long remained in doubt. The impoverished condition of the country, and the stagnation of its trade due to the recent revolution, compelled the government to abandon its original design of appropriating $100,000 to defray the expenses of an exhibit, but it is believed she will be creditably represented.

CHINA.—Owing to certain diplomatic troubles between the United States and China, caused by the exclusion of Chinese immigrants, it was doubted for some time whether China would participate in any way in the Exposition. But the government of the Empire, while giving no official countenance to the Exposition, it was understood, would assist private exhibitors substantially. Later on it was announced that China would subscribe $200,000 and $50,000 to defray the expenses of a private exhibit. The Chinese government authorized Tao Tai, the representative of the custom service at Shanghai, to remove all export duties on exhibits intended for the World's Fair. Later still the Chinese government announced through its minister at Washington that its Embassy to this country would eventually be made a commission to represent China at the World's Fair and see that the rights of its citizens were thoroughly protected. The general indications are that China will be represented in many of the important departments of the Exposition and will probably erect a building on the grounds.

COLOMBIA.—Colombia's display is particularly attractive. Its building is modeled after the capitol at Bogota. The exterior is in imitation of the sandstone of which the capitol is built, while the interior is finished in the valuable hardwoods of the country, comprising more than a hundred varieties.

COSTA RICA.—Among the first exhibits received in Chicago for the World's Fair of 1893, were ten cases of curios and antiques collected in Costa Rica by the Latin-American bureau. Lieut. Scriven was specially detailed to make the collection. It was valued at $500. This little Republic appropriated $50,000 t defray the expenses of her display. Her exhibits are to be found in nearly every one of the principal departments.

CUBA.—The exhibit from Cuba is principally remarkable for the wonderfu floral and horticultural specimens which it includes. These are to be found in the proper departments. Cuba also contributes to other departments of th Exposition, particularly to the manufactures, where her display of tobaccos an cigars will attract general attention.

DENMARK.—The Danish exhibit comprises contributions to nearly all de partments, and particularly to those of fine arts, agriculture and manufactures The sum of $55,000 was set apart by Denmark in order to show as a leading feature of its exhibit a Danish dairy complete and in full operation.

DUTCH WEST INDIES.—The Dutch colonies of the West Indies, composed c the Islands of Curacoa, St. Martins, Bonaire, Aruba, St. Eustache and Saba, ar represented by special exhibits in several departments.

ECUADOR.—The President of Ecuador early in 1892 decreed that the Gover nor of each state of the Republic should collect and forward to Quito exhibits c all kinds illustrating the riches and the productions of the country. The Consul General of the United States in Quito directed the Consuls and Vice-Consuls an Consular Agents at different points in Ecuador to assist the Governors of state in every way possible in the collection of articles relating to commerce wit! exterior countries. The best of these exhibits so collected and exhibited i: Quito during the National Exposition held there in 1892, were forwarded t Chicago. The President of Ecuador also named Commissioners to Chicago, an a sufficient sum was appropriated to meet the expenses. The state of Esme ralda makes a special exhibit of gold and gold ores from the mines of Ibarra rubber, and other lowland products. The department of Guayaquil also has special exhibit. Ecuador has her own building on the grounds. Ecuador i represented in many of the leading departments.

ENGLAND.—England made application for 200,000 square feet of floor spac for exhibits, or nearly five square miles. This was equal to the space asked fo by Germany, and indicated at an early day the international character of th Exposition. The exhibits from England are on a greater and grander scale tha were ever seen before outside of London Expositions. England contributes t every department of the Fair. It is unsettled, at this date, whether the Iris] exhibit shall be included in England's. The Scotch exhibit certainly wil Both of these kingdoms contribute very creditable displays.

FRANCE.—France asked for 25,000 square feet of space for its picture exhibit alone. The leading men of France became interested in the Columbian Expc sition early in 1892, and from that time on the collections made in France an forwarded to this country gave every assurance that France would maintain he pre-eminent position among the industrial nations of the world. France occu pies 100,000 square feet in the manufactures, 10,000 in the machinery, and 10,00 in the live stock departments. The first appropriation made by France for th expenses of the exhibit amounted to 3,250,000 francs, or about $650,000.

GERMANY.—The demand of Germany for 200,000 square feet of floor spac early in 1892 indicated pretty clearly the intentions of that empire with regar

VERMONT.

ARKANSAS.

MISSOURI.

MICHIGAN.

CONNECTICUT.

to the Columbian Exposition. The interest of the people of Berlin, Dresden, Leipsig, Stuttgart, Nuremburg, Hamburg, and, in fact, of all the leading commercial, manufacturing, art and educational centers of Germany, has been centered in the Columbian Exposition for over two years. The first appropriation made by the German government to defray the expenses of its exhibit amounted to 900,000 marks. This, however, was quickly swallowed up, and large additional appropriations became necessary.

GREECE.—The financial situation in Greece prevented that kingdom from doing what it would have liked to do in the way of sending an art exhibit to the Columbian Exposition. It proposed a display of casts and models of the Greek art schools, the value of which, it is said, can scarcely be overestimated, and asked that the Columbian Exposition Company pay a sum ranging between $20,000 and $200,000 for this proposed exhibit. This proposition is referred to under the head of Art department.

GUATEMALA.—Guatemala started out by appropriating $100,000 in gold to defray the expenses of its exhibit at Chicago. Later on an appropriation of $20,000 was added to pay for the erection of a suitable building to be used as headquarters for this republic. The greatest interest in the Exposition was manifested in Guatemala from the first. This country contributes its national band to the Exposition. It will perform daily. This band is the third largest in the world, that of Austria being first and the Mexican National Band being second. It is composed of 200 performers.

HAYTI.—The congress of Hayti appropriated $25,000 for its exhibits. Frederic Douglas, the celebrated American negro, is in charge of the Haytian display, which is a very creditable one.

HOLLAND.—The Netherlands not only contribute one of the finest collections of paintings from the Dutch masters, but are represented in the Liberal Arts and Mechanical departments quite fully. Some of the most unique and interesting exhibits displayed at the Exposition came from Holland.

HONDURAS.—The exhibits of Honduras are very attractive and interesting. One of the measures adopted in that country for raising the necessary funds was the establishment of a national lottery. The exhibits forwarded are classified under the heads Minerals, Wood, Agriculture, Drugs, Animal Kingdom, Ethnology, Industries and General Information, and include a geological collection showing the mineral wealth of Honduras in building stone as well as in such semi-precious stones as opals, etc.

INDIA.—No money was appropriated by the Indian government, but the viceroy declared he would encourage private exhibitors in every way possible. Indian exhibits began to arrive early in 1892. Several Indian princes will attend the Exposition.

IRELAND.—An effort was made by the Irish members of Parliament to separate the Irish from the British exhibit, and to secure an independent subsidy from the crown. Before this question was determined the Countess of Aberdeen, a patriotic Irish lady, took the matter of collecting an exhibit of Irish industries in hand, and raised between $15,000 and $20,000 in this country, her object being to have an independent room in the Women's building.

ITALY.—The United States was not on amicable diplomatic terms with

Italy in 1891, and there was no resumption of relations until late in 1892. This was the result of the Italian massacre in New Orleans. Accordingly it was feared that Italy would take no part in the Exposition. Commissioners Higginbotham and Bryan visited southern Europe in 1892 and paid particular attention to Italy. Before they returned an *entente cordiale* was established and they brought back assurances that Italy would do her part toward giving an international complexion to the World's Fair. The king has officially recognized the Exposition by the appointment of a World's Fair Commission Although no appropriation will be made, the government will in all probability transport Italian exhibits without cost to exhibitors.

JAPAN.—Japan leads all foreign countries in the amount of its appropriation for the World's Fair. The empire of the Mikado was willing to spend more money in making an exhibit in 1893 than many of the countries of Europe, so far as their appropriations were first reported. Exposition officials were both surprised and pleased to receive authoritative information that the Japanese Parliament had set aside $630,765 for a display at the Fair. It is thorough and shows everything of interest which the ingenious people of Japan manufacture or otherwise produce. In appropriating the money the Parliament took occasion to authorize its expenditure as follows : During the year 1891, $51,495 ; 1892, $313,098 ; 1893, $241,536 ; 1894, $24,636. Japan made a novel proposition for the consideration of the World's Fair management. It offered if a suitable location should be granted, to reproduce a building of the most ancient style of architecture of Japan, and make to the city of Chicago a gift of the structure at the close of the World's Fair. The offer to do this came from the Japanese government. The estimated cost, including the elaboration of the gardens about it, was figured at $100,000. This edifice, with all its surroundings, will be tendered to the city of Chicago as a permanent monument of Japanese architecture and landscape gardening.

Japan was given 40,000 square feet for the purpose indicated in the north end of the wooded island. In addition to this Japan consumes over 90,000 square feet ; in the Manufactures building, 35,000 ; Agricultural building, 4,000 Fine Arts, 2,000 ; Mines and Mining, 750 ; Forestry, 350 ; Bazaars, 42,000.

Japan makes a magnificent display in all of the principal buildings, and has a Japanese tea house on the lake front and a bazaar on the Midway Plaisance.

MADEIRA.—The Governor of Madeira accepted the invitation to participate in the Exposition early in 1892, and the work of collecting an exhibit began at once. The display made by this province is worthy of attention. There are numerous Columbus relics in the exhibit.

MEXICO.—The nearest Republican neighbor of the United States makes one of the most prominent as well as one of the handsomest displays in each of the great departments of the Exposition. It was announced quite early that $2,000,000 would be expended upon the exhibit of this Republic, and the fact that the first appropriation amounted to $750,000, which was intended merely to be preliminary, justified this prediction.

The Mexican exhibits are to be seen in nearly every department of the Exposition. The floral display of the Republic is one of the handsomest to be seen in the Horticultural Building.

MOROCCO.—The Moorish minister of foreign affairs communicated with the United States Consul at Tangier immediately on receipt of the invitation to participate in the Exposition and asked that space be reserved for Morocco. Hassan Ben Ali took charge of the exhibit. Morocco makes a very interesting showing in the transportation department, where some horses, saddles, and other equestrian equipments from that country are displayed.

NEWFOUNDLAND.—The colony of Newfoundland participates in the Exposition and makes an independent display close to that of the Dominion and other English colonies. It is also represented largely in the fisheries department.

NICARAGUA.—Nicaragua set aside $30,000 for her display at the Exposition. It is the best exhibit the country has ever made. Senor Don Sallaverri, who had charge of Nicaragua's exhibit at Paris, arranged the country's display here.

NORWAY AND SWEDEN.—The amount raised in Norway and Sweden, including government and private subscriptions towards defraying the expenses of the exhibit, was about $150,000. It is understood that Norway and Sweden will each have a building on the grounds.

PANAMA.—The little government of Panama is well represented in the different departments, especially in that of horticulture. The marble slab presented by the Empress Josephine to Panama, and many other novel and curious articles are exhibited.

PARAGUAY.—The government of Paraguay very speedily accepted the invitation to participate, and the president of the republic was authorized to use whatever public funds he deemed necessary to enable Paraguay to make a proper exhibit. The republic makes an excellent display.

PERSIA.—The government of Persia as a first evidence of friendship toward the Exposition lifted the export duty on all goods sent to the World's Fair and all goods which might be purchased and returned to that country by visitors to the Exposition. This was looked upon at the time as a most liberal concession. The most important portion of the Persian exhibit is to be seen in the Manufactures Building, where there is a magnificent display of carpets, rugs, shawls and fabrics from that country. Ivories, curios and contributions to the art and other departments are also numerous. The representative of the Shah of Persia is M. E. Spencer Pratt, formerly United States Minister to Persia.

PERU.—The exhibit made by Peru is certainly equal to that made by any of the Latin-American republics, with the exception, perhaps, of Mexico and Brazil. A national exposition was held at Lima in May, 1892. This was known as a "Congress of Producers." The exhibition continued several months, and when it closed the entire exhibits were shipped to Chicago. The first appropriation made by Peru amounted to $25,000.

RUSSIA.—Although one of the most dreadful famines of recent years prevailed throughout the Empire during the greater part of 1892, the interest of the Russian Government and people in the Columbian Exposition was not permitted to languish. The Imperial Government appointed a commission of which the famous Count Tolstoi, the novelist and statesman, was a member, and the work of preparation, though hindered by the depressed financial condition of the Empire, went steadily on. The Russian Government undertook to bear all expenses for transportation and insurance of private exhibits. Every e: hibitor, whether from European or Asiatic Russia, who had goods of histori artistic or economic value to offer worthy of a place in the Exposition wa encouraged to send them. Russia is represented in every one of the leading d partments in a manner befitting the greatness of the Empire.

ROUMANIA.—Roumania contributes exhibits to the Art and several oth departments. Her display is in every way more prominent than at the la Paris Exposition.

SAN DOMINGO.—Many interesting relics from this island are on exhibitio The most valuable and the most interesting perhaps is the first church be that ever rang out in the New World. It was presented to the colonists of th first settlement of San Domingo by Queen Isabella in appreciation of the fa that the first settlement bore her name. There is also an exact reproduction the cross which Columbus raised immediately upon landing. The material the cross is the same exactly as that which Columbus nailed up, having bee taken from the wood of a building erected in 1509. There are also in this co lection fac-similes of the doors which close the cells in which the bones of C lumbus repose. The collection of relics is very extensive and is contained i a building erected for this special purpose.

SANDWICH ISLANDS.—A separate building is devoted to exhibits of th government of Hawaii. The collection in the department of agriculture, fror these islands, include rice, arrowroot, sugar cane, sugar models and machiner for making sugar, photographs of mills, coffee in the berry, in the shell, cleane and growing. In the forestry department are shown trees of every descriptio and in the horticultural department a great variety of fruit. In the floricu tural department many beautiful palms are exhibited, and in the department viticulture will be found a display of grapes, preserved fruits of every descrip tion, dried or in alcohol or in syrups. The Islands are also represented by fisb fish products and manufactures, including gold ornaments, palm leaf, bamboc feather work, artificial flowers, seed work, etc.

SERVIA.—The kingdom of Servia sends a large and interesting display, great portion of which was taken from the government museums and stores and of articles such as ancient armor, tapestries.

SIAM.—The kingdom of Siam charged the commissioner of agriculture t charter one or more vessels and load them with the products of the farms mines, forests and manufactories of that country and ship them to Chicagc The exhibit which is made here eclipses that made at the Paris Exposition where it carried off the honors of the Oriental section.

SOUTH AFRICA.—The exhibits from South Africa include those of th British colonies, Orange Free States and other settlements. These are scattere through the various departments of the Exposition. Cape Colony alone appro priated $25,000, and the De Beers Company a like amount. Zanzibar exhibit among other things a score of pigmies from the east coast of Africa.

SOUTH AMERICA.—The exhibits from South America include those fron all of the so-called Latin-American republics, and are referred to here under th headings of the different countries represented. In the spring of 1892 commis sioners had been appointed and appropriations made to pay the expenses of rep

BRITISH.

GERMAN.

resentation of the South American republics which exceeded in the aggregate the sum of $2,000,000 more than had been provided up to that time by the United States, with Illinois excepted.

SOUTH SEA ISLANDS.—The South Sea Islands are represented at the Exposition. The nature of their display was not known to the Exposition management when this book went to press.

SPAIN.—It is but natural that Spain should have taken more than an ordinary interest in the World's Columbian Exposition, designed as it is to celebrate the most glorious achievement in the history of that nation—the discovery of America. For many reasons, however, but principally because the financial situation in Spain is depressed, the display made by that country does not compare favorably with that by other European nations. Spain is represented in nearly all of the principal departments. The Queen Regent of Spain sends a portrait of the youthful king. Many of the jewels and other possessions of Ferdinand and Isabella are exhibited in the Spanish collection.

SWITZERLAND.—There was considerable feeling manifested in Switzerland against the United States and the World's Fair, owing to the passage of the McKinley bill, which it was claimed would have the effect of depressing the trade of that country. Besides it was held that to exhibit the expensive and complicated pattern of embroideries would result in having the trade of Swiss manufacturers injured by cheap imitations, as had been the case at Paris. The sentiment in Switzerland, however, underwent a very decided change upon the arrival of the Columbian Commission. The importance of the World's Fair, and the gigantic nature of the enterprise having been laid before them, the manufacturers quickly decided to make an exhibit, and the government was called upon to make a suitable grant. Among the attractions of the Swiss exhibit is a magnificent display made by the watchmakers of that country. Switzerland is represented in nearly every department of the Exposition.

TRINIDAD.—Trinidad was the thirty-first nation to accept an invitation to participate in the Columbian Exposition. The display made by this little country is very interesting and creditable.

TURKEY.—Enthusiasm for the World's Columbian Exposition and material assistance in making it an international affair, strangely enough came at the beginning from nations that were not expected to participate to any great extent. This fact was particularly exemplified in the cases of Japan and Turkey. The Turkish flag was the first foreign flag hoisted at the World's Fair grounds. This event occurred on September 20, 1891, with appropriate ceremonies. The flag was raised on the site which Robert Levy, of Constantinople, secured for his Turkish specialties. The Sultan took a great personal interest in the Exposition, and gave orders concerning certain exhibits which make a showing of Turkish progress in science and education. He officially signified his consent to the erection of a mosque, to be used by Mussulmans for religious services during the Exposition. The supervision of the construction of the mosque was committed to the imperial Turkish commissioner and cost $3,000. The merchants of Smyrna occupy about 1,000 square feet of space in an exhibit of the finest Turkish rugs and carpets. Turkey is represented in nearly every one of the leading departments. The Turkish commissioner is Hakki

Bey, translator at the imperial palace, and Fahni Bey, of the general post-office, is sub-commissioner. In addition to these, other representatives of the Turkish government and Imperial Palace are daily on the grounds.

URUGUAY.—The display of the government of Uruguay is in charge of the rural association, and is one of the most interesting to be seen. The Rural Association of Paraguay is an important national organization, and has spared no pains or expense in making the exhibit creditable. This association managed the Uruguay display at Paris. The republic is well represented in the agriculture, live-stock and educational departments.

DEDICATION DAY PROGRAMME.—The dedication of the World's Columbian Exposition took place October 21, 1892. The programme agreed upon for the first three days devoted to the festivities was as follows:

1. March for orchestra. Written for the occasion by John K. Payne.
2. Prayer by the Rt. Rev. Bishop Brooks, of Massachusetts.
3. Report of the World's Columbian Commission by the Director-General.
4. Presentation of the buildings, for dedication, by the President of the World's Fair Columbian Exposition to the President of the World's Columbian Commission.
5. Chorus, "The Heavens Are Telling"—Haydn.
6. Presentation of the buildings, for dedication, by the President of World's Columbian Commission to the President of the United States.
7. March and chorus from "The Ruins of Athens"—Beethoven.
8. Dedication of the buildings by the President of the United States.
9. Hallelujah chorus from the Messiah—Handel.
10. Dedicatory Oration by the Hon. William C. P. Breckinridge, of Kentucky.
11. Dedicatory Ode. Words by Miss Harriet Monroe; music by E. A. McDowell.
12. "Star-Spangled-Banner" and "America," with full chorus and orchestral accompaniment.
13. National salute.

DEDICATION OF THE BUILDINGS, ETC.—In the dedicatory exercises on the 12th, the completed buildings were tendered by the President of the Exposition to the National Commission. President T. W. Palmer accepted them on behalf of that body and at once presented them to the President of the United States, who fittingly responded. The dedicatory oration followed. Much attention was given to the musical portion of the programme. This included the dedicatory ode and orchestra marches written for the occasion. These and other numbers, including "America" and "Star-Spangled Banner," were rendered with full choral and orchestral accompaniment.

In April, 1893, a grand international naval review, preliminary to the opening of the Exposition, as provided for by Act of Congress, will be held in New York harbor.

FIRE WORKS.—For a consideration of $25,000 Mr. James Payn, of London, gave a display of fire-works at the dedicatory ceremonies, that excelled in magnificence anything of the kind ever attempted. There were three displays on as many nights. The first night's programme included a salute of 100 aerial maroons, four and one-half inches in diameter, fired from iron mortars. Following this was a grand device, representing Chicago's welcome to all the nations of the earth. Then came Columbus and his departure from Spain, and a floating star-spangled banner, which remained in the air for hours.

On the second night a grand device in honor of the army and navy was given. A scene from the battle of Lake Erie was selected. After this was shown a prismatic fountain, a reproduction of the Capitol at Washington and many other equally striking and beautiful pictures.

On the third night was shown a reproduction of the facade of the Administration building and devices showing the portraits of the Exposition officials.

The grand display was closed with an illumination of the entire Lake Front from Van Buren Street to Jackson Park, together with the lagoons and the canal with a crowning device representing the Goddess of Peace surrounded by Science, Art and Literature, with glimpses of the Brooklyn bridge, the Eiffel Tower and other famous structures.

MILITARY DISPLAY.—Fifteen thousand troops at least, with all the crack artillery companies in the country, were present for the week of the World's Fair dedicatory ceremonies. The display of troops was particularly impressive, and there was the greatest display of artillery here ever brought together in one place in the United States since the close of the Civil War. Ohio sent 1,000 men, Indiana 500, Illinois 3,000, Missouri 500, Iowa 500, Minnesota 500, Wisconsin 1,000, Michigan 1,000. This makes atotal of 8,500 troops specially invited. In addition there were 5,000 regulars of the United States army.

The encampment lasted from Oct. 11 to Oct. 14 inclusive. The Exposition management furnished quarters and subsistence during the encampment. Beyond the number of men of the National Guard of the United States army indicated, the Governors of many of the States were accompanied by their guards.

The entire cost of the encampment is estimated at $30,000. The reasons for inviting the Governors of the States adjoining or near to Illinois to send the specified allotment of troops was because of their proximity. In the summer of 1893 there will be another encampment, when it is expected that troops from a distance will be present. Gen. Nelson A. Miles will have charge of the military display.

PROCESSION OF CENTURIES.—After months of deliberation the joint committee representing the National Commission and Board of Directors adopted twenty-four floats, which formed the procession of centuries. These floats were drawn around through the canals and lagoons of Jackson Park on dedication night. They were built at an average expense of $3,800 each, or a total cost of $91,200. Following is the list of floats :

1. The Stone Age ; representing the cliff-dwellers and the Toltecs.
2. The Bronze Age ; representing the Aztecs and the mound-builders.
3. The Aboriginal Age ; representing the American Indians.
4. Columbus at the Court of Ferdinand and Isabella.
5. Departure of Columbus from Palos.
6. The discovery of America.
7. Columbus before the Court of Ferdinand and Isabella presenting natives and the strange products of the new country.
8. English Cavaliers and the Settlement of Jamestown.
9. Hendrick Hudson ; Discovery of the Hudson river ; Dutch Settlement at New Amsterdam.
10. Landing of the Pilgrams.
11. Illustration of early Puritan Life.
12. Ferdinand de Soto ; Discovery of the Mississippi.
13. Père Marquette, Chevalier La Salle, and the Northwest.
14. Washington and his Generals.
15. Signing the Declaration of Independence.
16. Union of the Colonies ; the thirteen original States ; the sisterhood of the great Republic ; welcoming the Territories to the constellation of States.
17. "Westward the course of empire takes its way."
18. The genius of invention ; application of steam, etc.
19. Electricity and electric appliances.
20. War ; representing valor, sacrifice, power, death, devastation.
21. Peace ; representing tranquillity, security, prosperity, happiness.
22. Agriculture.
23. Science, art and literature.
24. Universal freedom of man ; equal rights ; law and justice ; liberty enlightening the world.

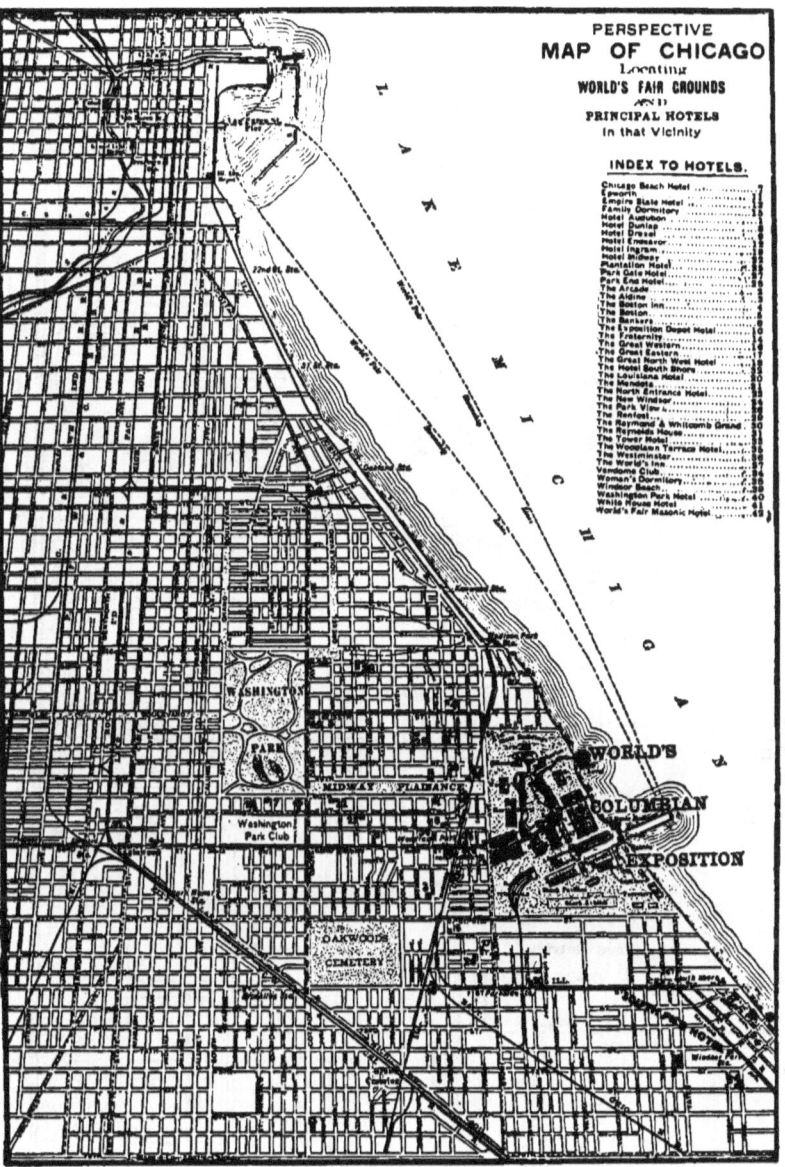

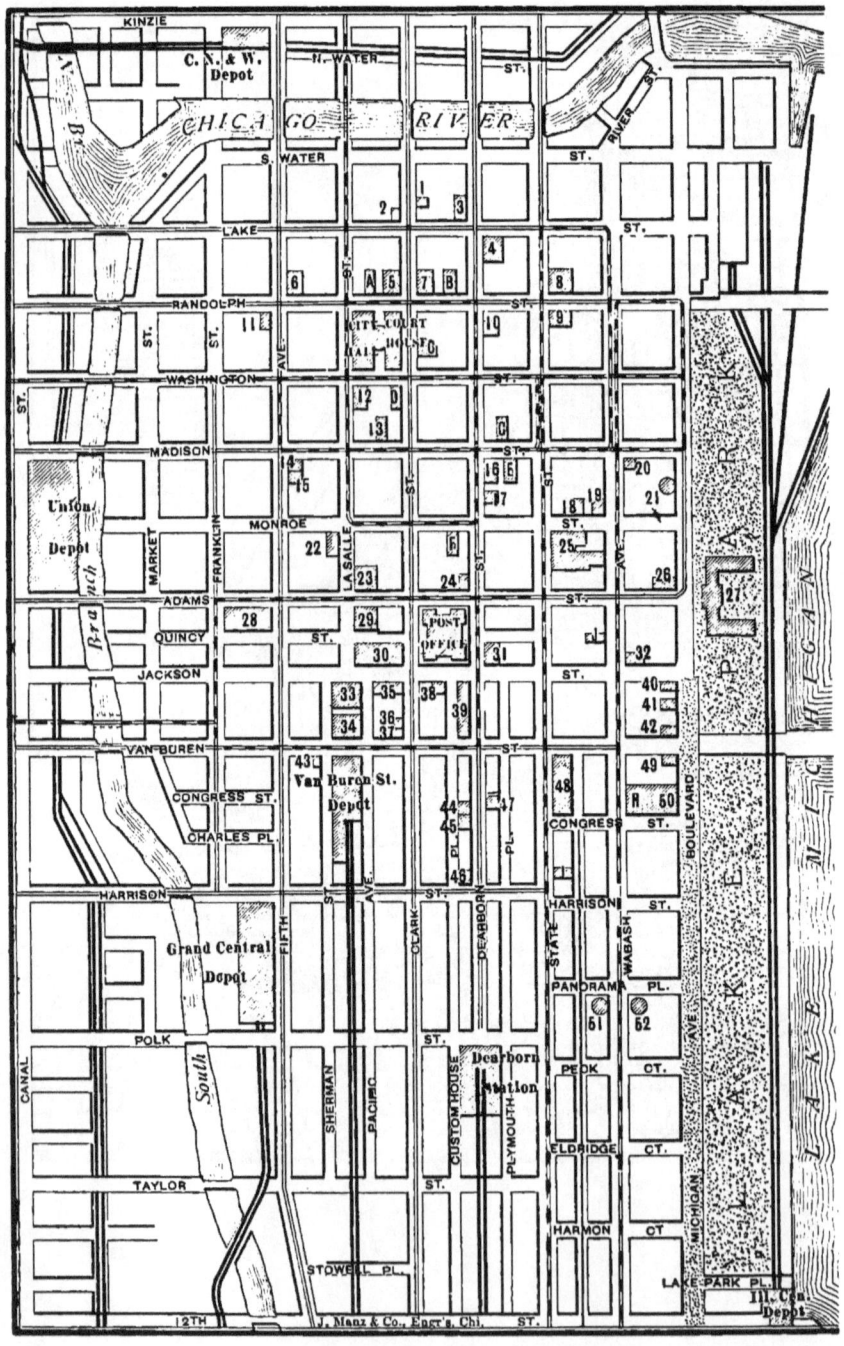

www.ingramcontent.com/pod-product-compliance
Lightning Source LLC
Chambersburg PA
CBHW021157230426
43667CB00006B/433